ANTHONY EDWARDS

# A TUGMAN'S TALE

*This book is a part of my book 'Paid to Live the Dream'. It was extracted especially for people who are interested in Steam tugs, and life in 1960's Gravesend. It could also be of interest to those visiting the steam tug Cervia now lying in Ramsgate and being restored by a dedicated band of volunteers being led by Mike Houckham, an ex tugman himself.*

A TUGMAN'S TALE



ISBN-13: 978-2956327905

https://anthonyedwards.fr

# DEDICATION

For my deceased parents who suffered so much in life and who involuntarily passed on the genes that enabled me to live such a wonderful, unconventional life of triumphs and mishaps.

# AUTHOR'S NOTE

This book is an account of my almost seven years working on Thames steam tugs in my native Gravesend. When I was just 15 years old, I was unexpectedly offered an instant job as cook with Ship Towage Ltd. In this narrative, I have endeavoured to capture the essence of life aboard with the tough, hardworking tugmen, the ever present potential dangers, the long hours worked throughout the days and nights in all weathers and the joys of living through the cultural and sexual revolution of the swinging sixties. I am deeply indebted to all of my fellow crew members for their comradeship; some are still living, but most have now sadly passed on to the great river in the sky. The names of the majority of these remarkable men are factual and just a small number have been changed. The names of the Thames tugs have not been changed.

# CONTENTS

I WOULD LIKE TO THANK THE FOLLOWING:

*MARJIE EDWARDS*, for her understanding, her patience and her invaluable assistance in the preparation for this book's publication. Without her contribution the book may never have been published.

*MIKE HOUCKHAM*, for giving me a guided tour of the Cervia in Ramsgate, the generous amount of time he spent with me afterwards and for his additional valued contributions.

*BOB MCKECKNIE,* for allowing me to access his amazing memory, for verifying the facts as I remembered them and for supplying me with facts that I had forgotten.

# STEAM

*There are many points in the history of an invention which the inventor himself is apt to overlook as trifling, but in which posterity never fails to take a deep interest. The progress of the human mind is never traced with such a lively interest as through the steps by which it perfects a great invention; and there is certainly no invention respecting which this minute information will be more sought after, than in the case of the steam-engine. – Sir David Brewster*

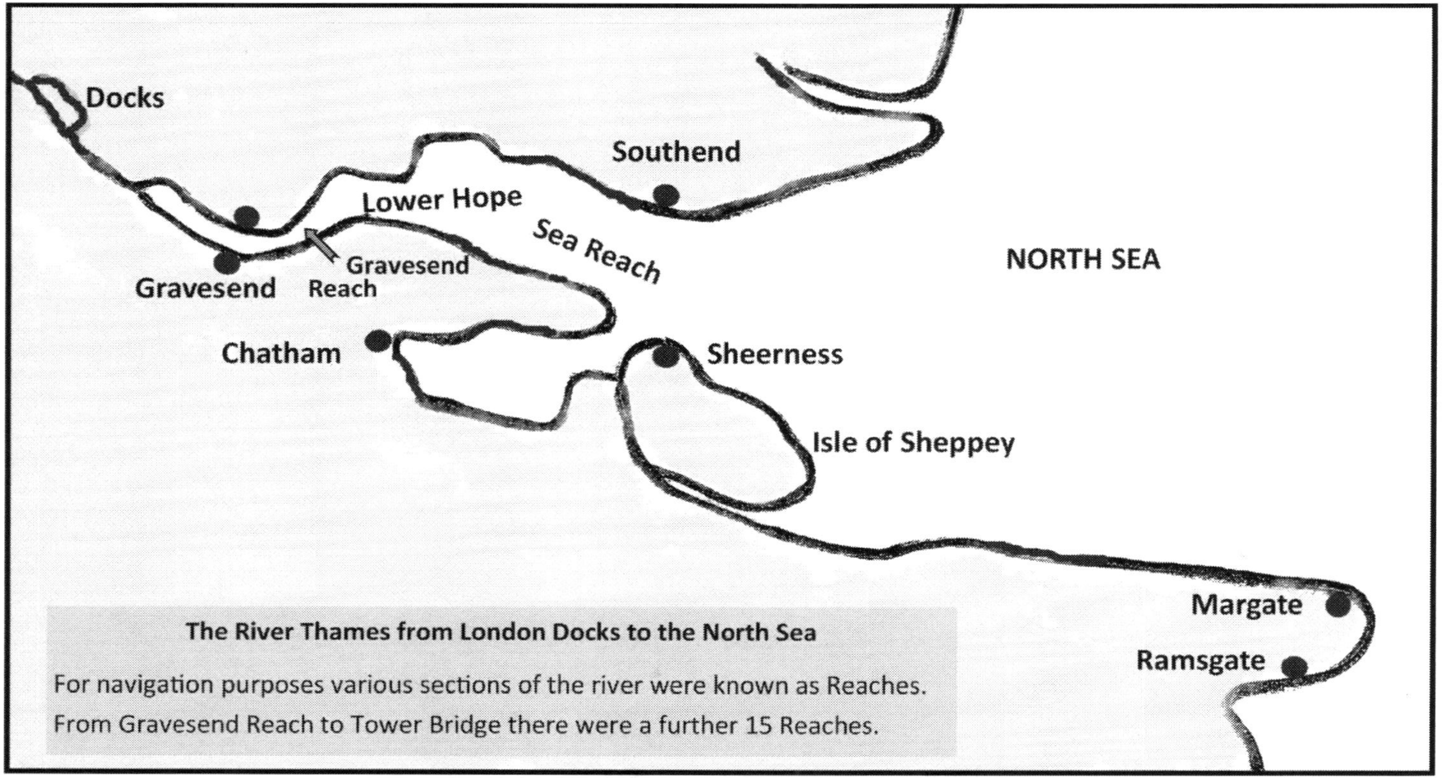


**The River Thames from London Docks to the North Sea**

For navigation purposes various sections of the river were known as Reaches. From Gravesend Reach to Tower Bridge there were a further 15 Reaches.

# CHAPTER 1
# SERENDIPITY

The design of Gravesend's Clock Tower was based on the Elizabeth Tower that houses Big Ben in the Palace of Westminster. It was dedicated to Queen Victoria to commemorate her 50$^{th}$ year of reign and was a focal point in the town. I was 15 years old, not long left school and wandering aimlessly early one afternoon when I stopped beneath it. I paused there momentarily as a thought flashed into my otherwise unoccupied mind. It's intriguing how an inner voice seems to sometimes communicate with a certainty that is hard to ignore. I hesitated a while, should I or shouldn't I? Oh go for it I decided, as Mahatma Gandhi once said, "The future depends on what you do today". Without further ado, I turned and strutted down Harmer Street. Although work was plentiful for school leavers in the '50s, I was looking for an exciting outdoor activity. I crossed into Royal Pier Road and at the end reached The Royal Terrace Pier. I faltered momentarily as a doubt crossed my mind, then plucked up the courage to continue. I entered and walked along the wooden corridor, glancing at the doors on either side. At the end on the right-hand side, I saw what I was looking for: a door with "Ship Towage Ltd" etched onto a wooden plaque. I tapped nervously on the door and went in. It was a spacious, untidy room with a window overlooking the lower reaches of the Thames and obviously a place of constant activity. A well-built, grey haired man was seated behind a large wooden desk shuffling through some papers spread in front of him. Behind him was a small, slim, dark haired man flitting from one side of the office to the other receiving and relaying messages on VHF radios in a nasally, whining voice. Tug Skippers were calling in to report their current situations and awaiting new orders and the two office agents discussed and made decisions quickly and easily despite the constant cacophony in the background.

Not being sure what to do, I stood motionless and when the grey-haired one, who had the air of being in command, glanced up at me I shyly asked him if they had any job prospects for me. There was no discussion whatsoever. He had barely raised his head as he occupied himself with more important issues and barked,

"Be back here at six o'clock tonight with your kit, you can join as cook." Then he turned to his colleague and gave out further instructions and that was it.

I was taken aback and then excitement took over. Oh, my God. I really wasn't expecting that! Not just a positive response but an instant job offer. I didn't know what kit I would need and didn't like to ask. I exited and rushed back up Harmer Street to the clock tower, turned left for the bus stop and could barely contain my excitement as I waited for the number 46 on the Maidstone and District line to get me home. The bus seemed to take an age to arrive and there were only a few hours remaining until six o'clock. Finally, it appeared in the distance and rolled to a stop where I waited. The queue started shuffling on and I felt like barging past them in my impatience to get home as quickly as possible.

The main economy of Gravesend was from the River Thames and maritime trade. Seventy-five million tonnes of shipping each year would pass through during the 1950's and 60's, importing and exporting around two thousand four hundred million tonnes of meat, sugar, grain, wool, tea, timber and other goods. The Port of London Authority has had a base on the Royal Terrace Pier since the 19$^{th}$ century and it is operational twenty-four hours a day. The pier was built in 1844 and was given the prefix "Royal" in honour of Princess Alexandra of Denmark who arrived there in 1865 on her way to marry the Prince of Wales, later King Edward VII. It had been and still is a departure point for pilot cutters carrying river and sea pilots to the ships sailing in and out of the Thames. The tug control centre was also based there and steam tugs had been operating from there since the mid-19th century. Gravesend also had a sea cadet training college, which was referred to as the Peanut Factory by locals and for some unknown reason, the trainee cadets were known as peanuts.

On the journey home, I was able to reflect on what had just happened. I knew that jobs on the tugs were highly sought after and stayed pretty much within families. Although I had a cousin who worked on them as Mate I had never thought to ask him to help me join the tugs since he was much older than me and for that reason, we weren't close. I also knew that the wages could be exceptionally good.

I was glad when the bus eventually turned into Old Road East where I got off and rushed home. I couldn't wait to tell my parents and start packing my kit. As soon as I arrived home, I immediately blurted out the good news as I rushed through the door.

"Guess what?" I spluttered, "I've got a job on the tugs. I've got to be back there tonight at six o'clock."

Dad was seated in his usual chair beside the fire and in front of the television. He was an Eastender, born in West Ham and spoke in cockney rhyming slang, a language that originated in London's East End around 1840. The reason for its development is not known for certain and many of its expressions are used in everyday parlance although most people are unaware of their origin. For example "Take a butchers" related to butchers hook, meaning look. Rhyming slang uses two or more words from a phrase, an event, a place name or a person's name where the last word rhymes with the commonly used word and then the last word is dropped. Dad, for instance, would always talk of his "titfa" meaning his hat, (tit for tat = hat). I never heard him say the word hat. He wore a whistle (whistle and flute = suit) and I had a skin (skin and blister = sister). I wonder how many people realise that when they refer to somebody as a berk that this is in fact from rhyming slang, the origin of which is Berkely Hunt, a famous fox hunt, which rhymes with a well-known four letter expletive. Blowing a raspberry is another commonly used phrase which is again rhyming slang, raspberry tart = fart. I grew up with this intriguing language, which wasn't widely used in Gravesend but was used by Dad.

Dad had spent years at sea down in the boiler room (stokehold) shovelling coal into the furnaces. When he settled down and took a shore based job, he ended up shovelling more coal into the furnaces at the local gas works. All those years breathing in the coal dust and fumes had left him with emphysema and on top of that, a terrible accident occurred at the gas works that had rendered him disabled. He was shovelling coal into one of the furnaces when it exploded and he took the full force of it. The powerful blast propelled the contents of the furnace straight onto him. Subsequently, he'd spent a prolonged period in hospital throughout much of my earlier years. I was never allowed to go to see him, his wounds were so terrible. He'd needed numerous skin grafts and suffered the loss of one eye, so hadn't worked in years. His movement was restricted due to his breathing difficulties so he didn't do much except bet on the horse races and watch on TV each afternoon to see if he'd struck lucky. How lamentable that after having lived through two world wars and survived two separate torpedo attacks that he should end his days thus. Overcoming challenges can make us stronger but it was not easy watching Dad end his days in that way. "Out of suffering have emerged the strongest souls; the most massive characters are seared with scars," said Kahlil Gibran, Lebanese poet and author of "The Prophet."

"Well done, son," Dad congratulated me, rising from his chair. He was genuinely pleased for me and straight away offered to rescue his old kit bag from where he kept it upstairs.

"I've got me old kit bag up the apples, I'll go and dig it out for ya," he said as he turned and went to get it.

Since he'd been discharged from the merchant navy a long time ago there was no chance of him ever needing it again himself. He soon came back carrying the soiled, white canvas bag. I went up to my room and brought down some clothes and when we'd finished piling them into the kit bag with some toiletries and food it was only one quarter full and looked a bit ridiculous. A smaller bag would have sufficed but I didn't want to disappoint Dad. Mum hovered in the background with a worried look on her face, not quite knowing how to react.

"Do you want something to eat before you go?" she said, wishing to contribute somehow and be a part of Dad's and my enthusiasm.

"No, I'm OK," I assured her as I rummaged around collecting any other items I considered necessary as six o'clock seemed to be approaching fast.

"You must have something," she insisted. "You must be hungry."

"No thanks, maybe later," I said. I was far too excited and anxious not to miss my deadline to think about stopping to eat.

"Shall I put the kettle on then?"

Mum's life was pretty boring so she didn't have a great deal else to think about. She'd spent most of her youth in hospital in her home town of Liverpool for reasons that were never discussed. I do know that for a long time she was confined to a Bath chair; consequently she'd had very little education. She could be belligerent and stubborn, which was difficult to accept and it was only very much later, almost sixty years on in my life that I understood what a cruel hand she'd been dealt in her own life. In addition to the extended hospitalisation and having an evil mother, she'd also had a child out of wedlock when she was twenty, something that was a disgrace in those days. The child was taken from her, never to be seen or heard of again, so she was basically an unhappy person. Because of her limited education, she lacked the knowledge and confidence to pursue any interests other than occupying herself with looking after the family and the home, but she was a loving mother. It must have been heart-wrenching for Mum to have lived all her life not knowing the whereabouts of her daughter and never daring to speak about her. I have been told that towards the end of her life when she was lying on her hospital bed, with tears in her eyes she said to the nurse "Who is looking after my baby?" At that time nobody understood what she meant. So throughout her life, she never forgot about her baby. I didn't learn of the illegitimate child until 2014, by which time her baby had grown into a 76-year-old woman who tracked me down and finally found her only blood relatives. If, when Mum left this three-dimensional world, her spirit made a transition to another dimension, maybe in that new dimension she is aware that the child she never knew has now discovered who her mother was and has made contact with the children of the mother she never knew. Maybe Mum is now at peace and smiling on us. That's a comforting thought and I have gained a sister. It pains me how much my parents suffered in their lives and to think that they may be reliving it all over again. Over the centuries, many brilliant philosophers in their search for an explanation of the universe came to believe that we return to live the exact same lives over and over again in an endless cycle known as the Eternal Return. This belief can be found in Indian philosophy, Ancient Egypt, Mayans, Aztecs, Pythagoreans and more recently Frederich Nietzsche. It is also implied by modern day quantum cosmology. A similar theme was used in the 1993 film Groundhog Day starring Bill Murray and Andie McDowell.

Mum met Dad when he was in Liverpool during the war as part of HMS Mersey, which was not a ship but the Royal Navy's depot where men of the merchant fleet agreed to serve aboard ships under the Navy to make up for the lack of manpower. They married in 1941 and later Mum moved to Gravesend, staying with one of Dad's six sisters whilst he was away at sea. I was born in 1943 and was two years old before Dad returned home and saw me. It was at that time that they moved in to the top floor of a two bedroomed semi-detached council house nearby, which they shared with another family who occupied the sitting room and kitchen downstairs. After that, the only other child they had was my sister who was born in 1948, by which time the other family had long since moved out.

After Dad and I had put together what we thought I'd need to be properly kitted out, I was ready for my adventure and thus began my seafaring days.

"Shall I make you some sandwiches to take with you?" said Mum as she stood by optimistically in her floral pinafore.

"OK," I eventually agreed. It seemed the kindest thing to do and off she went to the kitchen, happy in the knowledge that at least I wouldn't go hungry.

As Dad was such an experienced seaman it made sense for me to profit from his abundance of knowledge.

"Any advice for me, Dad?" I asked as I was leaving.

He stood before me and looked me in the eye as he searched his memory for the most pragmatic counsel that he could offer, then, in a serious voice, his words of wisdom came forth.

"If yer git seasick," he said, "and yer find a little red lump in yer mowf as yer 'eaving yer guts out over the side, whadever yer do don' spit it aht."

"Why not?" I questioned.

"'Cause it'll be the roof of yer arse," he said.

There is an English proverb that says, "Write down the advice of him who loves you, though you like it not at present" but I doubt that the author of that proverb had anything like Dad's words in mind when he said it.

So with Dad's philosophical offering I left, not forgetting, of course, Mum's sandwiches. On many future occasions, however, Dad's words of advice, although of no comfort or practical use, would echo in my mind as I hung vomiting over the ship's side wishing I could die.

# CHAPTER 2
# GALLEY DUTIES

*Relief Crew No. 4*

Feeling nervous and excited, with Dad's kit bag slung over my shoulder, I set off and took the bus back to the clock tower. My only previous knowledge of anything maritime was hiring a rowing boat on a nearby lake with my best friend Tommy for half an hour on Sunday afternoons. As for cooking, apart from helping Mum to shell peas in the kitchen sometimes, I was a complete novice. Mum cooked excellent meals for us, always using fresh ingredients and I'd enjoyed eating whatever she'd prepared. I was then and still am an enthusiastic eater and there was very little that I didn't consume with relish. I just loved food. Unusually, as a child, I'd enjoyed reading an old copy of Mrs Beaton's cookery book but that was probably due to the fact that it was the only book that I can ever recall seeing at home. Dad started working as a very young boy, so like Mum had little education and consequently little interest in reading anything other than the News of the World and the Herald for his horse racing form.

I trundled down Harmer Street for the second time that day, feeling self-conscious as I lugged the kit bag that was almost as big as I was. It must have been an unusual sight because very few people used wartime kit bags anymore but it was dark by then and there were few people around to notice. At 18.00 hrs exactly I was back in the Ship Towage office on the Royal Terrace Pier. The same two people were still involved in the same hustle and bustle of the office, issuing orders over the radios to the tugs. My excitement was so great that it overpowered my feelings of unease. Once again, there was very little communication from either of them, just a brief instruction from the grey haired one sat behind his desk. When the radio conversations fell silent for a second or two, he looked up and said,

"Go down to the pontoon and go aboard the Cervia, she's waiting for you."

Off I went down the brow, a sloping wooden walkway with iron railings either side, to the floating pontoon. I became aware of how much colder it was in the breeze the nearer I got to the river. Lights shone through the port holes of the Cervia as she lay moored alongside. I looked at the prominent black funnel with its red band a third of the way down, silhouetted against the backdrop of the night sky and the lights on the opposite shore. There was a solitary figure standing on deck by an open door. Lights were visible on the various craft making their way up and down river, with the occasional steam whistles screeching the intentions of each vessel to avoid collisions. The smells were a mixture of the sea and smoke. When I reached the tug she was moored facing up river against the tide, held alongside by creaking sisal ropes as they took the strain of the water rushing past at six knots. Strung around the black painted bulwarks were large rubber tyres to provide protection whenever she came alongside other craft and I could hear the throbbing of the engine. The man standing on deck was smiling; he greeted me and took my bag as I clambered over the side onto the steel deck. He was well built, balding and wore glasses. He introduced himself to me as Smokey. The smell of diesel accompanied by the rumbling and hissing of the steam engine became more prominent. As soon as I was aboard I heard the ring of the brass telegraph alerting the engine room to stand by. A Deckhand appeared through the open door.

"Let go," the Skipper shouted from the bridge and he leant over to watch the deck hand flick the mooring rope expertly from the mooring post.

"All gone Skip," the Deckhand said.

The telegraph rang once more indicating slow ahead and a corresponding needle on the engine room telegraph did the same. The Engineer opened up the wheel sending more steam into the cylinder heads and the engine thumped into life, turning the giant propeller and we steamed away from the pontoon heading out to the middle of the river. Smokey told me that we were going to the King George V docks in London and then he led me down the ladder to show me the cabin that I would be sharing with him. Only a few hours previously I had been strolling through town without a care in the world, never imagining for one moment that I would find myself in such a situation. I was jubilant.

The tugs in the fleet at that time were steam driven and mostly coal-fired. The Cervia was a relatively recent addition and was oil fired. She was built towards the end of the Second World War having been commissioned by the Navy but was never required, so became part of the Watkins tug fleet in 1946. Her gross tonnage was 233 and she was 34.4 metres in length. She was the first tug that I had ever been on and was one of the most modern of the fleet. In 1954, four years before I joined her, at eleven o'clock in the evening of 25 October, she was towing the P & O liner Arcadia stern first out of Tilbury docks. There were two other tugs in attendance on the bow. As the Cervia crossed the Arcadia's stern with a slack towrope, the ship put her engines into ahead to avoid a collision with another liner waiting to enter the docks. The towrope was pulled tight and the Cervia was girted (pulled over and sank) as a result of the towrope being unable to be released quickly enough. Five crew members, including the Captain, were drowned and the search for the bodies continued until dawn the next day. My cousin Billy was one of only three who survived. Two days later she was re-floated and taken to Ramsgate shipyard for repairs. Today, the Cervia is one of just two of the steam tugs remaining from the original fleet and was, in fact, the very last steam tug ever to operate in the UK. She is currently moored in Ramsgate Royal Harbour where she is being lovingly restored by a dedicated and enthusiastic team of volunteers led by Mike Houckham. Mike is an ex tugman himself, like his father and grandfather before him. He had also served on the Cervia whilst he was a member of relief crew No. 7. She is now one of the very few steamships still in existence and is open to the public.

Once we were under way, Smokey, the caterer and Leading Hand, began outlining my duties.

"This is your bunk." He pointed to the upper berth.

"You can sleep from ten o'clock each night until six in the morning," he told me.

The cabin was small, comfortable, deliciously warm and permeated with the smell of diesel, hemp and a mixture of other unrecognised odours. After Smokey left for the engine room, there wasn't much for me to do except unpack a few bits and pieces and wander around before getting into my bunk. I didn't sleep at all that night. As I lay in the darkened cabin, fully clothed, covered with a rough blanket, I could hear the deck crew running along the decks, tow ropes being hauled aboard, bumps and a slight roll each time we steamed alongside ships and lock sides. Steam whistles blew, communicating signals between ships and tugs and other ships. The telegraph rang over and over again; the Engineer increased or decreased the engine revolutions accordingly and the 1000 hp. triple expansion steam engine thumped and hissed. Occasionally the anchor chain rattled and banged as it shot out of the chain locker when the heavy anchor was dropped, and we heeled over at a steep angle each time the weight was taken on the tow ropes. Smokey came into the cabin to sleep for a few hours when the Chief Engineer relieved him, then left again when he was next on watch. I found the whole experience exhilarating and couldn't resist climbing out of my bunk from time to time to peek out on deck and soak in the atmosphere.

The next day at 06.00 hrs prompt, reality checked in. I was shown around the tug and my duties were outlined in more detail by the Mate, Ken.

"You can start by scrubbing the cabin floors and the table, then collect and wash up all the mugs and plates that are hanging around. We do our own breakfast and afterwards, you can clear away and wash up again. Smokey will see you later and explain what he wants you to cook for the midday meal." he said.

I was shown where to find a galvanised bucket, hot water, and scrubbing brushes etc. and told to get on with it - and I did exactly that. As I scrubbed the wooden floor and table, members of the crew came in and out of the cabin and chatted to me and I learned that I was now a member of Relief Crew No. 4. Nobody asked me my name. I was referred to only as "Cook" or "Cookie."

The total crew consisted of Skipper and Chief Engineer who had their own cabins apart from the rest of the crew. The Leading Hand and two Firemen completed the below deck crew and the Mate, Deckhand and Third Hand were in charge of above decks. Along with other relief crews, our role was to go aboard and take over the running of any of the fleet of tugs where the permanent crew were due time off. Time off, in those days, was sometimes three nights a week if we were lucky. We were supposed to work no more than 48 continuous hours without a spell ashore but this was flexible and always to the advantage of the company. What was referred to as a weekend off once a month could sometimes be from late Saturday evening until 06.00 hrs on Monday morning. Working hours had to be flexible to fit in with the tides and shipping arrivals and departures. As Cook though, I could at least curl up in my bunk every night from 22.00 hrs till 06.00 hrs and even if I didn't sleep too well because of the constant activity, at least I was resting.

The layout and accommodation on each tug varied. Very few had the luxury of the enclosed wheelhouse that was fitted to the Cervia. The other, older tugs had an open, exposed bridge with a small canvas dodger providing limited shelter from the elements but that wasn't to affect me until later when I was transferred to the deck department. My area of interest as Cook was the galley and each one had its own peculiarities. Some galleys were small with hardly any real work surfaces and just about enough room to turn around. The meals for the crew of eight strong, muscular tug men were mostly prepared on cast iron, coal burning stoves in a small, hot galley. Some crews would have a rota with each crew member taking turns as caterer. Sometimes one person would hold the position permanently and sometimes it would be the Cook himself who collected the money from all crew members and decided what would be on each menu. Everybody on board began on the tugs at a young age as Cook. I was fortunate to receive my initial training from Smokey, a keen caterer. He had an extraordinary interest in providing wholesome food and was a gifted and enthusiastic cook. Everything was bought fresh and prepared with no fancy gadgets. I learned a great deal from him and developed a real interest in cooking that has continued throughout my life. It still gives me great pleasure to prepare food of all descriptions and I enjoy devouring the results.

I only had to prepare the main meal at midday but other crews might expect the Cook to prepare more. Typical English fare of main course and desert was served; continental cuisine hadn't yet taken off in the U.K. in 1958, and even if it had it's hard for me to imagine the eight hungry, hardworking tuggies tucking into sole à la bonne femme in preference to a good meat duff. The main meal in the middle of the day had to be ready on time to facilitate the engine room crew's change of watch. Deck crew ate as and when they could relieve each other if towing or steaming up or down river. I was always expected to prepare lots of fresh vegetables and meat and standard desserts of that era. There was no thermostat on the stoves of coal burning tugs so controlling the heat wasn't always easy. I had to control the amount of coal I put in the firebox, adjust the airflow and lift and replace the hotplates. With the inevitable kettle of boiling water on the stove, plus a number of pots of cooking vegetables and maybe a roast or pie in the oven, it could get very hot indeed in the confined space.

To keep the fire burning, I shovelled coal from a coal bucket, a modified oil drum with a rope handle, into the fire box. Water was pumped up by hand to keep the kettle topped up as fast as the crew were emptying it for the endless pint mugs of tea and the saucepans were shuttled to different sections of the stove to try and get them either boiling or simmering. My body dripped with perspiration. The only respite from the heat was to stick my head out of the door and enjoy the cool outside air for a few minutes as I watched the towing process in operation. Working under the expert tuition of Smokey the caterer though, I became quite an accomplished cook and was then mostly left to my own devices. Much to my discomfort, the rest of the crew would occasionally tell me and members of other crews how good they thought I was. I would be overcome with red-cheeked embarrassment but secretly pleased and flattered and knowing how much my efforts were appreciated, I was encouraged to improve even more. I am so grateful to Smokey for his guidance and infectious enthusiasm. There is an Irish proverb that says, "Laughter is the brightest in the place where the food is." and when we were moored to the buoy between towing operations and sat around the table together for the meals, there was always an abundance of laughter and good humoured banter.

Washing up the mountain of crockery, cutlery and pots after meals was done in one of the all-purpose galvanised buckets using lots of soda. The bucket was filled with water using the hand pump and then I would plunge one of the cast iron hot plates directly from the stove into the bucket. The water sizzled and bubbled like crazy as it was instantly heated. An effective way of removing any obstinate or burnt areas from the pans was to scour them with ashes from the fire. To keep the stove hot, the coal bucket needed constant replenishing. I'd take it from the galley along the deck to the fiddley door, lower it on a rope down into the stokehold in the bowels of the tug for the Fireman to fill with coal and then I'd haul it back up and take it into the galley. If the Fireman was disinclined or if he was too busy feeding the furnaces, he'd refuse to cooperate, which meant that I had to descend the hot, metal ladder into the very hot stokehold and fill the bucket myself, then climb the ladder to haul it back up. This was exasperating when it happened in the middle of cooking a meal.

## *Traipsing the docks*

Shopping was time-consuming and tiring. Since I was only required to cook the main meal at midday, the caterer would give me the list of what was needed to feed the nine of us for the next couple of days and each individual crew member would add his own requirements for preparing the additional meals. When the list was completed I'd disembark with a hessian sack or two and set off in search of everything. We always needed lots of potatoes, fresh vegetables, meat, bread, cans, prepared food, bottles of drinks, newspapers, cigarettes and so on. The weight of the sack increased considerably as I continued on my way until finally, it was sometimes as much as I could do to carry it back.

Mostly the shopping would be done in our home port of Gravesend, where we had our own known suppliers. At other times, since we were constantly steaming up and down the Thames and locking into different docks, I would be sent ashore with my sacks in a place I didn't know at all. There were many working docks on the Thames in the 1950s and 60s covering a total of 2000 acres. They were originally built to accommodate the increasing amount of trade in the 19th century and locking into and steaming through them on the tug, passing through the various cuttings, looked complicated to me. I found out just how complicated when I had to find my way around on foot to do the shopping. I would steel myself for a long, perplexing, circuitous walk in search of the way out through the dock gates. When I eventually arrived at the exit, I would often be in a remote area nowhere near a town or shops, so that involved yet more walking or even bus rides. Sometimes, it would take so long that when I ultimately returned, tired, fed up and exhausted from carrying the heavy sacks on my back, I would discover that the tug was no longer where I had left her or where I thought she might be. She could have been ordered to another area in the same dock, or sometimes to a completely different dock. So off I'd go again, utterly disheartened, in search of her. I often didn't know where to begin looking. The worst case scenario, which was rare, would be that she had been ordered to return to the home port of Gravesend. Then I would have to find a means of getting from London to Gravesend before she left again for somewhere else.

On a dry or reasonable day it was bad enough trudging around loaded down with the weight of the shopping, trying to find my way through the gigantic concrete maze with my visibility virtually blocked by the huge ships moored to the quays and no way to contact the crew. When it was raining, windy, snowing, cold or any combination of the aforementioned, with my vision impaired, it was utterly wretched. I would walk what to me seemed like miles, getting soaking wet and cold, bent double with the weight of the sacks cutting into my shoulders. As the search continued, my fingers would get cramped from holding on tightly to the sacks, which got heavier by the minute and pressed me down. I often needed to stop and put the sacks on the ground to allow the blood to circulate through my fingers and shoulders before swapping to the other shoulder and continuing on what ostensibly could be a long haul. Sometimes I would be able to hitch a ride on another tug and even occasionally, a lighter, if the distance was too great to walk, such as when going to another dock. It was the task of the Lightermen to transport their cargos to their destination by any means appropriate, either using the current itself or getting a tow from a tug, so it wasn't a choice of preference for me, but rather one of desperation. With imagination and determination I'd eventually reach the elusive vessel. As soon as I'd boarded it would be straight to work unpacking and probably preparing mugs of tea for the crew. If I had been gone too long and meal time was imminent, there would be a ravenous crew to feed, so there would be no time to rest. The stove would need stoking, maybe coal to be got from the stokehold and inevitably a mess to clear away if the crew had been too busy to occupy themselves with galley chores during my absence.

### *No sympathy*

I very soon realised that my youth and inexperience didn't entitle me to any special privileges or sympathy. The bare wood mess tables were worn and grooved from years of being scrubbed. One morning whilst scrubbing rather too vigorously, the lateral edge of my thumb slid along the grooved surface and I winced from a stabbing pain as a splinter shot in underneath the nail. As the day wore on and the discomfort increased, the thumb throbbed, reddened and started to swell. That evening when we were moored up to the buoy, I was lying in my bunk nursing the painful thumb and stupidly made the mistake of mentioning it to the crew. I was immediately grabbed, pulled out of the bunk, stretched out and pinned down on the table while two of the crew took turns at trying to dig out the splinter, which was well and truly embedded. They had no possibility of removing it as it had penetrated too deeply. No matter how hard I struggled and yelled they kept me firmly on the table. I had no alternative other than to suffer and wait whilst they prodded and poked, which just made the pain even worse, much to their amusement. I learned very quickly to suffer in silence after that.

Fortunately, the next day we received orders to take the rest of the day off when the permanent crew boarded. The thumb was not looking good - it was terribly swollen and looking a strange colour. When I arrived home my worried mother decided that I should go to the hospital so off she trotted with me in tow. A lovely, gentle mannered nurse took me to a trolley, brought me a hot, sweet cup of tea then bathed my thumb for a while in disinfectant before removing the splinter. She was surprised at the length of it and so was I. It had travelled all the way to the knuckle and presumably broke off there because my thumb was bent over the scrubbing brush, preventing it from travelling any further. She placed it on a pad of cotton wool and gave it to me as a memento. In my ignorance, I took it with me the following day to show it to my fellow crew buddies. Nobody was the least bit interested. The general attitude was of complete indifference. All things considered, life aboard a Thames steam tug in the 1950's and 60's was hard work for a 15-year-old boy but I absolutely loved it! And as Benjamin Franklin once said, "It is the working man who is the happy man. It is the idle man who is the miserable man."

# CHAPTER 3
# DEATH AND SEX

*Man overboard*

We were moored to the buoy aboard the Challenge, which I knew well, having relieved the permanent crew many times. She was one of the Dick and Page tugs, built in 1931, and is the second vessel from the Ship Towage fleet that is still afloat and able to be visited by the public today. She is listed on the National Register of Historic Vessels and known for the role she played in Operation Dynamo, evacuating the Allied troops from Dunkirk in May/June 1940. She was converted from coal to oil burner at Sheerness in 1964, was laid up in 1971 and was the last steam tug to serve on the Thames. She has since been restored, is operational once more and has been exhibited in London, Liverpool, Southampton, Bristol, and other locations in the UK and abroad and is now owned and cared for by the Dunkirk Little Ships Restoration Trust. The most memorable thing about the Challenge was that she was inundated with cockroaches, more so it seemed than the other tugs. I made the mistake once of swigging from a can of Coca-Cola that I'd left lying around open and was rewarded with a mouthful of hard, lumpy cockroaches. Cockroaches were an annoyance generally, on another occasion at a later date when I was working on deck, I was in a hurry to put on my rubber gloves to manhandle a steel cable, this was necessary because any stray metal strands could rip your hands open as the cable slid rapidly through them. I'd left them in a warm place and a small colony of cockroaches had decided to make them home. When I shoved my hands in, the disgusting little creatures scrambled up my arms and I couldn't get the gloves off quick enough. Both occasions produced howls of laughter from the rest of the crew.

I was resting from my cook duties in the cabin of the Challenge when I heard the radio speaker crackle and was thrilled to hear the announcement that I was to join the Gondia temporarily as Junior Deckhand, commonly referred to as Third Hand. It was customary after a couple of years in the galley for Cooks to be promoted to Third Hand either in the same crew, or almost always a different one. The Gondia was a coal burning steam tug, older than the Cervia by twenty years and had been part of the Watkins fleet, which had amalgamated with Gamecock tugs and Dick and Page tugs to form Ship Towage Ltd. In total there were twelve Watkins tugs, five of them based at Woolwich, and the remaining seven moored onto a buoy upriver from the Royal Terrace Pier. The rest of the fleet, four gamecock tugs and four Dick and page tugs moored on two buoys downriver. The Gondia ended her days in 1966 when she was laid up and scrapped shortly after I left the service of Ship Towage Ltd. to seek a different lifestyle. My time on the Gondia was enjoyable as I learned the deck routine in the company of a fine bunch of men and working as part of a team I began to feel more like one of them. I did miss my old crew mates of Relief Crew No. 4 though. After having worked for almost two years in close confinement with such colourful men, it's inevitable that a rich sense of camaraderie would develop.

One particularly appreciated aspect of this move was that I would have my own bunk and a locker where I could leave my personal items whenever I went home for time off. Most permanent crew members would keep their lockers securely locked so the relief crews had to make do as best they could, carrying their gear with them wherever they went. All relief crews had access to a store on the pier where their basic food supplies - flour, sugar, tea etc., plus working clothes and wet weather gear were kept in a large communal box that had to be carried by two crew members to wherever they were sent. If they were ordered to London to relieve one of the London-based tugs, this large, heavy box had to be carried to Gravesend railway station to take the train to Woolwich and finally the ferry to Woolwich pier where the London-based tugs moored. If the vessel being relieved was in a dock, things became more complicated. For example, perhaps it would be necessary to get off the train at Greenwich, carry the box down the spiral staircase into the Greenwich foot tunnel and cart it all the way along to the next lot of steps going upwards and then on to wherever the tug happened to be.

It was on the Gondia that I had my first personal encounter with the danger involved in towing. This happened very late one night whilst towing a ship into the King George V dock. The blackness of the night was broken by an array of lights from the docks and passing shipping. The pilot on the ship's bridge blew his whistle to direct the tugs, that responded by blasting the same signal on their steam whistles. The Skippers swung the steering wheels over to take up their appropriate positions and rang the brass telegraphs to the engine rooms for the desired engine power. The propellers of the vessels churned up the water as the tow ropes were stretched to take the weight. Deck crews were in position on the aft decks wrapped in warm winter clothing and the Skippers were shouting out orders to them. The Gondia was positioned on the ship's port bow, one of the two bow tugs that were helping swing the ship around to starboard to enter the lock. Two other tugs were attached to her stern. Another ship was anchored just down river from us with tugs in attendance waiting to enter the same dock. Next thing we knew was that the open channel 16 on the VHF sets all around burst into life reporting man overboard. The towing cable on one of the stern tugs had snapped and like a demented snake, whiplashed back along the side deck at an unimaginable speed, snatching up a Deckhand and flicking him over the side before anybody had had time to take stock of the situation. All available tugs in the vicinity scrambled to the scene communicating with each other on the

VHF radios. It was pitch black apart from the navigation lights visible on dozens of craft navigating their way up and down river and the water was in turmoil from the wash of propellers and the six-knot tide ebbing out to sea. The search went on and on in vain. The Deckhand was never found. A hush persisted among us for some time after that as we worked throughout the night each in our own thoughts. As the river water ebbed away it took our colleague with it. "Disappearances happen. Pain goes phantom. Blood stops running. And people, people fade away." Anon.

*In flagrante delictco*

The refitting of our fleet of tugs was carried out at Ramsgate until 1961, after which time it took place at Sheerness. My first visit to the Ramsgate slipway was aboard the Gondia and I had the most wonderful time. We set off from Gravesend on a warm, cloudy day to navigate the confusing passage through the Thames Estuary where many buoys are used to mark the numerous, constantly shifting sandbanks. These buoys are regularly re-sited to correspond with the movement of the sandbanks and the channels between them are shallow. The tides are fickle and there are very few reliable landmarks because of the low lying land. By the time we'd cleared the estuary and entered into the gentle rolling of the North Sea swell, the sky had cleared. It was a beautiful, warm sunny day and when Ramsgate Harbour entrance appeared, we steamed to a safe distance and dropped anchor with the town in view. We sat on the aft deck sunning ourselves as we rolled gently,l waiting for the tide to turn in our favour so that we could proceed to the slipway. The town looked inviting from the sea and I contemplated the pleasures that may be awaiting me. Ramsgate has the United Kingdom's only Royal Harbour, that title being bestowed upon it by King George IV during a visit in 1821, as recognition of the kindness of Ramsgate's inhabitants. It served as a major departure point during both the Napoleonic wars and the Dunkirk evacuation and for many years has been a base for cross channel ferries. Ramsgate is well-known for its Ramsgate Main Sands that has attracted tourists since the 19$^{th}$ century when it gained a reputation as one of England's best-known seaside towns.

When the tide was right for us, we steamed into the harbour, heading towards the Clock House where we slowly nudged our way onto the waiting cradle. We were securely roped into position and hauled up onto the slipway. A number of spectators gathered to watch the operation. I was on the foredeck whilst we were being winched into position and noticed two attractive girls taking an interest in me. Before the winching was finished I'd already arranged a date with them for that evening, which impressed my fellow crew members. I knew straight away that I was going to enjoy Ramsgate. The Gondia was winched up to dry land; wooden posts were placed against the hull on each side and secured in position by hammering in wooden wedges. A ladder was placed in position and securely lashed. There wasn't a lot for the crew to do during the refit so they packed their bags and took the train back home to Gravesend until the refit had been finished. I, however, had no reason to leave. I didn't know the town and it beckoned me to come and explore. The slipway was ideally situated at the edge of the town, with pubs and shops directly opposite. My evening with the two girls was fun but that's all it was, one fun-filled evening. I was 17 years old, a young, virile teenager and it wasn't long at all before I'd met a young, pretty brunette called Sally. She was slightly smaller than me and had a well-developed body. She showed me around and shared with me my all too short stay. I had the time of my life.

The crew accommodation on the Gondia was in the fore part of the vessel. A door on each side deck opened into a passageway with the wood panelled Chief Engineer's cabin on the starboard side and the wood panelled Skipper's cabin on the port side. (The Skipper's and Chief Engineer's cabins throughout the fleet were opulent in comparison to the very basic crew's cabins.) The galley was amidships. Opposite the galley, a ladder descended forward into the crew cabin. My bunk was the top forward one on the port side and it was there that Sally and I would lie, enjoying passionate nights together in complete privacy. One night we were startled by banging and raucous shouting outside. Footsteps clunked on the rungs of the ladder, then on the steel deck.

We had invaders. The steel entrance door clanged open and a gang of noisy men spilled into the passageway above. We both shot bolt upright, horrified at what might be happening. Whoever they were, they were not only already aboard but were inside and descending the ladder into the cabin. I have never been the bravest person and the thought of having to defend the lovely Sally filled me with dread. Or had her father discovered our affair and sent in the heavies to deal with me? I quaked at the vision of them all snarling at me as I stood before them, a scrawny, naked teenager attempting to look threatening. I looked directly in the eyes of the first one.

"You dirty, lucky little fucker," said Fred the Fireman when he saw Sally and me in the bunk clutching the blanket around ourselves. The rest of the crew came down one by one. Feeling like a very naughty boy caught misbehaving, I gave them a nervous grin and they immediately erupted into a chorus of ribald comments, albeit in very good humour. Unbeknown to me the crew had decided to return in expectation of the Gondia's refit soon being finalised. The atmosphere became relaxed and light hearted from then on and the poor hapless Sally had little choice but to endure the ribald comments for another hour or so until they'd fallen asleep. The second Fireman, Reg, had the bunk below mine and thankfully he had the decency to pass us our clothes that we'd left on his bunk. With a combined effort, Sally and I, using a little ingenuity and contortion, struggled into our clothes beneath the blanket. It wasn't practical for Sally to make her way home alone so she stayed with me until morning when sadly I had to bid her farewell, as we were due to leave for Gravesend the following day. She was a lovely girl, and we'd had some good times together. We quietly crept out of the cabin and descended the ladder to the quay. We hugged and kissed one more time and then she turned and walked away, turning briefly to wave goodbye. I never saw her again. The American writer Henry Miller said "Sex is one of the nine reasons for reincarnation. The other eight are unimportant." From the deck, the Skipper, Cyril, saw us on the ground below and kept his council but I was later to find just how wary he was of me when I was in the vicinity of females he knew. Sadly, the next day, we rolled down the slipway and set course for Gravesend. From that moment on my reputation as a good cook faded into the distance of time and was replaced for the duration of my final years on the Thames steam tugs as a smooth operating lothario.

*Silly buggers*

My next temporary posting as Third Hand was on the steam tug Water Cock. The Water Cock was originally part of the Gamecock fleet. She was built in 1923 so was even older than the Gondia, slightly smaller, and equally relied on coal to power her boilers. She was also scrapped in 1966. I didn't spend long aboard this vessel but long enough to get to know and befriend John, one of the two Firemen aboard. We socialised and sometimes holidayed together. We were two young men, who did crazy things. We had many laughs on our escapades ashore but what happened on board one evening could have had serious consequences. We were moored on the buoy in the Gravesend Reach awaiting the arrival of a ship that we were to accompany to the London docks and tow into position. Part of my duties as Third Hand was to act as lookout and signal to the Skipper when the ship was in sight. This allowed the Deckhand and Skipper to rest before they accompanied the ship on the upriver run whilst the Mate and I slept.

It was a flood tide so we were bows on to the wide stretch of river from which the ship would approach. I was standing around shivering, wandering up to the foredeck from time to time to see if I could see the approaching lights. John was on his four-hour shift. To keep warm, we decided to hide away in the fore part of the vessel that was reserved normally for the Skipper and Chief Engineer. There were two entrances, one on the port side and one on the starboard side, with a central ladder leading down to the cabins below. There were no lights because we didn't want to spoil my night vision. We started blabbering away about mindless things, chuckling like a couple of silly little children and feeling mischievous. John disappeared to the crew cabin aft and came back with a large, grotesque rubber glove covered in hairs and warts and made up to resemble something out of a horror movie. If you were alone on a dark, tranquil night and you found that unexpectedly clamping down on your shoulder you could well be in need of a clean pair of pants afterwards. When we heard the Skipper coming up from his cabin below, we nipped out to the starboard side deck. The Skipper leant out of the port side to see if there was any sign of the ship approaching, obviously getting a bit agitated as the arrival time drew near. Seeing no sign of the ship, he turned to quietly disappear back down to his cabin.

Our focus on the hand and things supernatural must have opened up a channel invoking an impish demon to possess John because as the Skipper put his foot on the first step, John crept up behind him on tiptoes and clamped the repulsive looking glove on the Skipper's shoulder. In the security of his personal area, the unsuspecting Skipper stopped dead in his tracks, turned and saw the monstrous hand gripping him. He squealed and leapt sideways in horror banging into the support at the side of the steps. A little whimper was audible as his legs momentarily buckled under him from fright and he grasped the handrail to arrest his flight to the bottom of the steps. When he'd recovered from the shock and his face returned to its normal shade of pink, he composed himself remarkably rapidly and looked at John towering over him, his arm outstretched, wiggling the rubber glove with a triumphant grin on his face. I was expecting a vitriolic outburst with the threat of instant dismissal but the Skipper was surprisingly forgiving, no doubt a wee bit embarrassed. The only reaction was a feeble,

"Oh, you frightened me," then he descended to his cabin.

John came back out on deck and we both sidled off tittering childishly. He was the classic, tall, dark, handsome man who girls found hard to resist and he was great fun to be around. I can say, immodestly, that I was considered a good looking young man myself so got along well with the opposite sex. With other friends, we decided one time to take a holiday at Butlins Holiday Camp which, in the early 60s, bore no resemblance to today's Butlins. John had dated one of the Bluecoats almost before we'd finished unpacking. In fact, we all did rather well with the opposite sex that week. One of our friends convinced a waitress to move in with him. When we called by to check out what had been going on, we noticed that she'd left some clothes on the bed in her absence. As the conversation progressed, we began the inevitable chuckling and managed to coerce our friend to dress up in the female attire. The end result was a complete transformation. We encouraged him to parade around in an effeminate manner and as he reached the door, one of us quickly opened it and the rest of us shoved him outside, then slammed and locked the door. It was bad enough that he was standing around in a woman's clothes in full view of everybody but it didn't help his situation when he began banging on the door, shouting and pleading to be let in. That was a foolish thing to have done because it only attracted the attention of everybody who happened to be in their chalets. Well, I call them chalets but in reality, they more resembled prison cells. There were two rows of them, one on either side of the central recreational area and two tiers high. The resulting shouts, jeers and wolf-whistles only brought even more campers to the area to find out what the fuss was about. He had no other choice at that stage but to accept the adulation and put on a show for the enthusiastic observers. I don't know if he ever forgave us.

................

One time when we were moored up at the Royal Terrace Pier, we were the outside tug; the innermost tug was the Contest, with the Gondia between us. The Gondia had received orders over the VHF set to steam to Tilbury docks on the opposite side of the river to Gravesend. I heard her telegraph ring alerting the Engineer to stand by, followed by the answering ring from the engine room. Our Skipper went to the bridge and rang our telegraph for standby so that we could cast off allowing the Gondia to leave. I went to the foredeck to flick our rope off the Gondia's mooring post.

"Let go aft," the Gondia's Skipper, Cyril, ordered the Deckhand, then

"Let go Fo'rad," to the Third Hand. He leant over from the bridge to verify that we had cast off from him and saw me on the Water Cock's foredeck.

"Hello, you dirty little bugger," he said good-naturedly, remembering our time in Ramsgate.

"Hello Skip," I replied, smiling.

As he turned back to take the steering wheel and ring for slow ahead I happened to mention that I'd seen his daughter in town the week previously.

"Oh, I met your daughter last week," I said.

"Hold that rope, don't let go," he yelled to his foredeck hand. "DON'T LET THAT FUCKING ROPE GO!" he repeated even louder than before. He shot back to the side of the bridge and glared down at me.

"What did you say?" he demanded.

"I met your daughter in town last week," I said.

"Where, when, what did you say to her?"

"Nothing really, I just chatted with her for a while, that's all," I said.

"Are you sure?"

"Yes, I just spent a few minutes chatting with her, then she carried on down the street," I told him.

"Well, that's all right then and you make sure you stay away from her. I don't want you anywhere near her you dirty little sod."

By that time a few crew members from both tugs had wandered up to see what the holdup was and when they heard the conversation they looked at me with knowing smiles on their faces. Cyril, reassured that I hadn't tried to bed his delightful daughter, relaxed and smiled at me again before giving the orders to finally cast off.

# CHAPTER 4
# THE WAY IT WAS

*Carry on regardless*

After a few months, the time came for me to be transferred to another tug on a permanent basis and I was ordered to join the Atlantic Cock. Some of my most memorable times were aboard this vessel and the next tug that I would join, the Moorcock. Once again, more aged than the Cervia but rather more recent than the previous two vessels, the Atlantic Cock was built in 1932 and continued to operate until she was scrapped in 1970. She was also coal fired. As much as I loved the deck work, there were many times during the cold, sleepless days and nights when I envied the cook, snuggled up in a warm bunk or preparing meals in a nice warm galley. I often envied the engine room crew too as they had a shift of four hours on duty, then four hours off, whereas us Deckhands had to grab time off and sleep as and when we could, day or night. At that stage in my career, I could have chosen to either continue with deck work or join the engine room personnel as a Fireman. The advantages of the latter were the aforementioned four hours on duty and an assured four hours rest before going back down into the stokehold. The wages were also higher but neither of those perquisites, as appealing as they were, were enough to make me want to head in that direction. Deck work in the open air was always what had attracted me despite being forever tired due to the long hours and lack of sleep.

I had been a small, weedy teenager when I'd started on the tugs but as Third Hand, I started to develop muscles that I never knew I had and with that came an accompanying increase of strength and toughness. The outdoor life suited me well and has done ever since. My principle duties as Third Hand were on the foredeck operating the steam driven windlass and anchor. It was a very physical job, throwing and hauling hawsers, mooring ropes and heaving lines, especially when they were heavy with water, which they often were, either from the rain or because we'd failed to lasso a mooring post and the rope had fallen in the river. We had to then smash them on the decks to try and get rid of the excess water. One night, I threw a mooring rope and felt a sudden, sharp pain in my back. I froze solid, unable to move. I'd missed the mooring post and the rope had fallen in the water.

"Hurry up and get the rope out and take a turn" yelled Roy from the bridge. He needed me to make fast to control the bow so that he could manoeuvre the tug alongside. It's the stern of a vessel that moves, the bow has to be held fast with anchors or ropes to prevent it from swinging around. I don't know how I managed it because I was in pain but I quickly hauled the soggy, heavy rope in and threw it again. The eye fell neatly onto the other tugs mooring post, I quickly made it fast and Roy completed the manoeuvre. Safely moored, I walked with difficulty to the aft cabin, climbed into my bunk and tried to rest. I knew there would be no point in complaining. The rest of that night was agonising. Getting in and out of my bunk each time I was called was difficult and painful but when I threw and hauled in ropes it was infinitely worse. When morning came, mercifully, we were told that a relief crew would be boarding and we could go home until six o'clock the following morning. Later that day I went to see a doctor and when he asked me to bend forward to test my mobility, I found that I couldn't move at all. It took six weeks for it to heal and I've been troubled with it ever since, but fortunately not too often. If only osteopaths or chiropractors had been around in those days, I could have been back at work in no time. The only treatment the doctor was capable of offering me was rest and painkillers, in other words, not very much and nothing seems to have changed today.

When we were navigating up and down the river on the open bridge, the only protection we had to shield us from whatever the weather threw at us was a small canvas dodger. I can't say that it achieved very much. We worked day and night, mostly with very little sleep. It was considered a real bonus If we managed to get four hours sleep during a night. During daylight hours when we weren't towing, we were required to maintain the vessels, chipping, painting and polishing etc. and ropes needed splicing, so we often had very little spare time to ourselves. There were plenty of brass fittings that had to be highly polished once a week. The steam whistle at the top of the funnel, the bell, the portholes, the paraffin lamps, the binnacle and the voice pipe were all brass. Electricity was supplied by a generator but some cabin lamps and navigation lights worked on paraffin as an emergency backup. They had to be kept full, the glasses cleaned and the wicks trimmed regularly so that they worked well when needed. Each crew member had his own set of chores but when it came to bunkering, a filthy job, most of them joined in. When the coal bunker needed replenishing, we'd tie up alongside the coal barge, Artemis, moored in Gravesend Reach, make sure all the hatches, portholes and doors were closed to keep out the coal dust and remove the wooden hatches from the top of the coal bunker amidships. The crane would pick up and empty tonnes of filthy coal into the bunkers sending coal dust all over the place, which had to be washed away afterwards from every part of the vessel. It could be fun though and like most activities there was always plenty of joking and larking around.

## *The pendulous Skipper*

The Thames was considered difficult for navigation so pilots were compulsory. Part of our duties from time to time, when the pilot cutters were unavailable, was to collect the pilot from the Royal Terrace Pier and take him to the ship that was making its way up or down river. Once he was on board, we'd steam out to the ship and go alongside, matching our speed to that of the ship. The pilot could then grab hold of the Jacob's ladder and make his way up to the decks and onto the bridge. One day, as the pilot was clawing his way up the rope ladder, Tony, the Fireman on duty, for some inexplicable reason known only to himself, decided to throw a bucket of paraffin into the furnace. The Mate, the Deckhand and I were standing on the aft deck chatting when we heard a powerful booming whoosh accompanied by a scream at the same time as we were hit by a blast of hot air. We spun round in the direction of the whoosh in time to see a gigantic column of flames exploding out of the funnel. The pilot, halfway up the ladder, had let out the terrified shriek. He was spinning around clutching onto the ladder for all he was worth as the flames roared from the funnel and shot up in the air past his back. When the searing heat scorched his back, he instinctively spun around on the ladder to turn his back away from the flames. That just exposed his front to the heat so he tried to spin back again. We were gobsmacked, wondering what on earth could have happened as the pilot hung there scared witless with his eyes popping out of his head in terror. When the Skipper questioned the Fireman afterwards, he explained it away by saying that there was a compacted mass of coal dust in the furnace, which he broke up with his rake releasing the pent up gases that ignited and burst into flame. His doubtful explanation seemed to appease everybody, although whether anybody actually believed him is another matter. He later confided in us Deckhands about the paraffin, although he didn't tell us why he did it and we never found out how the pilot fared after his surprise roasting. He must have arrived on the ship's bridge blistered and in a state of shock.

With the pilot installed, we would accompany the ship to Tilbury or London Docks then steam up to the bows where a heaving line had to be thrown up to waiting seamen so that they could attach it to the towing hawser. Tossing the line wasn't always my finest accomplishment. I had the strength and determination but not always the ability and it would sometimes go wildly off course. I could see where it needed to go and the waiting seamen were eager to catch it. I would gather up enough coils of rope in my throwing hand, give a few very impressive swings back and forth to get a good rhythm and momentum, then let it fly upwards to the ship's bow or stern as the case may be, with as much strength as I could muster. The waiting seamen would have no chance of catching it. I'd heave the line and it would take on a life of its own snaking its way towards any unsuspecting sailor who happened to be anywhere other than the target area. There was every likelihood that he could be rendered unconscious by the Turks head that had been weighted with a piece of metal to give the line momentum. On the occasions when my line did land at the spot I'd aimed for I was elated at my accomplishment, discounting the fact that that was exactly what was supposed to happen every time. I would often delay reaching for the line in the hope that the Deckhand, Arthur, would get there first, which he almost always did and would send the line expertly to its intended target with a dexterity that I greatly admired. Over a period of time I became expert myself out of necessity.

With the heaving line tied to the hawser, the Skipper would increase speed to clear the bows of the ship as the tow rope was lowered to us. As the distance between us and the ship increased we'd haul like crazy to try to prevent the hawser from becoming submerged and made even heavier. The speed of the vessels through the water and the strong tide, which could be as much as 8 knots, would add to the weight. As many hands as possible would be needed, the Mate, Deckhands, Firemen and even sometimes, the Cook, to haul the tow rope aboard and manhandle it over the engine room casing to the towing hook. It would then be placed on the hook and a clamp pulled down to hold the rope in place, which was then locked in position with a pin.

"On the hook," Roy, the Mate, would call out to the Skipper on the bridge to let him know that he could increase speed.

The telegraph would ring and the engineer would open up the wheel to increase speed gently until the slack had been taken up on the tow rope.

"Coming up," Roy would cry out, as the towrope cleared the water, followed by "All tight."

That was the signal for the Skipper to ring down to the engine room once more to increase speed and keep the rope tight to start the towing operation.

When the ship entered the lock, the tugs on her stern would slacken the tow rope temporarily, allowing the deck crew to loop a stop rope over it, pulling it down and making it fast to the bits on the aft deck. This kept the main purchase on the towrope well aft so that as the ship's propellers thrashed when she moved ahead, the tug wouldn't be pulled over as had happened to the Cervia. Whenever the tow rope or stop rope were released all hands had to stand well clear to avoid getting hit or caught in any coils, the consequences of which could be dire. The grey haired office agent, Jack, who told me to be back at six with my gear, was a victim himself, which is how he came to be seated behind a desk and not on the deck of a tug. He was serving on the Gondia and made the drastic mistake of getting his foot caught in a bight of the stop rope as it flew through the bits, taking his leg with it and severing it below the knee. His father was one of those who perished when the Cervia was girted and his grandson later fell overboard and drowned in the King George V dock. You may wonder why I was so enamoured with such a dangerous lifestyle, but looking back on it 60 years later I would still do it all again. I have never since worked with such a tough, loyal, generous and fun loving bunch of men.

Deck crew stayed on watch during the towing operation which could last for hours, and the River Thames could be bitterly cold in winter, especially at night. During the big freeze of 1963, the river froze in places and the ice made it difficult getting alongside the ships. Dressed in thick sweaters, duffel coats, pilot boots and anything else we thought might keep us warm, we blew into our hands and stamped our feet to keep the circulation going and comforted ourselves by drinking endless pint mugs of hot tea sweetened with Fussell's condensed milk. It was always a relief to be able to go into the warm galley to make a brew. The Skipper didn't have that luxury because he was committed to staying on the bridge whilst towing, relieved only occasionally by the Mate and he had to rely on one of us taking a piping hot tea to him when he called down for one.

The Skipper was the only crew member supplied with a uniform and peaked cap. He would also have the benefit of a thick warm overcoat, which was very smart with a little half belt at the back. When towing, the Skipper had to turn and face aft sometimes to keep his eye on the towrope, reaching behind him to spin the small steering wheel. There were two steering wheels, a large one for sea voyages and a smaller, steam driven one attached to it for towing purposes. The Atlantic Cock's Skipper, Fred, was rather vertically challenged so stood on tip toes a lot of the time to get a clear view aft. Sometimes he even had to jump up in the air to see what was happening and assess the situation in a split second before landing back down. The Mate, Roy, Deckhand Arthur and I were standing by on the aft deck when we heard howls for help coming from the bridge. The cries were getting hysterical.

"Roy, Roy, Roy," he wailed in panic.

Roy charged up to the bridge and found the Skipper suspended in mid-air, swinging from side to side trying to free himself from the small steering wheel that he'd become attached to. He'd jumped so high that on the way back down, the belt at the back of his overcoat had hooked onto the uppermost spoke of the steering wheel, abruptly breaking his descent. He hung above the flybridge deck gyrating as he frantically tried to unhook himself. The pilot was blowing his whistle giving instructions to the tugs, and our Skipper, firmly hooked to the steering wheel, with his little arms and legs making useless movements at his sides, was unable to carry out the commands. The Mate took hold of him and lifted the little fellow off, placing him back in front of the wheel where he could carry on with his duties. Very shortly after that little fiasco, which was entirely unrelated, Fred was posted to another tug. Another Skipper, also named Fred, was ordered to join us as his replacement. The two of them couldn't have been more different. Little Fred who left us was a fun loving character who mixed with the rest of us at every opportunity. Our new replacement had the most fearsome reputation of the entire fleet and when the radio crackled and we heard that he would be joining us, nobody was happy, and we spoke of hardly anything else that day.

The towing hook was sited amidships, aft of the main casing and over the coal bunker. The upper section consisted of a hinged clamp with an eye that dropped onto the hook, which was held in an upright position by a locking pin. To release the towrope, the locking pin was removed and the vertical spindle on the clamp would be struck with a mighty blow from a sledgehammer. This released the clamp enabling the hook to drop down and the towrope to disengage and disappear over the stern in a flash. Everybody needed to be well clear of the rope when this happened to avoid being whipped overboard. The towrope had to be freed very quickly to avoid the tug being girted and sunk when the ship increased speed. Sometimes there would be so much weight on the taught towrope that it took more than a few hefty swings of the sledgehammer, called the knockaway, to free it, with the Skipper screaming “Let go,” “LET GO!”

If during towing, the situation looked so dangerous that the tow rope needed to be released quickly, the Skipper or Mate would order the senior Deckhand to stand by ready to strike the hook with the knockaway to prevent the tug being girted. It wasn’t an order that the Deckhand welcomed and it would be with considerable trepidation that he jumped up beside the hook with the sledgehammer at the ready. With the tug heeled over and the tow rope bar tight, it could be difficult, if not impossible to release it with the knockaway, so an axe was kept nearby for such an emergency and such an emergency happened once on the Ocean Cock. The ship she was towing was steaming ahead and the Skipper called to the Deckhand to let go the tow rope. There was so much weight on the hook that it couldn’t be released with blows from the knockaway. The order was given to cut through the towrope. The Ocean Cock was being pulled over by the ship. The Deckhand, Bill, took the axe and struck the towrope. It didn’t part. The Ocean Cock was heeled way over, almost onto her beam ends, with water gushing through the fiddley doors flooding the engine room and boiler room. The cook at the time was Mike Houckham, who is now responsible for restoring the aged Cervia to her former glory at Ramsgate. He was just fifteen years old and was trapped in the galley with water up to his chest. Bill slashed away at the tow rope as if possessed. Eventually the yarns started splitting and finally parted. The tug shot back to the upright position. It was singularly nerve wracking for the Skipper, Billy, my cousin, who'd already survived the girting of the Cervia. He had to be treated for shock afterwards. The water from the flooded engine room, boiler room and fore and aft sections was pumped out after it had found its way into the bilges. Danger was always present and in one particularly disastrous year, three tug hands were lost on three separate occasions. "You gentlemen of England, who live at home at ease, how little do you think on the dangers of the seas." - "The Valiant Sailors" – Martin Parker.

### *Rum and Grapefruit*

On a lighter note, there were occasions when we could profit from unexpected perks during our trips up and down the river. It once became known among the tug hands that moored to a buoy, was a barge loaded with barrels of rum, and that one of the barrels had been opened. It's intriguing how rapidly news of that nature becomes common knowledge. We felt it our duty as honourable citizens to stop off alongside said barge just to verify the facts. It was true, the barrel was open. Our next duty was to verify that it did, in fact, contain rum. We syphoned off some of the contents and tasted it and it was indeed rum. We decided that others may be tempted to over indulge and become inebriated if so much rum was available, so, being caring people we decided to remove some of the contents and therefore the temptation. It was comforting to learn that every other tug crew who called by carried out the same charitable act and that between us, over a short period of time, we'd removed temptation from the weak willed. The barrel was empty and the contents were safely stored at our homes where it somehow seemed to evaporate over time.

On another occasion, we were moored alongside a jetty at night and went off to check that the cargo that had been offloaded from the ship hadn't been tampered with. We came across opened crates of grapefruits and decided that they would probably attract vermin if they were left there and there were all sorts of other reasons why they should be removed. So again, being caring citizens, we set about the responsible task of lessening the attraction to the vermin. We couldn't hold many in our hands; the haul would be limited, so we stuffed our trousers into our socks and sea boots, undid our belts and filled our trouser legs up with the fruit. That was a good idea that enabled us to carry as many as possible but not such a good idea when we tried walking back to the waiting tug. As we set off, one of our number, the Deckhand, Arthur, stepped out a little too eagerly and the weight of the grapefruits lifted his trouser bottoms out of his sea boots. The grapefruits rolled in all directions and he scrambled around trying to recover them and at the same time keep the others in his trouser legs. We realised that more caution was required. It was a painfully slow progress as we made our way back to the tug, walking with stiff legged movements like robots, trying to keep the fruit in place. We looked utterly ridiculous moving along in slow motion, with our trouser legs bulging out and wobbling.

The goods we bought from the foreign and British seamen when we went alongside a ship were varied and cheap. We'd be offered or would ask for all manner of things, clothing, fishing equipment, crockery, alcohol and cigarettes, all at duty-free prices. Almost every tugman smoked. We were always so tired it was something to do to help keep us awake when we worked through the nights. The cigarettes would be sold to us in packs of two hundred, which encouraged us to smoke more than usual. Because of the tearaways I'd mixed with when I was at school, I'd started smoking at an early age and by the time I'd reached nineteen was smoking twenty Senior Service a day. It wasn't until my increasing coughing spells, the disgusting smell of the smoke on my clothes and the phlegm in the mornings that I realised the utter stupidity of swallowing mouthfuls of smoke, so I stopped, never to smoke again.

### *Some like it hot*

As a teenager I was already earning considerably more than most mature, married men with shore based jobs. It's true that our take home pay packets were well padded but we worked long, hard hours to earn them and it definitely wasn't a job for the weak and fearful. To put it into perspective, a 40 hour week was the accepted standard for an average shore based job, and we tugmen could be working an average of around 140 hours a week and much of that with very little sleep so we were constantly tired. Despite my poor relationship with Mum and Dad in those days, I did what I could for them out of the money I earned on the tugs. I paid for and redecorated the entire house for them, installing new carpets or anything else that I thought was needed and would please them. I was blessed to be able to buy, what for them, were luxury items that they could never have afforded themselves. I surprised Mum one day by having a refrigerator, a washing machine and a Flatley dryer delivered. We'd never had any of these in our council house until then. Mum had done the washing in the kitchen sink using a corrugated washboard and a large bar of soap. Once a week the copper boiler would be heated up and the bed linen etc. boiled. To remove the excess water after being rinsed, the washing was taken into the back yard and passed through a mangle before being hung out to dry. She was so happy and seeing her happy made me happy. As a family, before I became a tugman, we were far from well off, as Father hadn't worked for most of my life and I only knew him as an aged, disabled, unemployed and rather unhappy person who'd experienced a life of terrible suffering. I hadn't realised just how tough he must have been in his prime until I decided to go down into the bowels of the tug and try my hand at stoking the furnaces myself.

One of our Firemen, Norman, went on holiday for two weeks, so I volunteered to take over his duties as the pay was higher than for deck crew and I fancied a trial run at something I'd never attempted before. A replacement Third Hand came aboard to fill in for me.

A Fireman's task didn't look too difficult when watching the experienced hands shovelling coal into the furnaces but I soon learned why they were allowed to rest for four hours after having sweated away for the preceding four. I'd ventured into the boiler room on many occasions but to find myself alone in front of the three roaring furnaces, all hungry for coal to keep the boiler producing steam, was an altogether different state of affairs. Air was needed to feed the fire and to allow ventilation for the heat to escape, so at deck level, a framework housed an iron grating that extended across the width between the side decks to a door on either side that was kept open, this area was known as the fiddley. The Firemen were tough men but the deck work had hardened me into a tough little teenager too, so when I first heard the orders issued over our radio for us to get under way for a towing operation, I felt confident. Alone in the stifling hot boiler room, I stood before the furnaces with the shovel at the ready. The telegraph rang, the engine thumped into life and I was then responsible for supplying the steam to power us along. I scooped the shovel into the pile of coal that had tumbled out of the coal bunker and swung around to throw it into the first furnace. The shovel clanged as it hit the framework and spilt the contents onto the floor, sending shock waves along the length of my arms. Turning back to the coal bunker, I quickly shovelled some more and clang went the shovel again and the coal spilt onto the floor adding to what was already there. I started to get concerned then; I hadn't been very successful at feeding one hungry furnace and there were two more waiting. The pile of coal on the floor grew larger as I continued shovelling frantically, striking the side of the furnace and spilling more coal. I was convinced that the shovel was too large to fit into the mouth of the furnace. It was a special skill to be able to twist the shovel whilst throwing the coal the length of the furnace but I mastered it as time went on. In addition to shovelling the coal into the furnaces non-stop, I had to gather up the spillage at the foot of the first furnace because it was hindering me. It was all very discouraging to begin with because it was looking increasingly unlikely that I would ever be able to get enough fuel into the furnaces to supply sufficient heat to produce the steam required. Even when I did master it and the coal landed at the back of the furnace, it disappeared in a puff and more was instantly needed - and that was just one furnace. Keeping all three going at once was hot, back-breaking work. When the tug was running at full speed, the furnaces were hungrier than ever and there hardly seemed time to stop for a second. I found myself shovelling away at breakneck speed, with perspiration oozing from every pore of my body just to keep them going. What a relief it was when we finally stopped and moored up.

The fires needed to be cleaned out regularly. For this a long handled metal rake was used to pile the fire to one side of the furnace and then with an equally long handled slice, the clinker was removed. When that was done, the fire was moved to the other side and the clinker removed. I kept this up for the two week period and became a proficient Fireman but at the end of it was glad to be back on deck. In reality, I was lucky to have lasted for so long because one night, moored alongside the pier at Woolwich, I was so tired that I went back to sleep after I had been woken to start my shift. The radio burst into life and we received orders to cast off and head to one of the docks. The crew were roused and started to prepare. I rushed down to the engine room to get the furnaces fired up and was horrified to see that the fires had gone out. We therefore had no steam and no power to move. My heart sank. I was so worried, I grabbed hold of some paraffin soaked cotton waste, threw it into the furnaces, set fire to it, piled some coal on top and blew and blew in desperation, frantically trying to get the fires going. It was never going to happen; it takes 24 hours to build up the steam. In truth, I don't understand why I wasn't sacked there and then. I felt for the Skipper who had to report to the office that we respectfully chose to decline the offer of towing the ship. I was embarrassed and ashamed to face the rest of the crew. I felt like squatting down in the corner of the stokehold where nobody could see me and hiding away forever. There was a consolation, however, in that we had an enforced day of rest.

It was not just the arduous work of a Fireman that caused me to oversleep; the situation was compounded by my nocturnal activities when I was ashore. I was hardly ever home, so partied and clubbed into the early hours. I played hard and it took its toll. "Do not feel embarrassed by your failures, learn from them and start again," said Richard Branson, but I'd decided that I would never again attempt to be a Fireman and I wonder now if this had ever happened to any other Firemen in the past.

................

The first known use of steam to provide motion goes back to the $1^{st}$ century AD. However, the first commercially successful steam engine was used in 1712, to pump water from mines and it wasn't until 1802 that it was adapted for maritime use. The world's first viable steamboat was built in 1807. As technology developed, steamboats were used successfully on canals, rivers and for short coastal passages with the first Atlantic crossing taking place in 1819. Later that century, in 1850, the first iron hulled ships were seen, which over time replaced the wooden hulls and screw propellers began to replace the paddles. From 1870 onwards, the much stronger steel hulls replaced iron. As the ships became larger they required more efficient and complex engines, hence the development of the compound engine. The original steam engines used the steam once before recycling it back to the boiler; compound engines recycled the steam into larger, lower pressure cylinders before returning it to the boiler, thereby gaining more energy and enabling ships to be faster and more economical. The steam tugs were fitted with triple expansion engines, which were compound engines that expanded the steam in three stages through a Scotch boiler fitted with three furnaces. Scotch marine boilers were used in steam ships internationally. They were short, large diameter boilers with furnaces beneath and the larger and faster the ship, the more boilers were fitted. The Titanic had a total of 29 boilers, each with three furnaces.

# CHAPTER 5
# ON STANDBY

*The first door*

The knockaway was sometimes used maliciously by certain crew members for perverse entertainment. The toilet compartment on the Atlantic Cock was the first door on the port side deck immediately forward of the coal bunker and just a few feet from the towing hook. Once in there, you were confined in a steel enclosure with very little space and in a constant state of agitation. If you were seen sneaking in there for a "tomtit," you could expect at any moment to have every cell of your body reverberating from the holy terror of having the sledgehammer smashed down onto the steel roof. When this happened, the tremendous shock caused your whole body to shake, rattle and roll. The crash of the sledgehammer smashing down on the steel roof was magnified in the empty toilet compartment. Even the metal plates from which it was constructed vibrated. You would stumble out trying to maintain your balance, quivering all over as if your whole body had been turned to jelly. Your ears would be ringing, head spinning and teeth chattering. If anybody had difficulty passing a motion when they entered it was a sure way to loosen everything up. We had to devise ways to divert attention and one cunning ruse was to nonchalantly stroll along the opposite deck on the starboard side under the pretence of going to the galley for a mug of tea, avoiding eye contact with whoever was standing near the knockaway. A few clanging sounds were made in the galley in the hope of deceiving anybody who was eyeing up a victim then you would sneak out and head to the fiddly door leading into the stokehold. Nipping in quickly, you could then dash across to the port side and slide along to the toilet door, quietly open it and creep in. Feeling triumphant to have made it undetected thus far, trousers could be safely dropped and the required position assumed. Mostly this worked but if you gazed up at the porthole and saw a malevolent, grinning face eyeing up its prey, that's when you braced yourself, gritted your teeth and waited for the inevitable bone-rattling crash. Mercifully, this antic came to end after an overzealous crash with the hammer one day shattered the deckhead light in the toilet, showering the occupant in shreds of broken glass.

There was no such luxury as a flushing loo. Flushing was done by using a draw bucket. This was a galvanised bucket attached to a length of rope. The procedure was to hold the bucket in one hand and in the other, coil the rope so that there would be enough length to throw the bucket over the side into the river. The bucket would be thrown in upside down, whilst holding onto the rope with the other hand. As the bucket hit the water, an upward flick of the rope would tilt the bucket, filling it with water. It could then be quickly hauled back up and tipped into the toilet. That was easy enough even with a strong tide running but when the tug was steaming through the water at twelve knots, things got a bit more complicated. Then, you would have to calculate carefully, throw the bucket well forward of where you were standing to allow for the forward motion of the vessel, hoping that the bucket would be full and in the upright position, ready to be hauled up as rapidly as possible at the precise moment it was immediately below you. If you failed, your arms were suddenly jerked almost out of their sockets by the jolt as you took off and were dragged, skipping and hopping along the deck towards the stern, all the time trying to pull the bucket back up. All in all, going to the toilet could be both frightening and exhausting.

Peeing, (Jimmy Riddles) was always done over the side at the stern and downwind. One day, as we were steaming up river towards the London docks, I was in the galley making a mug of tea when nature called. I went out on deck and too idle to go aft, thought I'd pee over the side as there wasn't much wind and nobody around. The contents of my bladder was instantly whisked around behind me, missing me by millimetres.

"You fucking filthy, disgusting little bastard," screamed Tony the Fireman, who had decided to come up for a breath of fresh air and had popped his head out of the engine room entrance hatch. He had turned to look at me at the precise moment that the wind caught the steaming stream of urine, whipped it aft in a warm spray hitting him square in the face. I turned to see him frenziedly rubbing his hands over his face. His glared at me first in disgust then anger as he exploded into a torrent of unrepeatable profanities. Once he'd exhausted his vocabulary of expletives he screamed them at me for a second time before he disappeared back down the hatch. It took some time before he forgave me and I always pee'd over the stern after that.

### *Passing the time*

The Skipper and Deckhand navigated the upriver runs as I've said before, whilst the Mate and I slept, despite the rumbling of the propeller shaft rotating directly beneath the cabin floor and the clanging of heavy chains that ran along the scuppers to the quadrant that turned the rudder. When Roy, the Mate and I did the downriver runs we had plenty of opportunities to chat, exchange ideas and get to know each other better and I like to think that we became friends despite the age difference. He taught me a lot. He was built like a bear but was a kind, considerate, gentle and a very forgiving man who was very aware of other people's feelings and would be deeply upset if ever he thought he'd embarrassed or hurt anybody in any way. He was also very much a team player as indeed we were all obliged to be. He'd not only join in with the rest of us in our onboard leisure activities but equally our socialising events ashore. He'd spent several years at sea in merchant vessels and had so many interesting tales to tell. Throughout my six plus years on the tugs, he is one of the people I most remember because of his gentleness, kindness and intelligence, yet he was as tough as they come. The down river runs were enjoyable but it was miserable cowering behind the dodger in bad weather. However, it was as it was and we just got on with it. Worse was the fog. The Thames in those days had a huge volume of shipping and with visibility down to virtually zero and ships blowing their horns alerting other vessels of their whereabouts, it was unnerving watching all the blips on the radar as we steered our way past them.

When the towing had finished, if we didn't have another assignment, we would either tie up at Woolwich pier or more frequently return to Gravesend where we had three mooring buoys. When we reached the buoy, if nobody was already moored to it, the Mate would steer alongside and I would jump on it, quickly thread the mooring rope or steel cable, depending on how long we would be staying, through the eye and get back aboard as quickly as possible to make the rope fast to the tug's mooring bits on the foredeck. If there were several other tugs already moored to the buoy, as the Mate steered towards the outer one, I'd throw a rope to lasso its mooring post then make it fast to our own mooring post. This helped the Mate manoeuvre to a position alongside it. The most difficult and scary part followed, for which I relied on the Deckhand for help. Once moored alongside the outermost tug, I'd clamber across them all until I was on the one that was the closest to the buoy. The next stage could be tricky, especially in adverse conditions, wearing thick winter clothes. I'd climb over the bow, and hold onto the stem whilst balancing myself on the large rope bow fender. The next undertaking required an athletic manoeuvre. I had to drop onto the mooring cable leading from the bow down to the buoy and balance in a horizontal position across the cable at a 90° angle, with it passing under my stomach. Face down, with my hands gripping the cable tightly on each side of me, I'd work my way down the taught wire, swaying one way then the other to reach the buoy, and holding on for dear life. The more I slid down the cable towards the buoy and the closer I got to the river, I'd straighten myself out as much as possible to keep my feet out of the water. Once on the bobbing, wet, slippery buoy, I'd sit down and make myself as safe as possible by planting my feet on the other mooring lines. The Deckhand would throw me a heaving line attached to our steel mooring cable and shackle. I'd haul these to the buoy and with the shackle, fasten the cable to the buoy. To do this, I had to lean forward at a frightening angle because the mooring ring on the buoy would be almost at water level with the weight of several tugs pulling on it in the strong tide. Once the shackle was firmly fastened, I had to go through a reverse performance to get back aboard my own vessel. This mooring procedure was to be prohibited in later years due to Deckhands falling in and drowning, but I found the danger exhilarating.

If there was no more towing for a few hours and if it was cold, the coal burning stove in the cabin would be rattled into life and the cabin hatch closed. If there was to be a prolonged period of inactivity at night, the dynamo generator would be shut down to prevent it using steam. In the boiler room, the coals would be drawn to the front of the furnaces to stop heat getting to the boiler, furnace flaps were put on to stem the air flow and the funnel damper would be closed. The paraffin lamps were lit and the stove stoked up to the limit. Those of us who chose not to sleep would gather around the wooden table and enjoy hours of joking and laughing, smoking, playing cards, chess, doing crosswords, reading or whatever each person preferred in the warm ambience of the smoke-filled cabin. Some of us would spread a blanket on the table and set up a card school. I learned and enjoyed playing a variety of games, poker, brag, shoot, solo, rummy and a host of others. The stakes could be high and more often than not I managed to supplement my wages with the winnings. Whilst I was briefly acting as Third Hand before joining the Atlantic Cock, a mature Cook, Bill, joined temporarily. As a teenager, he'd served a short spell in prison as punishment for stealing cigarettes. His only request whilst serving time had been a pack of playing cards. I thoroughly enjoyed his company. He was a card fanatic and exceedingly competent when playing or performing card tricks. He had me hooked in no time. I enjoyed it so much that I would take books out of the library to learn as much as possible and spent a lot of time practising, learning how to cheat and deal from the bottom and the middle of the pack and do card tricks. This I would do only for my own amusement and to entertain others, it never occurred to me for a moment that I would ever actually cheat. In fact, I didn't need to because I usually did well enough, especially at poker.

As well as perfecting my card playing, fancy dealing techniques and a host of card tricks, I became enamoured with chess. Roy was a keen and accomplished chess player so the two of us would spend many hours engrossed in games which would sometimes take place over a period of days. I found this to be a very enjoyable way to spend some of my free time. Another interest I had was in making bell ropes. It was Roy who taught me how to play chess and initially taught me how to make the bell ropes. As my interest and ability in the latter increased so did my desire to try more elaborate and complicated designs. I found an excellent book in the local library and became fairly accomplished at producing wonderfully decorative ones. It was a satisfying way to pass away free moments in the limited space of the cabin and is a pastime that had obviously originated from sailors spending lonely hours in tiny spaces during long sea voyages. Rope work is a natural and essential activity for sailors. Every Deckhand would be efficient at long splicing, back splicing, eye splicing, weaving Turk's heads and I took it a stage further. My skills in making bell ropes introduced me to some cleverly designed knots, such as pineapple knots, diamond knots, eight strand square sinnets and so on. Traditionally, bell ropes would always be painted to protect them from the ravages of the weather and mine were no different. All of the finished articles I ended up giving away as presents but I wonder if these gifts were ever appreciated or even wanted, apart from the one that hung on display in one of our local pubs, the Greyhound. Anyway, the objective was for me to have an interesting and constructive way of passing away my free moments. The Greyhound was one of the nearest pubs to the Royal Terrace Pier and consequently a regular for us as soon as we came ashore. The second pub, even closer, was The Crown and Thistle, commonly known as "The

Crown and Crumpet". The landlord, Fred, behaved as if he was one of us and we had many a riotous time in both of the establishments.

One crew member who joined us temporarily had his own peculiar form of entertainment on board. He took a special delight in setting light to his farts. Suddenly, at any time of the day or night, whenever we were together in the cabin, he would shout out,

"Quick, somebody get a match, hurry up."

At the same time, he'd get into position, lying on his back, he put his hands behind his knees and pulled them up to his chest to stretch his orifice open to achieve maximum propulsion of gas. Usually, one person would oblige him by scurrying off in search of a box of matches, then position himself with arms outstretched waiting for the signal to place a lighted match against the expulsion point. When the moment was exactly right there'd be a shout.

"NOW!"

The match would be struck as the gas was released with an explosive sound and we would be exposed to a mini pyrotechnic display when it ignited. I hasten to say that not everybody was amused at his choice of entertainment and fortunately he didn't stay with us for very long. "Home is where the heart is, home is where the fart is. Come let us fart in the home. There is no art in a fart. Still, a fart may not be artless. Let us fart and artless fart in a home," - Ernest Hemingway.

The accommodation on the Atlantic Cock had the Skipper and Chief Engineer in their comfortable, wood-panelled cabins and dining room at the forepart of the vessel and the rest of us in the stern. Our bunks were set on either side of the cabin. We didn't have the luxury of wood panelling, just the riveted metal hull plates that were painted with a special paint containing cork to help prevent condensation and it was for the same reason that the steel decks above the fore and aft cabins were laid with teak planking. The hull plates were bitterly cold in winter and piping hot in summer but the section below the water line, always cold, was a useful place to keep perishable food. There was a long wooden table and wooden benches at the forward end of the cabin with the coal burner in the centre. The entrance ladder was at the stern end. It was referred to as a ladder but it was not how a ladder is usually visualised. It was actually a steep wooden stairway, rather like a cross between the two. Access was through a hatch from the aft deck. Because the ladders were steep, we were taught to always go down backwards, which was the sensible thing to do. That allowed you to place your foot on the full expanse of the step and hold on to the rail. Going down frontwards limits you to having just your heel on the step, with the step above that cutting into your calf and nothing to hold on to, unless you happen to be a contortionist, or, as a ballet dancing acquaintance of mine was capable of doing, turn both feet outwards at a 90° angle, a feat he was proud to demonstrate whenever the mood took him. I didn't know any burly tugman who'd ever had the inclination to ballet dance so the motto was, always go down backwards. When I was once in a hurry, I decided to neglect this sound advice and paid a painfully heavy price. I dropped down the hatch and started to descend frontwards and it didn't take very long before I found myself lurching forward into space. I flung my hands out in front of me and grabbed the first thing available to break my fall. I wished I hadn't done that. I yelped as my hands sizzled from being firmly clasped around the coal fire's blisteringly hot funnel that momentarily broke my fall until I released my hold in a flash and hurtled headlong downwards, landing with a painful crash on the wooden floor. I lay there for a while in shock. I was in pain from the fall and didn't quite know what to do with my smarting hands that had turned to an impressive colour red. Fortunately, nothing was broken except my spirit and I was so pleased that there had been no witnesses. I never told anybody what had happened; it would have produced howls of laughter. Aware that I would get no sympathy, I just got painfully on with my job, suffering in silence as if nothing had happened. My own stupidity had caused it and I had learned a useful and costly lesson. "A good scare is worth more to a man than good advice," – E. W. Howe

Another time when the crew's lack of sympathy was well demonstrated had to do with food – or lack of it. We were around the dinner table tucking into one of the renowned meat duffs. I salivated at the thought of sinking my teeth into the scrumptious plateful before me. The rowdy chatter and storytelling had gained momentum with much hand gesturing being used for emphasis. I got a little too excited, slammed my hands down onto my plate, which flipped over spilling the contents of the hot steak and kidney pudding, with its thick gravy and all the accompaniments, into my lap. This provided a wonderful source of amusement for the crew as I leapt up, tipping my longed for dinner all over the floor. Every one of them roared with laughter at my distress. The misery was amplified by the fact that before I'd sat down I was ravenous. I must have looked a pitiful sight standing there forlorn, a huge, hot stain spreading around my crotch area as I stared down in disbelief at all the lovely food splattered at my feet, knowing there were no seconds. I had to resort to heating up a packet of dehydrated Vesta curry that I had as a standby.

*Don't panic!*

Another lesson I learned from painful experience was that when disaster strikes, it's every man for himself. The old adage of women and children first in times of crisis is fine and may or may not be adhered to if women and children are present. However, when seven men are shut into a confined space and something happens that signals danger, anything goes and it's a case of survival of the most brutal and determined. It was a still, foggy night with visibility restricted so much that no shipping ventured on the river. We'd dropped anchor in a safe place to wait for the fog to clear and settled into our bunks to take advantage of the break in activity. It was deathly silent apart from the gentle lapping of the water against the steel hull, the hissing of the coal burner and the occasional fart or snore from the crew members. All was calm and peaceful and we appreciated being in our bunks, snuggled up under our rough blankets in the warmth of the cabin. All of a sudden there was a loud thump and the boat shuddered. Some of the crew instinctively leapt out of their bunks and onto the ladder as fear and panic spread. I decided I'd better do the same. I jumped down out of my bunk and rushed to the ladder where there was a writhing mass of fear filled humanity scrambling over each other intent on being the first one through the hatch to safety. Seven panic-stricken men could no way fit through one small hatchway at the same time. In desperation they were determined to prove otherwise. There were far too many at the top of the ladder so nobody could actually squeeze through. Each person seemed to be on the back of another. I got to the ladder but couldn't go any higher because I had somebody's arse in my face as another terrified individual with his head between my legs was doing all he could to shove me up further. Somebody else was climbing over my back. My fingers were gripping tightly onto something or someone and were being crushed so much I thought they'd break. Nobody wanted to be the last one out. In the ensuing havoc, hands were grabbing anything they could get hold of to gain enough purchase to smash their way past everybody else. We ultimately finished up on the aft deck dazed, scared and covered in scratches and bruises but somehow, we'd made it. We stood there shoeless, huddled in a group on the aft deck shivering in the cold, wondering why everything was exactly as it had been when we'd last stood there. We weren't sinking. Nothing but a ghostly silence and stillness in the dense, damp fog, and then somebody noticed in the murky darkness, a large piece of wood drifting away from our stern. The tide had carried it past the hull after it had bumped against it and created the panic in the cabin. We were so relieved to discover that the whole thing was just a false alarm and that we weren't going to be plunged into the icy cold, polluted water of the Thames. Had anybody landed in the water they would have had to be taken immediately to hospital. The pollution levels were so high that in 1957, the river was declared biologically dead. The only safe time to go in the water was during the brief period of slack water on the high tide.

I'd been through a similar event when I was ten years old. One of the older boys I knew promised to take us young ones to a popular cave that he knew somewhere near Northfleet. We'd heard other boys talk about crawling through it and so we were excited and raring to go. It was a nice sunny day when we set out on foot, filled with a sense of adventure. Northfleet was a five mile walk but then we walked everywhere in those days without giving it a thought. I would often walk to visit relatives in Northfleet and sometimes I'd walk the ten miles to Chatham to visit relatives. On arrival at the location in some barren land, we descended into a large, deep-set, sunken area similar to a quarry. We found the cave, which was set in the side of the steep bank, and we ventured inside. The older boy, Eric, carried a torch and led the way. The cave gradually got narrower until we were crawling along on our hands and knees in what was little more than a small tunnel. The rest of us followed the light up ahead and it was disappearing rapidly as the older boy, knowing the cave well, rushed off ahead of us four younger ones. Eddie, my best friend at the time, was in front of me and two more were behind me. Suddenly it was total darkness. We had no idea what lay ahead and no idea where Eric was. Eddie knew the leader well and called out but there was no reply. He started to panic and his cries were getting more desperate as he got closer and closer to tears. Still no reply came back so he started to cry and plead and this affected the rest of us. I'm not the bravest person but I wasn't overly concerned until my friend started crying and the two behind me began letting out little whimpers. Then Eric finally called out to us from somewhere way ahead.

"This cave is haunted and the ghost always grabs the boy at the back," he called.

Terror took hold. I wasn't sure about the existence of ghosts but being cramped on hands and knees in pitch darkness, with no room to move up, down or sideways and the possibility of being grabbed by some demonic apparition can be pretty upsetting. All of a sudden all hell broke loose. I'm proud to say that initially I wasn't too bothered until the other three went haywire. My friend at the front was now bawling and crying out for the light to be put on as he scampered ahead blindly on all fours. I didn't want to be left there and neither did the two behind me but the major factor that caused the ensuing mayhem was that none of us wanted to be at the back. The unfortunate boy who found himself there screamed out and tried to flatten the boy in front of him so that he could scramble over his back. The boy behind me was determined to do whatever was necessary to keep the boy at the back where he was and at the same time was doing all that he could to push me further into the ground so that he could scamper past me. I was whimpering then and kicking him back. Fear and panic had consumed us all - no, more accurately, it was blind terror. Our vision was absolutely nil. We swore, punched, kicked and scratched each other in the confined space of the black, narrow tunnel as we simultaneously scrambled onwards. None of us wanted to be the last one in reach of the ghost. Incredibly, the boy behind me, with staggeringly brute force and ingenuity, somehow made me disappear and got past me. That placed me one from the back! The fight that followed in the ridiculously confined space was savage as we scrambled onwards. Up ahead I heard a scream and we soon found out, painfully, what the scream was about as we tumbled headfirst on top of each other into a hole. It wasn't a very deep hole but at the time it felt like a bottomless pit. We were writhing around in an attempt to extricate ourselves from the mass of tangled limbs when the torch was switched on. Eric shone the light on us. We were dishevelled, tearful and bleeding. The torch beam was flickering to and fro as Eric tried to contain his laughter. I didn't go back into the cave after that. "I have, indeed, no abhorrence of danger, except in its absolute effect – in terror." - Edgar Allan Poe.

### *Bluetown*

The towage company had stopped using the Ramsgate slipway so all refits were thereafter carried out at the Sheerness dry dock, or at least that was what we called it. In fact, the refits were carried out close by at a naval yard in Bluetown, which had developed around the time of the Napoleonic wars. The name derives from the wooden houses that the inhabitants had painted with blue paint. It was strange how as more and more houses were painted blue, less and less blue paint could be accounted for at the storage in the dockyard! Bluetown is a suburb of Sheerness on the Isle of Sheppey, at the mouth of the River Medway and around 20 nautical miles from Gravesend. The first building ever constructed at Sheerness was a fort that was built by order of King Henry VIII to protect the entrances to the River Medway and the Chatham Dockyards from coming under attack by enemy ships. A restricted depth at Chatham Dockyards, meant that vessels needing repairs or to replenish supplies could be delayed for considerable lengths of time awaiting favourable tides. So with this in mind, Samuel Pepys, the Secretary of the Admiralty, ordered the construction of the Sheerness Dockyards as an extension to the Chatham Dockyards. The town didn't achieve official status until near the end of the 19 century.

In 1944, the SS Montgomery, a United States merchant ship carrying a large cargo of explosives, ran aground on a sandbank 250 metres from the Medway Approach Channel. When the tide went out, she broke her back and now lies 15 metres below the surface with her masts still visible. The excessive cost and danger involved in attempting to salvage her and her cargo were considered too great so she still has 1400 tons of munitions in the hold. If they should ever detonate for whatever reason, apart from damaging buildings on the shore, the explosion would send an enormous column of water in the air and probably cause a mini tsunami. It was with that comforting thought in mind that we cast off from the Royal Terrace Pier and steamed down Gravesend Reach into Lower Hope on our way to Sheerness for our refit. The voyage was a gentle one all the way and as we steamed into the final stretch of the Thames Estuary known as Sea Reach I started to look forward to my stay there.

As soon as we were moored up in the dry dock and were able to get ashore, Roy went directly to the blacksmith's workshop and asked him to make up some harpoon tips, which he managed to do in double quick time. We attached these to broom handles and waited for the water level to go down enough for us to wade in in our sea boots and spear the fish that had been trapped in the dock. We were rewarded with a few fine specimens, one of which was a beautiful sea bass, which we enjoyed later that day along with the remainder of the catch. That night the crew went back to Gravesend and to their families. Some of them returned the following day to carry out maintenance work and that was the routine they followed until the refit had finished and it was time for the tug to be re-floated and sailed back to Gravesend. At lunch times we had fun filled moments in the local pubs. I stayed there for the duration and had a thoroughly enjoyable time.

It was on the last night before we left that some crew members, everybody in fact except the Leading Hand, the Skipper and the

Engineer, joined the Cook, Alan and myself for a final celebration in one of the local pubs and it was there that Alan and I had a close encounter with two locals youths who would have dearly loved to make mincemeat of us. We were sitting around a table when I noticed two pretty girls standing at the bar eyeing me up and probably Alan as well since he, like myself, was as enthusiastic and successful with the opposite sex as I was. Alan and I were keen to make a move but hesitated because the girls were with two rather large men who were giving us menacing looks. Their intentions were unmistakable should we dare to return the girls' glances but the challenge was too great. The inviting looks were irresistible and so, emboldened by a few pints of beer, Alan and I decided to risk the wrath of the two bruisers at the bar. We strolled up to the flirting girls and engaged them in conversation. As expected, their male companions didn't take kindly to our intrusion. They pushed between us and the girls and stood directly in front of us. Their aggressive looks and threatening language left us in no doubt what their intentions were but we stood our ground, encouraged by the fact that the girls made it obvious that they would prefer to be with Alan and me. Peter, a Fireman in our crew, saw the altercation taking place and marched up to the bar and asked if everything was alright, at which point the two losers withered away. It was well worth the risk we took because when we left with the girls later that evening everything we'd hoped for came to fruition. They helped make the refit at Sheerness so memorable that I couldn't wait for a return visit.

# CHAPTER 6
# FAREWELL TO STEAM

*The agony and the ecstasy*

Since school days I'd dated a girl, Kate, on and off. As she matured, she developed into a beautiful, curvaceous young girl and I found myself becoming ever more attracted to her. She was a little smaller than me with shiny, wavy black hair, dark, laughing eyes, full, luscious lips and slightly coffee coloured skin, a throwback from her Maltese ancestry. We began dating more regularly until one day, I realised just how much she meant to me. It's strange that it seemed to happen quite suddenly. We were playing around and laughing and as I looked at her lovely, laughing face and bewitching dark eyes I became conscious of how much I enjoyed being with her and she felt the same way about me. We decided that neither of us wanted to be with anyone else and as time went on we both fell madly in love. The love I felt was so intense it was almost as much as I could bear, as happens to some teenagers when they fall in love for the first time. From that moment on I devoted myself entirely to her alone. "No there's nothing half so sweet in life as love's young dream." –Thomas Moore.

We became ever closer the more time we spent together until it became clear to us both that we never wanted to be apart so I proposed to her and she accepted without hesitation. I bought a ring for her and with friends gathered around to celebrate with us, I placed it on her finger. She cried tears of joy, and we hugged and kissed and were blissfully happy. Our engagement lasted for a year. I loved my fiancée very much but we had different ideas on which direction our lives should take. She wanted to settle down and have children, a natural thing for most women to want, I suppose, especially back then in those days. She would have been perfectly happy living in a council house with lots of children around and as long as I knew her, she was never enthusiastic about getting a job. I was more ambitious. I had been bitten by the travel bug and wanted to visit different countries and I could never envisage myself working on the tugs or remaining in Gravesend for the rest of my life. I'd decided a few years before whilst waiting at a bus stop in the cold rain that I wanted to go and live in an exciting, warm country. It didn't make sense to me that I should suffer bad weather when better climates were on offer. I equally could not imagine myself doing the same thing day in and day out for the rest of my working life. My friends seemed happy enough with their lot, going to the same pubs, meeting the same people, doing the same things that they did the day before and would do the same things the following day and so on. There were far too many other interesting adventures awaiting me and regrettably, my Kate was not prepared to move on. She was not interested in travel or leaving Gravesend or improving her education or seeking a better life in any way, all of which I was unaware of when I'd asked her to marry me. I agonised for a long time before telling her that I thought it better if we parted. I knew it would be painful for both of us but it was far worse than I'd expected. I could never have foreseen what the outcome would be.

I broke the news as gently and as rationally as I could. I felt wretched watching her hurting inside as she looked up at me pleadingly, her intoxicating, dark eyes filled with tears and her warm arms clutching me so tightly. My mind was in turmoil. I held her close and different emotions arose within me. As they melded together I became confused.

I loved her so very much and yet I just knew deep inside that I could not spend the rest of my life in Gravesend. We stayed together for the remainder of that evening and made love with such an intense passion that I was tempted to reconsider. I was overwhelmed as I held her warm, young, naked body next to mine, that beautiful body that she surrendered to me so willingly. We lay silently, hugging each other. I was tormented inside. I imagined how the rest of my life would be with her and convinced myself that it would be better for us both if we each went our own way from that moment on. I walked her home. Outside her house, we stood clutching each other tightly and then, finally, with heavy hearts, we said our goodbyes. For a long, long time afterwards, I was haunted by the image of her walking away from me.

It was some time later that I had a message from her mother telling me that my dear, sweet ex-fiancée was so distraught and so ill that a doctor had been called in to see her. I was filled with remorse. What had I done? I went to see her and was pained when I saw her sitting curled up on the settee, her lovely face looking hurt and dispirited. I sat next to her for a while and when she seemed more relaxed I left her with the promise that we would stay in touch. A few days later things got worse. Her mother sent a message to me to say that after my darling had described her dreams and nightmares to the doctor, she had been placed in a psychiatric clinic. I was shocked. I felt responsible and didn't know how to respond. I sent a message back offering to visit her at the clinic and her mother agreed that it would be a good idea. We arranged a day and went there together. It was horrendous. The patients could be heard wailing and crying and the atmosphere was incredibly depressing. When Kate appeared, looking distraught, my heart ached for her as she sat before me with tears streaming down her cheeks, pleading to be taken back home. When her mother and I rode away together on the bus, she said that if I would take her daughter back the doctor thinks she would be better and could be sent home. Whether this was intentional emotional blackmail or a genuine plea for help I don't know but after a few days reflection, I felt I had no choice but to agree. She came home and we continued as we were before the split. I had mixed feelings, I wanted to end our relationship because long term I could foresee difficulties and yet I loved her so much.

As time went by, little by little, we both came to the understanding that we would eventually drift apart but it wasn't easy. Even after we'd officially split for the second time, I couldn't stay away from her completely and she felt the same. She lived in a street parallel to where I lived and although it was further for me, I'd go out of my way to walk past her house on my way home late at night. I never knew which nights I would be on leave but whenever I walked past her house, she was always there, waiting at the window. She'd open the door silently to avoid waking her parents, I'd go in and we'd spend heavenly moments in each other's arms and we'd make love. Sometimes her mother would call down to ask what she was doing or to tell her to come to bed.

"Kate, get up here at once," she called down.

"I'm just coming," Kate shouted between her heavy breaths and groans of ecstasy. It was a most appropriate thing to say, considering the activity we were engaged in at the time.

It was never easy saying goodnight, except on one occasion when her mother called to ask what she was doing downstairs so late at night and started clomping her way down the stairs to check on her. We were in the process of making love on the settee. Horrified at the thought of being caught, I jumped up and feverishly searched for my shoes in the dark, falling over in the process because my trousers were around my ankles. Whilst I was stumbling on the floor on hands and knees, I found my shoes. The clumping on the stairs left no doubt that Kate's mother was getting dangerously close. I had one hand clutching my shoes and the other trying to pull up my trousers as I attempted to run as fast as I could with ridiculous little movements because my feet were so restricted. I hopped my way through to the kitchen and fumbled in the dark for the door handle. I got the door open as I heard Kate's mother enter the sitting room. I dashed through the back door with just my socks on my feet. I hobbled into the alleyway between her house and the neighbour's and cried out in pain when I trod on something sharp in the process. Panting from the panic and the pain, I propped myself against the wall, pulled my trousers up put my shoes on my smarting feet and snuck out into the street and home. Our clandestine meetings went on for quite some time until I'd walked past several times and realised that she would no longer be there for me. I was devastated that it was finally over but at the same time pleased that we could get on with our lives and that the ultimate decision was hers. I have never forgotten her and she will forever have a place in my heart. "Ever has it been that love knows not its own depth until the hour of separation." – Kahlil Gibran." It could well be that when the life force has left our physical bodies and our spirits transcend to whatever realm exists after death, we may well meet again. Cosmology, physics, astronomy, philosophy, religion, many quantum physicists, forward thinking scientists and others such as renowned theoretical physicist and cosmologist Stephen Hawking, hypothesize that there is a Multiverse. If then, our universe multiplies into copies of itself at every quantum event, with copies of ourselves living out every possible outcome of every possible situation, then somewhere in that infinite number of universes, Kate and I are at this moment entwined in each other's arms, deeply in love and living in perfect harmony. And yet again in another of those universes we've never even met.

## *Precognition*

During my engagement to Kate, I'd been promoted to Senior Deckhand aboard the Moorcock, the newest tug in the fleet. Built in 1959 (and scrapped in 1981), 272 tonnes, 113' long with a draught of 12' and with a 1280 hp. 8 cylinder diesel engine. She was so different to the old steam driven tugs. Instead of having a Third Hand (Junior Deckhand) and Deckhand (Senior Deckhand), she had two Deckhands, which for me meant another increase in salary. The Moorcock was absolute luxury compared to the coal burning steam tugs. The accommodation was forward and well thought out. The Skipper's night time cabin was on the starboard side of a through passageway at deck level, with his day cabin on the port side. Between these two cabins, a ladder went down to the Chief Engineer's cabin to starboard and the Mate and Leading Hand's cabin to port, with the rest of us forward from there. Leading aft from the passageway, the galley was to port with a diesel fuelled cooking stove. Opposite the galley, stairs led up to the wheelhouse and aft of that the showers and washbasins were to starboard and the toilet to port. After that there was a door leading into the engine room. It was such opulence compared to what I'd been used to. Everything was inside and to have a real flushing toilet and hot water showers was bliss. On the old coal burners, when we needed to wash, we each had a galvanised bucket that we filled with water then either plunged one of the hot plates from the stove into it to heat it or we carried it down to the engine room and heated the water from a steam jet then carried it along the deck and down into the cabin. We'd then place it on the wooden benches around the dining table, strip off, wash and prepare ourselves to go home. The Moorcock was fitted with a refrigerator, another luxury that hadn't existed on the coal burners where we'd had to make do with a safe on the boat deck, which was a simple wooden framework with wire gauze on the sides and doors to allow air to circulate. I'd always believed that I'd eventually be promoted to this tug. It was what I'd hoped for and would constantly say to my crew mates that I would be ordered one day to join the Moorcock. When it happened they wouldn't believe that I hadn't had prior knowledge. The vision I'd created in my mind had materialised into fact.

I was delighted to be on the Moorcock. No more misery enduring the effects of the cruel elements on the runs up and down river. Instead, the trips were made in a comfortable, heated wheelhouse without any need to go outside. The bunks were far more comfortable than they were on the old coal burners. Everything was new, clean and civilised. This fine tug was fitted with powerful water cannons and we were the duty tug for the Gravesend area, which meant that we were called upon to assist the fire service when required. The Kent and Essex councils subsidised this operation and firefighting officers would occasionally come on board to train us in the art of firefighting and instruct us on the correct procedure. Fortunately, the fires were few.

The crew on the Moorcock were a lively bunch and we got on well together. The Skipper, Arthur, was an interesting character. He had a French background and unusual for a tugman in those days, he liked to have the occasional bottle of Beaujolais when we were moored for the night. Apart from that, nobody drank much whilst on duty. One day, the Mate, Eddie and I were in the snug wheelhouse on the down river run, which meant that the Skipper was off duty. Approaching Gravesend Reach, he appeared on deck with a shotgun. He looked up at us like a naughty boy with a mischievous grin on his face, then he lay down on the foredeck with the barrel aimed through the eyes of the vessel and pointed towards a mallard floating up ahead. He fired and despite the spread of the shot, only injured the poor creature. By this time the blast of the gun and the slowing of the engines had brought some of the other crew members on deck. It was pitiful to see the wounded duck flapping around helplessly in the water. We stopped engines, drifted alongside it and hauled the poor creature aboard. We all wanted to end its suffering quickly - not so easy if you'd never done it before. Buck, the Engineer, tried breaking its neck by twisting it but only managed to strip the feathers and skin from the muscles and expose the red flesh beneath. Next, Chunky, the Leading Hand, had an equally unsuccessful attempt. One of the Firemen, Jack, took hold of its feet and with a couple of swings smashed the poor things head against the engine room casing. It was distressing to watch but nowhere near as distressing as it was for the now terribly injured bird. It was all done with the best of intentions but we were inexperienced animal killers. One final twist of the neck ended its life. Everybody was upset. Nobody wanted any more to do with it. I couldn't bear the thought of all that suffering for nothing so I took it, plucked it, cleaned it and roasted it for my dinner that evening with a few vegetables. When I sat down to eat it all by myself the rest of the crew, unable to comprehend how I could do such a thing, stared at me in disbelief as if I was some sort of heartless monster. At least the ill-fated bird didn't suffer in vain.

Fog was often a problem on the Thames and when we anchored and waited for it to clear, one of us Deckhands would keep watch and from time to time go outside and ring the ships bell to let other shipping know our whereabouts and listen for the sound of their horns. If we heard three short blasts from one ship followed by the same from another ship, it meant that each ship was going astern and a collision could be imminent and that meant salvage. We would also be permanently tuned into the open radio band 2182 kHz. This was the frequency used for “mayday” calls when ships were in distress. Mayday originates from the French “m’aidez” meaning “help me”. The financial rewards for salvaging could be substantial for the company and the crew. The company share was 75% and the remaining 25% was shared out among the crew on a sliding scale, with the Skipper being given the highest share, five parts plus sixpence in every £1. The Engineer received four parts, the Mate and Leading Hand three, the Deckhands two and the Cook one. The total amount awarded increased for the first tug to get a tow rope aboard the stricken ship. As soon as we heard the mayday call and ascertained where the ship was, the Skipper would be alerted. The trouble was, so was each of the other Skippers. It would be a free for all among the tugs available, each one determined to be the first. There would be a wild scramble with no niceties as the rewards could be so high. Even being the outside tug on the buoy or the pontoon didn’t necessarily provide an advantage because if you weren’t quick enough off the mark you risked being cast adrift or dragged along with whoever managed to cast off first. All available tugs would charge towards the prize at double full speed. It was all very exhilarating. During my time on the Atlantic Cock, we once came across an abandoned, burning ship by chance. We went alongside and I jumped on board amidships and ran along the smoking deck with the tow rope, attached it to the foredeck bollards before running back and leaping back aboard the tug. Meanwhile, we’d informed the office at Gravesend and before we knew it other tugs, eager to be a part of the action, heard our call and started appearing from nowhere. It was a pleasant surprise when I received a cheque for a substantial sum of money eighteen months after I’d left the tugs.

## *The singer not the song*

I went back to Sheerness dry dock on the Moorcock and had another memorable time with other crew members who’d stayed behind with me. Eddie, the Mate, had been posted to another tug and was replaced by Bert. Some evenings, he and I would fill in time waiting for the clubs to open by going to a local bingo hall and always won enough to partially or totally pay for the evening's entertainment. There was a holiday complex nearby so we never lacked a place to go for amusement. Ken, the second Deckhand and I went there one evening and drank more than we should have. We met a couple of girls who'd invited us back to their chalet for the night. One of them was more attractive and friendlier than the other and when the time came to go to bed she stood and said, "Right who's coming with me?" We both shot bolt upright at the same instant without the slightest hesitation and leapt towards her. Ken was a good deal larger and far stronger than me and pushed me back down onto the settee before disappearing into the bedroom with her. I sat there feeling dejected. By that time, the second girl was dispirited that neither Ken nor I were as eager to go with her so she refused to let me accompany her to her bedroom. I sat down alone on the settee wondering what to do next. After a while, Ken's girl came back out to see me and invited me to share the bed with her and him. I declined her offer but she didn't want to accept no for an answer. I assumed that Ken had passed out because she tried several times to persuade me but I refused and left, sulking my way back to the Moorcock. When Ken clambered aboard around breakfast time he had an anguished look on his face.

"What happened to you, you look dreadful?" I asked

"I feel sick," he answered.

"Why?" I said

"Ooh," he groaned "I was disgusted and felt sick when I woke up and saw her."

"Ha-ha, serves you right," I said showing no sympathy for his self-inflicted plight.

"Ooh, I feel sick. When I saw her in the daylight she looked fucking awful. She was covered in sores and, oh, it was just so fucking horrible," he said as he ran to vomit.

It's surprising how much perception changes the more you have to drink. It's like the best of the wine always being in the bottom of the bottle. Anyway, when he'd finished being sick he was so upset he decided to go straight home. The whole thing was compounded by the fact that he was married and felt so ashamed. Embarrassingly, on the way home, he had to ask the bus driver to stop twice so that he could step out and vomit. What I thought at the time as bad luck turned out to be good luck for me.

I was in the ballroom of the holiday complex on my own one night when I became entranced by the pretty redheaded singer. Not only was she pretty, she also had a good voice, getting plenty of applause for her interpretation of Barbra Streisand songs. As soon as she came off stage I rushed over to her side and engaged her in conversation before she became surrounded by other admirers. Naturally, I emphasised the brilliance of her remarkable vocal ability. She was a lovely girl and we both felt a connection. I discovered that she lived in London's East End and as that was one of my regular haunts we were able to continue dating for a while. We would meet up at the King's Head in the Old Kent Road where I'd been a regular visitor for some time. The entertainment there made it well worth the trip from Gravesend. There were musical nights, comedy acts and so forth. The pub would be packed solid, so much so that it paid to estimate how many pints of beer you wanted to consume and buy them all at once because it would be almost impossible to get back to the bar a second time. We were packed like sardines in the smoke filled bar and even the pavement outside was filled with people. Those were good days. I was also a regular visitor to the greyhound race tracks. Roy, the Mate on the Atlantic Cock had introduced me to the sport and we'd often go together wherever the races happened to be on our time off, be it Wembley, East Ham, Catford, Crayford or anywhere else. I found it more and more difficult to keep meeting up with the songstress in London and the affair gradually fizzled out when I met other girls closer to home.

# CHAPTER 7
# THE TRAVEL BUG BITES

*The weaker sex they're not!*

With plenty of money to spend, I made the most of my days off and the annual holidays. My first trip abroad was in 1960. I went with my friend Tommy to Lloret del Mar on Spain's Costa Brava when travel was more complicated than it is at the time of writing. The plane landed at Perpignan in Southern France and then a coach took us on a lengthy ride to the resort. I loved Spain. I loved the food, the sunshine, the people, the language, the Flamenco, the Spanish girls - even though I spent the majority of my time there romancing a lovely wanton German girl called Marina who was staying in a hotel not far from where we were staying.

Tommy and I had great fun playing practical jokes on the young chambermaid each time she came into our room. There was a time when Tommy hid under the bed and I let her in. Thinking it was safe to carry on, she started her chores and as she walked past the bed, Tommy flashed his hand out grabbing her ankle. She let out a piercing scream at the sudden fright. Later, at lunch, she and a group of her fellow chamber maids were peering through the window at us, giggling whilst we ate. When lunch was over, we left the dining room and headed to the exit to make our way to the beach.

"Pssst," I heard. A young boy grabbed my arm and indicated that something was amiss and that I should follow him. Concerned, I did as he bade, and he led me upstairs all the while beckoning me to follow him. He took me to my room and with a worried look and using sign language, implied that I should go in. I went in and immediately the door was slammed behind me. I was trapped in my room with a gang of young Spanish chamber maids intent on doing heaven knows what to me. A couple of them leapt at me. I dodged them and as more came at me from another angle, I briskly avoided them too, escaping to the other side of the bed. They ran around to try and seize me. I leapt across the bed and made it to the door and escaped. When I arrived at the hotel exit, Tommy was still waiting for me oblivious to what had been going on. Now, before any testosterone filled males start wondering why I didn't just take advantage of the situation, let me say that this wasn't the first time I'd been assaulted by a group of girls and in reality, whilst it wasn't entirely unpleasant, it wasn't good to feel powerless and at their mercy. In those days it was unthinkable for a man to strike or hurt a woman, which limited my self defence.

It happened to me once at a party. I'd become friends with a girl who lived on a different estate to myself and there would often be several of us teenagers at her home. Her father was mostly away working and her mother, being left on her own, would allow us kids to meet up and play rock and roll music and jive and generally enjoy ourselves, even joining in herself. As well as the usual teenage chatter, there would be plenty of sexual talk, confessions, boastings and fantasies spoken of and the mother encouraged some of it. As kids were coming and going in different rooms or the garden it wasn't easy to keep track of who was where. One girl invited me to go upstairs, so naturally, I obliged. When I went into the room, I was grabbed and pulled onto the bed by a group of squealing and playful young girls. Together they were surprisingly strong and some of them had definite intentions of a sexual nature. I do not intend to divulge in detail what happened next and leave my readers to draw their own conclusions; suffice to say that some of them were very inquisitive, experimental and resolute in satisfying their curiosity and desires. Why me, was I emitting some sort of aberrant pheromones that enticed the opposite sex to attack and take advantage of me? Anyway, I eventually staggered back downstairs dishevelled, exhausted and a little shocked. I can imagine what an outcry there could have been if an equally large gang of boys had assaulted a girl in the same manner! Even earlier I was the victim of a similar incident at the infants' school. It happened that once I was the last boy to leave the classroom and six girls were standing in a group nearby looking at me and giggling. They ran over and cornered me, got me on the ground and held me down whilst they took turns trying to kiss me to death. Of course, the Costa Brava incident had a perfectly logical explanation, revenge, albeit a playful one and it never happened to me again after that. As for the assault at the party, there were further developments. The mother once called by my home and asked for me. My parents had an inkling of what had been happening; it is difficult to keep such things quiet, especially if there's a likelihood of scandal. Anyway, she was standing outside and they forbade me to go with her. Later, for whatever reason, the police became involved and when the husband discovered what had been going on, they separated. Two years later, I met the daughter at the bus stop and we started chatting about the past. Her bus arrived before mine and just before she boarded she shoved a key in my hand.

"I'm at home alone tonight, come and see me about half past seven," she said and quickly got on the bus leaving me dumbstruck, holding the key.

That was the last thing I'd expected. However, the offer appealed to me so I pocketed the key and that evening duly went to her home. I hesitated at the door, instinctively. I had doubts about the wisdom of letting myself in, not knowing what the outcome might be, so instead of using the key, I knocked on the door. What a lucky escape I had because the door was opened by her father. We eyed each other up for a while. I don't know if he recognised me but I certainly recognised him and I felt very uneasy. I asked for his daughter and when she came to the door, she apologised, I handed her the key and we never saw each other again.

But back to Spain. I loved travelling abroad. I had well and truly been bitten by the travel bug. The following year, I went on my own to Torremolinos. The name means "Tower of the Mills". The Moors, who were of Arab and Berber descent, crossed the strait of Gibraltar in 711, and established the mills after they'd conquered Spain. The tower and the Alhambra Palace were both built during the Nasrid Dynasty, which lasted from 1230 until 1492, when they surrendered to a Christian Spain at the fall of Granada. Torremolinos was looted and destroyed by an Anglo-Dutch flotilla during the War of Spanish Succession and was rebuilt, together with the mills, in the early 19th century. The mill industry began to decline in the 1920's and Torremolinos became a poor, little known fishing village until it became the first tourist resort on the Costa del Sol in the 1950's. When I was there it was still a small resort and market day was a lively affair with the locals singing and dancing flamenco and the mules and donkeys attired in brightly coloured garments. Any small bar I visited would invariably have somebody singing and dancing flamenco and I've been passionate about the music ever since.

I took a bus to explore Malaga and having heard and read so much about bull fights decided to see what it was all about. The bus trip became interesting when locals boarded and took short journeys with their livestock. The prices of the tickets for the bull fight varied considerably and much to my regret, I chose to pay the cheapest price, which meant I spent the entire time in full sun envying the wealthier and more knowledgeable spectators who'd paid the higher price for the shade. The bull fight was horrendous. I am flabbergasted that such atrocities are still allowed to take place in the 21$^{st}$ century and I wonder how anybody could find it entertaining to watch a magnificent animal being tortured to death for twenty minutes.

I had a gratifying time with a mature woman for the first week and then I met a lovely, dark haired Irish girl. We spent wonderful romantic evenings alone on the beach and had such a good time together that our relationship continued in the UK for a while until she surprised me one day by talking about marriage as if it was a foregone conclusion. The thought had never crossed my mind, so I extricated myself as gently as I could.

My next trip was Paris. Paris in the sixties was an exhilarating place to be and I would go there as often as I could. Although my weekends and days off were infrequent and rarely consisted of a full two days, I would sometimes take the train from London to Paris so that I could spend a night and as much as possible of what remained of the my spare time there, rather than go on pub crawls with my friends in Gravesend. It was a 12 hour journey each way; leaving London Victoria at nine o'clock in the evening and arriving at Paris Gare du Nord at nine o'clock the following day. I visited as many of the famous sites as possible and I loved ordering interesting meals in restaurants. I wanted to taste everything new and felt as if I was floating through it all in a wonderful dream. It was the first time I'd had onion soup and I got into a right mess with it because I hadn't realised that there was a soggy mass of melted cheese at the bottom of the bowl. I plunged my spoon in and it came back up looking like a gooey yellow lollipop, making it impossible to scoop up any of the soup. When I tried to bite some of the cheese off and pulled the spoon back out of my mouth there was a lengthy stream of sticky cheese between my mouth and the spoon that I tried to separate with a fork. That just made matters much worse because I then had strands of molten cheese spreading out from both utensils as well as the bowl. It would have been funny if I'd been with friends but sitting on my own, I was mortally embarrassed and was sure that the eyes of the whole restaurant were riveted on me. Who was this idiot who didn't know how to eat soup?.

I particularly enjoyed the nightlife and the sounds of live jazz bands blaring out onto the street as I walked past the bars with their outside terraces thronging with life. I was supremely happy and somehow felt that I really belonged there. I have never lost my love of that wonderful city and of France itself. At that time I wouldn't have thought it possible that at a future date I'd be Captain of a beautiful eighty-foot motor yacht based on a mooring just outside the city centre.

## *Christmas Eve in custody*

I had some terrific friends in Gravesend and would regale them with the delights waiting in Paris for a single young man. I convinced them that they or any single male should never consider marrying until they'd experienced at least one weekend in Paris. My enthusiasm influenced them so much that six of us decided to go there for Christmas one year. On 24 December, we took off from Lympne Airport in Kent for a flight to Beauvais. Lympne Airport had been chosen as the landing site for the arrival of a Focke-Wulf 200 on 25 March 1941. It was Hitler's personal plane and his pilot, Hans Baur, had indicated that he wanted to defect and fly the plane to England with Hitler on board. This audacious kidnap plot, however, did not happen because at the last minute he changed his mind.

Our flights had been booked with Skyways, which was the world's first low-cost air coach service. It was established in 1946 and the flight that we took from Lympne to Beauvais was a far cry from modern day transport. The aircraft was a Dakota, a smallish, twin propeller craft that carried only a limited number of passengers. Dakotas had been used as transport aircraft during World War II and were one of the first commercially viable planes to carry passengers. Thousands of them were converted for use as civilian passenger planes by virtually every airline company after the war because they were cheap and easy to maintain. We had an exceedingly bumpy flight in this aircraft and spent most of the time wishing that we hadn't drunk so much before we left. If the wartime pilots had suffered half as much as we did on that flight we may have lost the war. Each of us tried to act as if we didn't have a care in the world, snickering at the plight of the others until we started to turn a strange shade of green. The interior of the plane was small and very basic. We were a total of 12 passengers with my pals and I seated behind the pilot. Our fellow passengers looked uncomfortable from the buffeting we were being subjected to but they didn't seem as distressed as we were. We were pleased when we landed at Beauvais airport, 85 kilometres NNW of Paris. During the German occupation in World War II, this airport was captured and used by the Luftwaffe, principally as a bomber base. Later, the bombers were moved away and interceptor fighter units were stationed there to defend the airport against constant daylight bombing by the American air force. Consequently, the airport suffered sustained bombardment to keep the interceptors pinned down. It was liberated on 03 September 1944 by the allied forces and after the unexploded munitions and wartime wreckage had been removed, it was opened as a commercial civil airport in 1956.

It was late when we finally staggered off the plane and onto the coach which took us into the centre of Paris. We found our way to the hotel that we had pre-booked, wasted precious little time unpacking and headed off in search of the pleasures to be found in that amazing city. It was Christmas Eve and after our nerve wracking flight we were ready to celebrate. We didn't get very far. On the opposite side of the road to the hotel, we walked past a small family run bar/restaurant. It was a bitterly cold night and the warm glow of the interior lights attracted us. We peered inside. A middle-aged couple and some attractive young girls were singing, dancing, drinking and surprisingly, not a single male was in sight, with the exception of the proprietor. We stood gazing through the window and when the occupants saw us gawking they beckoned us in. To say there was no hesitation would be an understatement as we rushed to squeeze through the door as one. My companions must have thought that I'd brought them to wonderland. We did have a most entertaining evening joining our new found friends in their celebrations. We'd ordered a meal to begin with, accompanied by copious bottles of wine that we were more than eager to share with our hosts. After the meal, we went to our hotel and brought back the bottles of duty-free booze that we'd bought at the airport so that we could share them with our fellow revellers. Our new friends spoke no English and none of us spoke any French, although my pal Paul had given us the impression that he had some knowledge of the language; we soon found out that he was somewhat delusional. It didn't matter; we had a marvellous evening. We joined in singing with them, making up our own words as we didn't have a clue what they were singing about. We danced with the girls until sadly the time came when everything ground to a halt and we asked for the bill, which was placed before us. *It was one hundred times what it should have been!*

We were aghast and sat staring at it with horrified expressions. Naturally, we refused to pay and it is regrettable that the situation became increasingly unpleasant. We'd had an unforgettable time with wonderful, hospitable people and now it was utterly ruined. Heated words were exchanged with wild gesticulations. Nobody comprehended in the slightest what the other was saying or attempting to convey by frantic arm waving and an exhaustive panoply of facial expressions. The only word we understood was "Gendarmes" that cropped up every now and again and we repeated it back, it being one of the few French words we knew. Anyway, we knew we were being ripped off, so had nothing to fear. How wrong can one be?

One of our group, Derek, went outside, presumably back to the hotel. Shortly afterwards the door burst open and in rushed several gendarmes. Without further ado, they surrounded us, shoved our arms up behind our backs, bundled us into the waiting van and whisked us off to the police station. They made us stand up against the wall for over an hour. Standing upright for a lengthy period is not easy when you are inebriated and tired. I was standing to the left of my friend Sid.

"Pssst," he whispered.

I swivelled my eyes in his direction. He surreptitiously cast his eyes down to his jacket pocket on the side closest to me. I followed his gaze. He then looked straight ahead so as not to attract any attention and gently eased part of an apple up to the top of his pocket.

"I stole it," he mumbled.

"When?" I asked.

"When they overcharged us," he whispered. "I picked it up from a bowl of fruit, I hope they won't notice it," he whispered again, obviously worried, though why anybody would be so concerned about a single apple at a time like that was hard to imagine.

He let the apple drop back into his pocket. I snickered and that seemed to ease his fears because then a smile replaced his worried expression. The smile broadened. He looked at me and the sight of me stifling a giggle made him start to giggle.

Paul, feeling confident that with his spattering of French words he could ease, if not even resolve the situation, walked over to the group of gendarmes.

"Er, excusez moi," he slurred.

The next moment he was lying flat on his back on the floor. One of the gendarmes had socked him one and flattened him. The rest of us stared in disbelief. He was our only hope and he'd blown it. Sid and I looked at each other and I motioned with my eyes to the apple in his pocket with a worried look on my face. He almost wet himself.

Paul came to and stood up dazed, blinking his eyes. He was forced back to the wall with the rest of us and that's where they made us stand for the whole of the rest of the night. It wasn't how we'd imagined that we'd spend Christmas Eve. Before we left Gravesend, I'd convinced them that they'd have an unforgettable time in Paris, which was turning out to be true, but not in the way that any of us had expected!

Seven a.m., Christmas Day. We were sagging and still not allowed to move when in walked the proprietor of the bar from the previous evening. He went straight to the desk and slammed down his bill. The Gendarmes conversed with him for a while. There were a couple of nods and hostile glances in our direction. One of the Gendarmes went over to Paul. Paul quivered and went a strange colour as he was grabbed and pulled over to confront the bar owner. They chatted among themselves for a while then they broke into smiles and Paul was nodding and saying "Oui, oui." We understood that.

A few years previously, in 1960, the French franc had been revalued. The new French franc was valued at one hundred old French francs with the latter becoming centimes. In spite of that, the French population still quoted in old francs. In fact, this carried on until the introduction of the Euro in 2002, and even the younger generation who'd never known the old franc insisted on using them. It was very confusing to visiting foreigners. When dealing with matters with which one wasn't familiar and had no idea of the true cost, it could be startling to be told the figure in hundreds or even hundreds of thousands. That's what caused our misunderstanding in Paris. As soon as the misunderstanding became apparent, of course, we paid immediately and everybody was happy. Well, the bar owner was happy. We were thirsty, hungry, tired, fed up but most of all, relieved. After the bill was settled the Gendarmes metamorphosed into kindness itself. There was much laughing, no doubt a lot of it at our expense. We were escorted back to our hotel in the back of the police waggon and during the drive back they couldn't do enough for us. We arrived wearing their kepis and surprisingly they even gave us their guns to amuse ourselves with. We said our goodbyes with the customary French handshakes and went up to our rooms. Derek had spent the night alone having no idea what had happened. He'd looked through the bar door and not seeing us there, went to his room and slept. He was flabbergasted when we related our little saga to him.

From that moment on, things got better and better and everything I'd promised them came to fruition. We had a wild, hilarious, unforgettable time and the memories provided us with laughter whenever we met in the years that followed. Almost our entire time there was spent in the Pigalle area, famous for the Moulin Rouge and the Can Can, a dance that had originated there. It was the place to be to experience Paris by night with its night clubs, topless and nude shows, and live jazz and in one area, it was reminiscent of present day Amsterdam. We stood outside staring in amazement as four provocatively dressed prostitutes sat at a window looking out shamelessly at passers-by. We weren't saying much, just ogling and then we were surprised to see Derek stroll across the floor towards one of them. He had a habit of sidling off to do his own thing without discussing anything. It was the reason that he wasn't arrested with the rest of us on Christmas Eve, having decided to disappear to the hotel. He stood before the attractive girl that he'd slyly chosen whilst the rest of us were merely watching. There was a brief nod of their heads, then she slid from her stool and walked off bidding Derek to follow her. He glanced over his shoulder and looked at us with a lascivious grin. We gave him the thumbs up and a cheer then wandered over to the bar on the opposite side of the road to wait for him. It wasn't very long before he came over to us looking more than pleased with himself. We bombarded him with questions. We wanted to know everything that happened, all the minutest details. The more we quizzed him, the more excited he got as he relived the ecstatic time he'd had as he glanced continually across the street to the girls in the window. He got so excited in fact, that he couldn't contain himself any longer so he rushed back over there for a second go. So, we had to wait again. The second time he was even quicker and he came back subdued. He had been too hasty, allowing his enthusiasm to get the better of him and after having paid he was unable to perform. We then each went our own way. Paul and I stayed together and met two Parisian girls who took us back to their flat for the evening.

The next evening we went into a bar hidden in a dingy side street, and the only customers were attractive, scantily clad girls. We couldn't believe our luck. We discovered that they were performers in a strip joint close by and we had the most fabulous evening with them. At times, one or more of them went next door to the club to perform and when they came back another one or two would go. They were totally uninhibited and wild. One of them took a particular fancy to Sid, the apple thief and he couldn't take the smile from his face as she fondled him in front of the rest of us. We stayed there enjoying their raucous company for a long time that evening before we went around the city to see what else it had to offer us and we weren't disappointed. The trip turned out to be everything I'd promised my friends it would be. It was indeed unforgettable. After our time in Paris life seemed flat once we'd returned to Gravesend and I resumed my life on Old Father Thames.

## *A small role in history*

Thirty million years ago, before Britain became an island; the Thames was a tributary of the River Rhine. Around 10,000 years ago, after the ice age, the melting ice swelled it to ten times its current size and about 3,000 years ago, it took the meandering course it has today. Men have traded on the Thames since the Bronze Age and when the Romans arrived in London and established a port, they discovered that the flood tide could carry them from the North Sea 50 miles up the Thames. At the spot where they came to a halt, they built the first bridge, which is the site of the current Tower Bridge. The only times we went upstream of the Tower Bridge was with one or other of the two ships operated by

Naviera Aznar SA, the Monte Ulia and her sister ship Monte Urquiola. They were the largest ships to pass under Tower Bridge, carrying produce and passengers from the Canary Islands and would berth at New Fresh Wharf close to London Bridge.

The Thames is Britain's largest river and the most important gateway to the London docks. Gravesend, on its Southern shore, has been a town of considerable maritime activity for centuries. In 1401, a Royal Charter gave the men of Gravesend permission to carry passengers to and from London and it soon became a popular alternative to the dangerous route along the Dover to London road, which crossed Blackheath that had a reputation for its infamous highwaymen. Four hundred years after the Royal Charter was granted, the first steamboat began making the journey to and from London, which brought increasing numbers of visitors, making Gravesend one of the first English resorts for tourists.

On 21 March 1617, a ship left London carrying John Rolfe and Princess Pocahontas, bound for Virginia. Pocahontas was the daughter of Chief Powhatan, the predominant chief of around thirty minor tribes of the Tidewater region, Virginia. She had been taken captive and held for ransom during the Anglo-Indian war in 1613 and converted to Christianity whilst in captivity, taking the name of Rebecca. At the time of her release, she chose to remain with the English and in 1615 married a tobacco planter named John Rolfe, which helped bring about an end to the war. They went to London in 1616, where she was introduced to English society as a "civilised savage" and became a much-feted celebrity. Pocahontas, however, was unwell, and by the time the ship reached Gravesend she had fallen gravely ill. She was taken ashore and died of unknown causes very shortly afterwards at the age of 21. She was buried at St George's church at the bottom of Gravesend High Street where there is a life-size bronze statue in her honour. She is most famous for reputedly saving the life of Captain John Smith, a colonist who, with one hundred others, settled in Virginia in April 1607. In December of that year, he was captured by a Powhatan hunting party and when threatened with death, it is said that Pocahontas placed her own head in the way as the club was raised to shatter Smith's skull. Her story has been portrayed in numerous films and literature over the years.

Mary Shelley mentions the town in her novel 'Frankenstein', as does Charles Dickens in at least three of his novels. He lived at Gads Hill Place, two miles east of Gravesend and close to where I lived there was a pub was called the Dickens Inn. There is also a Dickens Road. General Gordon also lived in the town from 1865 – 1871 during the construction of the Thames forts that guarded the river downstream from Gravesend. One of them, Shornemead, was an artillery fort that was abandoned in the 1950's and we boys would go there regularly to use it as a playground. General Gordon decided to improve the lives of disadvantaged boys, supplying food and clothing from his army wages and installing a Sunday school. In his memory, Gravesend Promenade is known as the Gordon Promenade and the secondary school that I attended was also named after him.

In 1932 a civilian airport was established on the eastern outskirts of the town that became a Royal Air Force fighter base in 1939 and was heavily bombed by the Luftwaffe during WWII. In 1944, when the Nazi's began deploying the V1 flying bombs, the forerunner of today's cruise missiles, the danger was considered too great for flying operations so the airport was used as a base for barrage balloons instead. Although I could only have been 11 months old, I have a clear memory of being carried under the table in my mother's arms to shelter from a V1 that landed in Gravesend early in June. It must have been a truly terrifying ordeal to have had such a deep impact on my memory. I never discussed the circumstance with my mother but I know that there was another woman in the room who joined us under the table. Over the next three days, seventy-two V1's hit London and the South, killing and wounding hundreds of people. On 18 June, one landed just 100 yards from Buckingham Palace, killing 144 people and in total, almost 10,000 were launched from France. A fifth of them apparently either crashed on take-off or malfunctioned but nevertheless, approximately 100 a day hit Britain, killing a total of 22,000 and wounding 6000. The bombardment continued until the allied forces captured the launch pads in October. Hitler then began using the far more lethal V2 rockets.

Over the next few months over 1400 were targeted on the U.K. with the last one striking on 24 March 1945. These deadly rockets had a range of 200 miles, flew at a speed of 3500 mph and were the prototypes for today's space program. Two of them hit Gravesend, one landing close to the Fort Gardens less than two miles from where we lived.

I'd been born just half a mile from the Royal Terrace Pier, in Gravesend Hospital, 500 feet from the edge of the polluted river Thames. In his novel "Little Dorrit," Dickens wrote that the Thames was a deadly sewer and in a letter to a friend wrote, "I can certify that the offensive deadly smells, even in that short whiff, have been of a most head-and-stomach-distending nature." And a journalist, George Godwin in a reference to the Thames foreshore, wrote, "in part, the deposit is more than six feet deep". Between 1831 and 1854 there were three cholera outbreaks and over 30,000 people had perished as a result of the horrific pollution. Raw sewage and discharges from factories and abattoirs had been pouring into the river since the 17$^{th}$ century. It reached a critical stage in 1858, the year of the "Great Stink", when an exceptionally hot summer sent the temperature to 35° and the level of the river, which was in effect nothing more than an open sewer, fell lower than normal, leaving piles of effluent on its banks. The smell was so overwhelming that in June, the curtains in the houses of parliament were soaked in lime chloride in an unsuccessful attempt to mask the stench and parliamentary members were unable to carry out their duties. Up to 250 tons of lime was spread onto the sewer outlets and onto the river banks at low tide to try to eliminate the overpowering smell. The civil engineer Joseph Bazalgette instigated a new system of interconnecting sewers to take the effluent clear of the city of London, which prevented further cholera outbreaks and saved thousands of lives. He also built the embankments over the foreshores, narrowing the river, which increased its flow, enabling it to more effectively remove the ever increasing amount of rubbish thrown into it. The embankments concealed the pipes for the new sewage system and allowed roads and raised walkways to be built. In 1878, the pleasure steamer SS Princess Alice collided with a Collier close to the sewer outlets and 650 people died mainly as a result of the toxins in the river. During the war, German bombs destroyed some of the Victorian sewage systems and post-war Britain lacked the funds or the inclination to restore them. When I joined Ship Towage, the Thames had been described as a "Badly managed open sewer" and "A vast, foul-smelling drain". The river didn't begin to breathe again until the late sixties then the sewage systems were improved as part of the post-war recovery.

I have played my small role in Gravesend's history and the history of the Thames, which provided us tugmen with our livelihood and sadly, all too often, an untimely death. I am privileged to have been a part of it and of the steam age. It's unbelievable the amount of power that was produced by boiling water. Those magnificent steam engines were built of high quality steel and polished brass, with wheels, valves, levers, dials and a maze of pipes carrying the steam to perform different functions to power the mills, agricultural machinery, trains and boats. I was also fortunate to have shared it with such wonderful, tough, hardworking, generous, and colourful characters. I'd learned a lot, and I'd had a good time but couldn't see a future for myself as a tugman and was ready for something new - so in the autumn of 1965, I left. Thus began a regular pattern throughout my working life. Every six or seven years or so, whether I was employed or had my own businesses, I would move on to seek a new experience.

# CHAPTER 8
# LOOKING BACK

*All the fun of the fair?*

My childhood days began on a rundown council estate where a lot of my former friends and their brothers and fathers had ended up in prison. When I began attending the infants' school, I became friendly with a boy, Eddie, who lived in the same street as me, just a few houses away and I was captivated by the tales he used to tell me. He would go eeling with his father and uncle on the disused Thames and Medway canal, which was originally built to link the River Thames to the River Medway at Strood, to avoid the sailing barges having to navigate around the Hoo peninsular and the Thames estuary. It was conceived in 1799 and was finally completed in 1824 but was a commercial failure so was sold to the South Eastern Railway Company in 1846 when it was filled in and a railway line built over it. The only section that remained navigable was between Higham and Gravesend and that was closed in 1934. Eddie's Dad would stretch nets across the canal, and then with his brother went a good distance away before wading in and walking back towards the net thrashing the water with eel beaters, which were basically long poles, driving the eels into the net. When they were gathered up they were piled into a barrow, which was wheeled around the neighborhood where the contents were sold to eager purchasers and I would sometimes accompany Eddie.

He also told me tales of rabbiting. His father kept ferrets and they would go to the marshes a few hundred yards from where we lived and send the ferrets into the entrances to the rabbit burrows after placing nets over the exits. The panic stricken rabbits scarpered to what they thought was safety only to be gathered up in the nets, killed and sold on to the local population. The same marshes provided an endless supply of turf, which Eddie and his brothers and other locals would dig up and sell on. They were a close family and his father and elder brothers taught him so much. Not only was I enamoured with the stories he told me, I also envied his close knit family so spent a lot of time in his company and was always thrilled when I was allowed to join them in their escapades.

I was initially a clever lad in school, always among the top few boys but as time went on and I hung around with Eddie and his cerebrally challenged, tearaway friends, I wanted to be accepted as part of the clique and allowed myself to be influenced too much by them. It was evident where their futures lay judging by the behaviour of the older youths. I used to wonder frequently why I allied myself with them as I stood back and watched another nose being broken in a drunken brawl or another burglary being planned or another innocent person being tormented and beaten up for the sheer, misguided pleasure of the unenlightened perpetrators. I felt such deep sorrow for the victims and I never participated in their brutal forms of amusement but did suffer the consequences when I was badly beaten up at a fairground one night.

The secondary modern boys' school I attended was next to the girls' school. They were in the same building and during the lunch break both sexes would meet up in the recreation ground behind the public swimming pool on the opposite side of the road. One particular girl was by far and away the most stunning in the school and all the boys would talk about her and hope to date her. I was the lucky one. When we stopped seeing each other she found another boyfriend from a different school. He was a nice boy and I had no hard feelings. One evening when I was out and about with two of the gang of lawbreakers, we saw the boy get onto a stationary bus.

"That's the boy who's dating my ex-girlfriend," I said as a simple matter of fact.

"Right, we'll sort him out for you," they said.

"No, I'm not with her anymore, it doesn't matter, he's OK. I quite like him," I tried to reason with them.

They ignored my protestations and just laughed when I tried to stop them. They rushed upstairs on the bus and proceeded to pummel the poor unsuspecting boy. I stayed on the pavement, ashamed to be involved. He looked out of the window when they came back down to join me and because we were all together, he naturally assumed that I had put them up to it. I deeply regretted what had happened but knew I would never have been able to stop my friends from passing up the chance of a punch up - especially if it was in their favour, two against one. It so happened that the boy's brother was an amateur boxer. He came across me one night at the fairground, accidentally I thought, but in reality, he'd been seeking me out as I learned later. He challenged me to a fight and I didn't stand a chance. I was with my friends who'd created the problem. They'd attacked the boy on the bus but it was me who was to pay the price. My opponent, surrounded by his band of eager supporters, stood facing me with a hostile stare, swinging his muscular arms in anticipation and almost drooling at the prospect of smashing me into a pulp. It was dark and a crowd had started to gather. There was a smell of hot dogs and onions, the fairground music blared, generators whirred, lights were flashing and I heard the screams and laughter of the crowds having fun as I was pushed forward by my friends. I don't really recall much of what happened after that except the cheers of encouragement from the baying crowd. At one stage there was an extra loud cheer and I have no idea if I'd managed to clobber him or if he'd landed yet another expertly timed and placed punch into my face – almost certainly the latter. I have never been a violent person and hadn't been involved in a fight before then or since, so I didn't stand a chance. Thankfully, my next door neighbour, a huge, tough character, happened to hear the commotion and rushed over and flattened my punisher and then turned on the rest of the onlookers.

"Ain't you bleedin' big enough to stop this?" he said as he floored the biggest of them.

They all disappeared rather rapidly after that, even my so-called friends. Bill, the neighbour, tended my wounds. When he had stopped my nose from bleeding and finished wiping away the blood from my face, I made my way home. By the time I arrived the blood had covered my face once more. Fortunately, Mum and Dad had already gone to bed.

I didn't commit any criminal offences myself but often stayed out late with some of the boys, occasionally all night. There was a riding stable close by and from time to time we'd sleep in the hay loft waiting for the horses to be put out in the fields very early in the morning. As soon as the stable hands had departed, we'd pick up the rough bridles we'd made up from bits of rope, go to the field, catch a horse, slip the bridle on and have terrific fun riding around on their backs before going home to get ready for school. However, these escapades were short lived because a group of boys from a nearby estate set light to the hayloft and the whole barn burnt down. Mum and Dad were not happy with me for staying out all night and also because of the type of delinquents I was associating with, but I was terribly unhappy at home and welcomed any excuse not to be there.

### *A traumatic time*

Mum and Dad were stuck in an ill-fated marriage but in those days divorce was rarely an option and it would never have occurred to either of them to do anything other than make the best of a worsening situation. After Dad received his compensation for the loss of his eye, "mince" Dad would call it, and other injuries, he took to drinking heavily. He was awarded £2500, which was a considerable sum at the time when a house could be purchased for a couple of hundred pounds. He gave half to Mum and the rest he squandered on booze and what he thought at the time were his mates, "china's" he called them (china plate = mate). It will come as no surprise to learn that they faded away at the same time as the money. I don't know what happened to Mum's share but that too disappeared quickly. I lived in fear during those years, dreading Dad coming home drunk and creating hostile scenes, especially when he was accompanied by his objectionable, scrounging, so called friends who were equally smashed out of their heads at Dad's expense. I used to plead with Mum to leave home with me before he returned and she always refused, which only made matters worse for everybody. Mum was a fiercely stubborn, independent woman who had no qualms about telling people what she thought of them, which resulted in her having very few friends. She neither smoked nor drank and was determined to stand her ground against Dad. She would berate him for his drunken behaviour and he, in turn, would retaliate and I hated every minute of it. Dad had married late in life so my cousins from his seven sisters were all adults; consequently, I had nobody to turn to for guidance or comfort. I once went to a pub where I knew he would be and begged him to come home. His response was to offer me a glass of beer and encourage me to drink it. It was repulsive to my young palate and I showed my disgust at the vile tasting liquid by spitting it out and grimacing, much to the amusement of Dad and the drunken spongers surrounding him. The emotional wounds from those years pierced deeply into my heart and took a long time to heal and the scars remain. On reflection, Dad did what worked best for him at that time. He'd suffered much in his life and he was stuck in an unhappy marriage. My sister is five years younger than me so she was spared the pain of those tumultuous years. However, whatever perceived faults my parents had, I never heard either of them swear and the only time Dad ever hit me was when I swore at home when he and Mum had guests. After that I never swore at home again throughout my childhood and adulthood. They drummed into me over and over again not to lie or steal and begged me to sever my ties with the delinquents, and I appreciate the fact that they tried so hard to protect me. Under the influence of my friends, I once stole some paints from school because I so wanted to paint pictures at home and we couldn't afford to buy them. Mum and Dad were horrified and insisted that I return them the next day.

They had each suffered harrowing lives. Mum's Mum, Nin as we called her, the only Grandparent I knew, was a positively evil woman. She lied and concocted all manner of schemes to cause maximum hurt and embarrassment to people, so heaven knows what she had been through herself to make her behave in that way. She lived in Liverpool and when she became homeless, Mum and Dad paid for her to come to Gravesend. They welcomed her into our home and cared for her selflessly. I was in the sitting room with her one day whilst Mum and Dad were in the kitchen, preparing our meal. The meal was brought in and placed on the table and my parents returned to the kitchen. The next instant, Nin called out to them and when they both came back she told them that I had stolen food from her plate, which was a malicious fabrication. Mum and Dad insisted that I apologise, except that I hadn't done anything wrong, so I refused. I pleaded my innocence and the vicious old woman beside me contradicted everything I said. It was a stalemate. Neither of us budged in our story and that placed Mum and Dad in a tricky situation. When neither of us gave in, Mum and Dad went back to the kitchen and left me with the hateful old hag.

Sometime after accepting Mum and Dad's hospitality, she moved in with a family a few doors away and we heard that she was telling lies, wicked lies, about Mum and Dad. What makes some people so hateful, I wonder? Without knowing their full history it is unwise to attempt to pass any form of judgement on them but being on the receiving end of their behaviour is difficult. All of my childhood experiences though have helped form my present personality. It was as it was and it is no more. I have no cause to complain now; had it been otherwise, I probably wouldn't have had the wonderful experiences of my later life. The crime writer Sue Grafton put it well when she said, "People who've had happy childhoods are wonderful, but they're bland. An unhappy childhood compels you to use your imagination to create a world in which you can be happy. Use your old grief. That's the gift you're given."

### *Beefy Banks's barrow*

I had no trouble with the 11 plus exams and should have gone to grammar school but chose to go to the same secondary modern as my wayward friends. The headmaster of my infant's school was not happy and summoned me to his office to explain myself. I got no encouragement from my parents.

"If you don't go to grammar school, you'll be able to leave school and can start earning money a year sooner," was Dad's only comment. Consequently, my education didn't advance as well as it could have. At the Secondary Modern, I was one of six boys chosen to attend free lessons at the art school on Saturday mornings but once again my parents showed very little interest in my work. I quit and instead delivered newspapers for a local newsagent each morning before school. On Saturday mornings, I also collected the money for the week's delivery, which took a lot longer. I had one of the two largest rounds, which meant that I earned a little more than the other paper boys but it also meant that the bag filled with papers was that much heavier and it took much longer to deliver them on the circuitous two-mile hike. On Sundays, with the papers being much thicker, the bag was even heavier but mostly I had the use of my bike. I had to get up and be at the newsagent by five o'clock each morning to sort out which papers I needed and mark them with the addresses before piling them into the bag in the order that I would need them. I have vivid memories of arriving home cold, wet and tired and Mum having to dry out my clothes and shoes in front of the fire so that I could wear them to school. The newsagent eventually found himself in trouble for allowing me and the other schoolchildren to start so early in the morning before school and was told to cease doing so, but my paper round was so huge I had to continue beginning at an unearthly hour.

Although I hung around with the wrong crowd because we were in the same class at school, my main friend was Tommy who was a year older than me and lived just a few houses away. For many years we were inseparable and he was so different to the others, who to my knowledge never read books or took much interest in anything other than fighting and other mindless activities. Tommy, by contrast, was intelligent and like me, artistic, so we passed many hours drawing, painting, reading, modelling, cycling and any number of imaginative and resourceful pursuits. For my thirteenth birthday, Dad had bought me an old second hand bike from one of his nieces, for a token price of half a crown. Tommy was one of eight children and his parents couldn't afford to buy him one, so we went off together on mine. We took turns, with one of us standing peddling and the other sitting on the saddle.

We both had a love of the cinema and because neither of our parents were wealthy, Tommy and I would find ways to make enough money to indulge in our passion for films. Friendly neighbours would sometimes buy my paintings and in those days, empty beer bottles were returned to the pubs and for each one returned there would be a payment of one penny; we would collect them whenever and wherever we could until we each had enough to earn sixpence (a tanner), which was enough for us to go to the children's Saturday morning matinee. Sometimes we would pilfer empty beer bottles stored in crates in the back yard of one pub and then take them to another pub and collect the money, which was the closest I ever got to criminality. We would also knock on doors in the neighbourhood, asking if anybody had any old rags that they didn't want. When we'd collected enough, we'd borrow a barrow from a friendly neighbour, a man called Beefy Banks, and pushing Beefy Banks's heavy barrow, we'd set off on the two mile hike into town to exchange the contents for money with the rag and bone man. I was impressionable and immersed myself into the films, partly to escape the unpleasantness of being at home. I loved the glamour and the lure of the exotic locations. I have colourful memories of Gregory Peck and Susan Hayward in The Snows of Kilimanjaro, Burl Ives and Christopher Plummer in Wind Across the Everglades, Burl Ives, Alec Guinness and Maureen O Hara in Our Man in Havana, Stewart Granger and Deborah Kerr, trekking across Africa in search of King Solomon's Mines, Humphrey Bogart in Casablanca and Jack Hawkins and Joan Collins in Land of the Pharaohs and a multitude of other films. I longed to visit those places. I wanted to cross the desert, to see the pyramids, to trek through the jungle, to go on safari, to browse in the souks. Coming from a poor family living on a rundown council estate I could never imagine it happening. Now, however, I've not only visited them all but many, many more fabulous and compelling countries.

### *Under arrest*

When we moved to a new area, although it was still a rundown place to live, it was infinitely better than where we'd been previously and I was away from the bad influence of my former friends. My life changed for the better once I'd started working on the tugs and spending more of my free time with Tommy and more balanced people but I would still spend as little time at home as possible. On the few days or nights that I wasn't working, I'd rather be with other people, either drinking with friends, nightclubbing, going to the greyhound races or the cinema or indeed anywhere but home and in any case the vast majority of my week was spent with my fellow tugmen.

I'd stayed clear of the criminal activities of my school friends but that didn't prevent me from being thrown into a cell one night. It was around one thirty in the morning and I was on my way home with an acquaintance that I'd met during a fun evening at the South Bank Club. We'd stopped to peer innocently through the window of a car showroom.

"Copper," my friend hollered and scarpered off before I could react. Why he did that has always remained a mystery because he never gave a satisfactory explanation. I presume he thought we'd be in trouble for wandering the streets at one thirty in the morning. I wasn't even aware of a policeman until the constable grabbed me by the scruff of the neck and marched me off to the nearest police phone box. These were painted blue, placed in strategic positions around the town and were linked directly to the police station by a telephone accessible from the outside via a hinged door. The interiors had enough space to enable the police to make out reports or even hold prisoners temporarily. They were phased out in the 1970's when two-way radios were being issued. I struggled and complained to no avail whilst he called the station. After a brief discussion with whoever was at the other end of the line, he bundled me off to the police station. I was forcibly pushed into a tatty room with painted walls and shoved down onto a wooden chair next to a desk. There were two policemen. One was the arresting officer and the other, who wasn't wearing a uniform, was large, loathsome and clearly ruthless. He had a round, pimply face and grotesque blubbery lips that had spittle around them when he spoke. They thought my friend and I had intended to break into the showroom, though what we would have done in there I can't imagine. I was ordered to empty my pockets, which I obediently did. They both fired questions at me over and over again, trying to get me to admit that I had been up to no good but I couldn't give them the information they'd hoped for because I was innocent. I started to get annoyed and back answered the loathsome one. He responded with a violent smash of his hand on my jaw.

"You call me Sir when you speak to me you miserable little sod," he yelled. I guess that maybe he didn't overly like himself and took out his self-loathing on others and that night it sadly turned out to be me. I refused to call him Sir, which didn't help my predicament. He fumbled through the contents of my pockets hoping to find some incriminating evidence and found pictures of some of my past and present girlfriends.

"How many of these have you poked?" he said.

"None," I protested.

"Don't give me that load of bollocks, how many?"

"None," I insisted.

"Why have you got all these pictures if you haven't poked any of them?"

"I just have."

"And I suppose you're going to tell me you've never stolen anything either."

"No, never."

"You're not telling me that you haven't taken the odd thing from Woolworths at times," he said

"No, never," I said. Try as he did, he had nothing on me and never would have because I wasn't guilty of anything.

"Lock the lying little bugger up," he told his associate.

I was led to a cell, shoved in and the door was locked but not before the thin, brown blanket was taken away from me. I spent a cold, lonely night on a horrible thin, green plastic mattress, locked in the stark, bare cell. Shortly after daybreak, they let me out, returned my possessions and sent me on my way. When I got home nothing was discussed because Mum and Dad had got used to me staying out and I probably wouldn't have told them anything anyway.

### *Ali the Imam*

Some of my happiest childhood years were spent in Liverpool. I don't know why I was sent there. I have a memory of travelling on the train with my Aunt Ethel, Mum's sister, with whom I stayed. She was married to a Muslim, Ali, and I adored him. She had converted to Islam when she married her first husband, also called Ali, with whom she had three children, Ali, Amina and Norma, who were all cared for by the second husband along with two adopted children, Maria and Mohammed. I shared a room with Mohammed. My Uncle Ali was an Imam and in addition to the five children, the large house where I stayed with him was always filled with other Muslims coming and going about their business and prayers. These were very happy years for me, living in a calm, loving, happy environment. I never witnessed any anger or heard a raised voice. Because of my Uncle Ali's status, he regularly received important members of the Muslim community and once I was asked to wait in a separate room because he was to receive King Hussein of Jordan.

As well as other properties, he also had a few halal butchers' shops and personally killed all that was on sale. I was taken by him to the abattoir on more than one occasion and accompanied him whilst he slaughtered the sheep that had been set aside for him. The noise was disturbing and the smell was nauseating as he took me on a tour of the various sections. The pigs that we wouldn't go near, squealed, the cattle bellowed and the sheep bleated in panic as they stood crammed in their pens awaiting their brutal slaughter. He took me up alongside the executioner and I watched as the terrified cattle were prodded into the tight enclosure. Unable to move, the executioner placed the gun on their foreheads and fired the bolt into their brains. As the animal collapsed in a lifeless heap, a trapdoor was opened sending it crashing to the floor below where somebody would shove a rod into the hole left by the bolt and turn its brain over, which cause the beast's legs to lash out. A team of men would then start ripping out the innards. We sloshed our way through blood and guts to Uncle Ali's area. His sheep were brought to him and placed on their backs in a rack one at a time with their heads pointing towards "Qibla," the direction that Muslims face in prayer. With the knife held behind his back, he would invoke the name of Allah, "Bismillah," then with one swift, expertly executed motion, slice through the carotid artery, oesophagus, trachea and jugular veins, leaving the nervous system intact so that the unfortunate beast would bleed to death. The consumption of blood is forbidden In Islam. The sheep were then not allowed to be touched until all life had drained away. To westerners, this seems a barbaric method of slaughter but they have no moral high ground to stand on. Despite this horrific experience, I never wanted to leave his side and I loved everything about his lifestyle. I loved the communal meals with so many people laughing and chattering away around the huge table as the bowls of food were passed around and we scooped the portions up with our fingers. I loved the frequent trips to Wales and other places in his Ford Consul, and to hear Uncle Ali singing in Arabic as he drove. We never had any family outings at home. (I can only remember one occasion when I was taken out with Mum and Dad as a family.) I loved it when visitors would arrive and Aunt Ethel would go to the back yard, pick out a chicken, kill it, pluck it and prepare a meal. The hospitality that they offered to everybody was overwhelming and the house was always full of love and laughter.

### *The gene drd4-7r*

The time came, sadly, for me to return home to Gravesend. After Mum and Dad had squandered every penny of his compensation, Dad stopped getting drunk and his true character of a quiet, gentle man was revealed. This meant that Mum wasn't nagging him so much. Being at home became more bearable and the mental pain and turmoil I'd suffered lessened. We were still not a close family though and never had been. A couple of years after I returned, my sister went to Liverpool to stay with Uncle Ali and Aunt Ethel. She stayed for a few years and went to school there. By the time she came home, I'd begun working on the tugs so we never really had a childhood together; we had such totally different characters anyway. I'd inherited Dad's wayfaring genes,

I looked the spitting image of him and just like him, I respond to confrontations or stressful situations calmly or not at all. I am a risk taker and crave constant changes in my life, whereas my sister has fallen heir to Mum's behaviour patterns, neither of them ever had any inclination to travel or even obtain a passport or driving license. It is intriguing that my half-sister has also never travelled.

For many years I resented the fact that my parents didn't do more to guide and inspire me but now I have no regrets. I would have been thoroughly unhappy had I qualified at something boring and spent my life in a conventional job year after year with not very much to look forward to other than a nice pension (although a nice pension would be much appreciated now!) I enjoyed my freedom as a youngster and on reflection wouldn't have wanted it any other way. It's made me what I am today. Mum and Dad may not have lived up to my expectations and I probably didn't live up to theirs, but they did what they felt they had to do in the circumstances and despite Dad's drunkenness in the early days, he was never violent and I love and miss them both. Scientific research has concluded that approximately 20% of the population have the gene DRD4-7r, which is linked to curiosity and restlessness and by association travel. It would seem that Dad passed that gene on to me and that it has been activated. My strong desire to travel originated in my childhood imagination and that gene has no doubt enhanced the desire and motivated me to constantly move on and seek new experiences. After I left the Thames tugs and Gravesend, I entered the blood tingling and sometimes hair raising world of sailing and fulfilled a wondrous dream.

*Like all author's, I would really appreciate it if you could find the time to write a review on Amazon.*

If you would like to continue following my adventures, they continue in 'Paid to Live the Dream'. I become bitten by the sailing bug, and end up skippering yachts in the Mediterranean. My first command was an ill-conceived new motor yacht, - the cause of many disasters and hilarious incidents which deserve to be told and were indeed 'stranger than fiction'.

The story of this boat was the initial reason for my putting pen to paper.

## ABOUT THE AUTHOR

Anthony Edwards was born in Gravesend, but since 1975 has lived mostly in the South of France. In 1980 He bought a ruin on three acres of land near a Provençal hill village. Together with his wife he renovated it and turned it into a self-sufficient organic smallholding. He went on to study complementary medicine and established a successful practice as a Kinesiologist, Hypnotist and Psychotherapist, and has made guest appearances on several radio programs in France and the U.K. He later moved to his present house, where he now lives with his wife and thoroughly spoilt, self-opinionated cat.

To see photos and get more information, go to my website at:-

https://anthonyedwards.fr

30538432R00065

Printed in Poland
by Amazon Fulfillment
Poland Sp. z o.o., Wrocław

# Always Mine

Scarlett Avery

Edited by John Hudspith

Proofread by Jamie Betts

Cover designed by Murphy Rae

**Always Mine © Scarlett Avery™**

**It Was Always You series**

ISBN 978-1-77498-144-3

# Dedication

*To those of us who want to be broken by a love story and then put back hole again...*

*This one will stay with you for days.*

Author's Note: This story touches on sensitive topics that might cause bad memories to surge for those who have been in a similar situation.

# Chapter 1

## *Roderick*

Someone barges into my office.

I shift my eyes from my iMac Pro screen—and all the priorities demanding my attention—to the tall man standing in front of me.

"I've had it up to here," my business partner says.

I frown. "What now?"

"This younger generation is useless. Useless." Loki's hands go flying over his head and land in a loud thump against his thighs.

"Says the twenty-nine-year-old."

Loki narrows his furious eyes at me. "Don't you dare compare me to Mr. Woo-woo Pixie Dust, Rod."

"You kill me with that nickname," I say with a laugh.

"It suits him. He's a chronic complainer who lives in an imaginary world where money grows on trees and gold paves the streets."

"Auburn Sorrel is at it again."

The irony is both names mean reddish brown. Our blue-eyed replacement video-director-slash-producer is as blond as a Viking.

"He's driving me to drink."

"Our temperamental temp is on another one of his legendary rants?"

"Yup."

I lift a hand up. "Let me guess. 'His chakra isn't aligned with the volume of work we demand', or is it, 'His qi isn't responsive to extra hours', or 'Working more than three hours a day is poisonous to the soul', or maybe 'He refuses to be a slave to capitalist bullies'?"

"All of the above. The idiot can't fucking decide."

"The guy is delusional. And lazy."

"My parents instilled strong work ethics in my sister and I. We don't expect to coast by like Auburn. Whatever happened to taking pride in an honest day's work?"

He's right. Loki's parents are amazing. I wasn't as lucky.

"Where did he drop the ball this time to get you this worked up?"

"Have you seen Unmerciful Fury's video?"

Auburn is working on the video for the group's comeback song.

"Not yet."

"It's crap. I mean, a five-year-old could've done a better job... even blindfolded."

"Yikes."

"How the hell did Auburn manage to graduate from film school with such mediocre editing skills? And who on God's green earth are these people who gave him all those glowing references? Lies, I tell ya." Loki jams his hand in his hair and pulls hard.

He looks like he's about to blow a gasket.

"Not everyone has our high standards," I say.

"Apparently not."

"I thought Auburn was supposed to make all the changes the band required and include our feedback. We sat down with him on Tuesday and spelled it all out... for three hours." I thought I was going to put a bullet to my head at some point. It was excruciating.

"He did." Loki's face is beet red. "His third take is still garbage."

"Get him to do a fourth one. We need a stellar video by next Friday. I don't want to let Unmerciful Fury down."

"Trust me, I know. I'm as unhappy as you are we're stuck with a crybaby wailing about working extra hours and demanding more work-life balance. This is the music biz. There is no such thing."

"Maybe if Auburn knew what he was doing, he would've nailed it the first time around."

"Right?" Loki says.

"Where is he now?"

Loki's lips twist. "Gone for the day."

"What?" I check the time on my phone. "But it's only twelve."

"He mumbled something about not being able to stay past four o'clock because of an ultimate tournament scheduled weeks ago."

I'm incredulous. "Our reputation is on the line and he needs to leave early to play Frisbee in the park with some friends?"

"The guy is twenty-seven, but a stupid game of ultimate is more important than his career. Go figure." Loki shakes his head. "Talk about having your priorities screwed on backwards."

"Jesus Christ. He needs to get his butt back here."

"I fired his ass," Loki says. "I told him to pack his belongings and get the hell out of my sight. I even had security escort him out. I don't need that shit. I called Unmerciful Fury's record label and told them we might not have anything to show them until later next week."

"What did they say?"

"They're okay with it. As long as we deliver a finished product by next Friday."

"Good call." I nod my approval.

Lochlan Berkshire and I own Pending Inference Productions. We pride ourselves on our creative and edgy music videos. In the past three years, we've worked with some of the biggest singers and bands in the industry. Yeah, we've been lucky. Believe it or not, this is my second career.

"This is all your fault, Rod." Loki shakes a warning finger at me. "The next time Dom is away, we'll stick to hiring pros or we'll schedule work around her absence."

Auburn is the third video guy we've hired in the last six weeks. That's what happens when you get used to working with the best.

"You won't hear any arguments coming from me." He places his closed fists to his waist. "I never thought giving a chance to up-and-comers would come back to bite me in the ass."

"Speaking of which, when the hell is Dom coming back from Europe? I can't handle hiring another amateurish and untalented editor. We'd have to go with a top editor, but that'll eat into our profits since we've wasted money on three incompetent idiots."

Dominika Jacek is my best friend. She's also a kick ass video-director-slash-producer.

"She got back in the middle of the night. She'll be here on Monday."

"We *need* her back, Rod."

"And I said, she'll be back on Monday."

"Are you sure she's back in LA? She hasn't seen her family in a while. What if she decides to extend her holiday? Have you heard from her?"

"Calm down, Loki. I texted her last night but I haven't heard back from her yet. The jetlag is going to be a bitch and I'm sure she'll feel it."

"Call her." Loki points to my phone sitting on my desk. "Make sure she's okay. How many people catch nasty airborne viruses on a plane? It's like a fucking germ factory. Maybe she's sick and bedridden."

"Good point, Doctor Berkshire."

He rolls his eyes at me. "If it's jetlag, I'll get my executive assistant to send her whatever kind of medication she needs. We'll pay. We need Dom back on Monday, Rod."

My best friend has her own company—independent from ours—but you'd never know listening to Loki.

"Yes, boss. I'm right on it, boss. Anything else, boss?"

He rubs his hand over his face. "I'm sorry. I'm overreacting. I'm stressed out. Call her, Rod."

"Don't worry, I will."

"Let's hope her time away will have cleared up whatever tension that's been playing out between the two of you in the last few months."

*He's never brought this up before.*

"What are you talking about?" I choose to play dumb.

"The way you've been acting around each other, you'd never know you've been best friends for the past twelve years. You've been bickering like an old married couple."

"I'm sure she was overwhelmed with all her projects and her pending trip. And I've been knee deep as well."

Loki pins me with a suspicious stare. "Let's hope that's all it is."

"Why do I feel you're accusing me of something?"

He arches an eyebrow in response.

*Whatever.*

"The yacht party will lighten your mood," I say to change the subject.

"Having Dom back is the only thing that will put my mind at ease. However, I'm looking forward to it. After all, nobody throws a party like Eddie Michaels. What a way to kick off the weekend."

"That's for sure."

Our buddy Eddie is what you call a triple threat in show-biz. He started out as a heartthrob popstar with some impressive dance moves before taking Hollywood by storm.

"The guy always parties hard, but now he has a good reason for celebrating."

"And that means a bevy of smoking hot women for all of Eddie's friends," I say.

"The guy sure knows how to attract 'em. Not that you have anything to complain about. Hanging out with you is always a blessing," he says. "Well, last night being the exception. Maybe we'll get luckier than we did last night." He grimaces.

"One would hope so, but who knows with Eddie's entourage."

Loki and I hit a few clubs last night. He ended up with a sexy petite redhead. I hooked up with her friend—a stunning blonde with brown eyes and spectacularly enhanced DD tits. We went back to her place. As things were getting hot and heavy, she excused herself. I never expected her to walk back into the bedroom carrying a platter of uppers. She claimed speed kept her thin, happy, energized and horny. That's a deal breaker for me nowadays. I kicked my drug habit to the curb and I'm not going back. No pussy is worth a relapse. I zipped up and got the hell out of there. Turns out Loki was in the same predicament.

"All right. Eddie's yacht sails at three. Let me tie up a few loose ends and we'll head out to the port."

"Sounds good."

"In the meantime, call Dom."

"Go back to your office." I wave him off.

Loki is right. Things have been pretty weird between my best friend and I. It seems like everything about me irritates the hell out of her. The problem is, I don't know why. Maybe it's a natural progression when people have been this close for this long. I've been tiptoeing through it like I'm walking on glass, careful not to make matters worse. I can't afford to lose her as my best friend. She means too much to me. Whatever it is that's caused this friction between us, I hope her time away will have mellowed her out. Eager to hear all about her trip and catch up, I dial her up. She answers on the first ring.

"Hey, Dom, you're back."

"Rod, how are you?"

"Good. Did I wake you up?"

"No, I've been up for a while. I got your text message. I was going to answer after coffee."

"No problem. I'm sure you're still a little tired."

"That's the understatement of the century. I'm so jetlagged, I don't even know what planet I'm on. Is this Pluto or Mars?"

I laugh. "I hear you. When I came back from Australia two months ago, I thought I woke up on Jupiter. Are you going to be able to stay awake until tonight?"

"I might have to take a nap if I want to make it to Zoe's birthday party. I wasn't planning on going since I just landed, but she insists. She also invited me to dinner along with her best friend before we head out to her party. Something about thanking me."

"It makes sense. You're responsible for her big break."

"It was an introduction. Nothing more," she says.

"It's much more than that and you know it."

Thanks to Dom, Zoe secured a phenomenal job at my brothers' TV production company. Dom would never take credit where credit's due. She's so self-effacing.

"Will you stop by Zoe's party?" She changes the subject.

"I'll head there the second Eddie's yacht docks."

"I don't understand."

"Remember how Eddie proposed to the so-called love of his life after a three-day sex marathon?"

"Don't tell me. It wasn't love ever after."

"It was a quickie Vegas wedding that lasted seven days. The six-month waiting period has elapsed and his divorce was finalized on Monday. Since she's loaded, she didn't ask for a dime, so it ended up being a smooth divorce. Eddie says her father is relieved."

"I don't blame the man. At least she isn't pregnant."

"Yeah, I don't see Eddie as the father type. The guy isn't wired for commitment."

"One could say the same about you, Rod."

"I never professed otherwise, Dom," I say. "Anyway, back to the divorce. Eddie invited a bunch of us to celebrate his newfound freedom by chartering a yacht."

"The usual suspects will be present?"

"No doubt."

"Kudos to Eddie. Nothing like getting back on the horse," she says.

"Yeah, well, Eddie loves women—"

"As much as you do."

It's not like I can deny it, but her snarky tone annoys me. She's been throwing these digs at me since before she left. I thought we were past that.

I let it slide. "How was the training?"

"There are no words to describe how amazing it was. I'm now armed with even more cutting-edge skills. My head is filled with ideas. I can't wait to put them all into practice. Thanks again for pushing me to apply." She clears her throat. "And... thanks for helping me get there."

I detect a touch of shyness in her voice. Even after all these years, Dom doesn't accept gifts easily.

"It would've been a shame if you'd missed out," I say.

"Yeah, well, it cost an arm and a leg."

I paid for it.

I didn't care how many times she protested. She was going to be part of that group of eight.

"It was worth it?"

"It was so much more than I expected."

"That's all that matters."

"Thanks again."

Dom is so freaking talented, it's ridiculous. She makes good money, but she's still a freelancer and she doesn't have a previous multi-millionaire career to fall on. When the opportunity came for a handful of professionals to be part of an advanced month-long video production program offered by Pepperdine University's Communication Division, I pushed her to apply. Since the training started in LA—New York was next—and ended in London, I nudged her to stay in Europe and play tourist. She didn't fight me.

"How was it seeing your mom and cousins?"

We've been relying on texting since she left because the time difference was challenging. I've also been catching the highlights of her trip on social media, but it doesn't compare to hearing all the details from her.

She lets out a long sigh. "I don't miss living an ocean apart from my mom." No chances my mother would've ever won a Mother of The Year award. Neither would Dom's. "Seeing my paternal grandparents is always weird. Are they still family when your father abandoned you as a kid?" It's a rhetorical question. "It was awkward. The language barrier doesn't make communicating easy since my German is rusty. And how many times are they going to apologize for my father's behavior? Their only son and he turns out to be a disappointment."

"Parents aren't always biological, Dom. You and I both know it."

"Isn't that the truth," she says.

Despite all the rotten and shitty things she's gone through in her childhood, she's always managed to maintain a cheerful facade. She knows how to keep her pain buried deep.

I, on the other hand, was a hellion growing up.

Some called me the devil's child. With good reason. I wore my anger on my chest like armor. It scared the shit out of most people.

Not Dom.

She's always accepted every part of me and she always knew how to turn my foul moods around. Until recently, that is. Lately, our bickering gets me all riled up.

"You turned out great," I say.

"Thanks to you. And so did you."

"Damn right I did."

"Roderick Wolfe. Always Mr. Humble."

"I'm a former rock star. I don't even know how to spell the word."

"No, you don't," she says with a laugh.

I love it when she's lighthearted like this.

Maybe we're back to being Dom and Rod.

"Other than family reunions, what kind of wild and reckless adventures were you on? European men must be grieving your departure."

Don't ask me why I'd dig my own grave by poking into her love life. It's not like I want to know she's been with other guys.

"Reckless adventures? As in vacation flings?"

"Yeah."

She laughs.

"What's so funny, Dom?"

She hasn't been in a relationship in so long.

The last idiot was a dickless mama's boy. I guess, in many ways, I should be grateful because I don't have to worry about some jerk disrespecting her or treating her badly. She's yet to date a guy worthy of her.

*Shame.*

Dom is gorgeous. Her jet-black hair and blue eyes against her luminous complexion is every man's dream. Her full lips could drive a guy wild. Other than for a dye job, she's all-natural. She wears a minimum amount of makeup. And in a sea of silicone, her tits are real. Bonus, she never uses her body as if it were her only asset. She doesn't have to.

She's super smart, too—in high school, she could solve complex math equations that stumped some of her teachers. To this day, she's still a math whiz. She's also vivacious and fiercely loyal. She's the whole package. Not that I'll ever tell her, but I've harbored a secret longing for my best friend for a while now. However, I have no intention of screwing up what we share with sex. Crossing that line could potentially be lethal.

"That's your department, Rod," she says.

I guess I spoke too soon. She still has a bee in her bonnet.

"After all, you're the self-indulgent bad boy who still—after retiring—gets women to drop their panties on command. I'm a good girl. Thank God I don't have a dick between my legs *dictating* my every thought."

What can I say? There's an abundance of gorgeous and willing women in LA. Add the former rock star factor and getting pussy is a joke. That's why I subscribe to the 'once and done' school of thought. It's best that way. Women can put too many expectations on a relationship and that screws everyone up. Mom was a prime example. But coming from Dom? It slices.

"Is that your way of saying you got zero action in Europe? Because it sounds like you're still a bundle of nerves."

If she wants to go there, I'm game.

"Fuck off, Rod."

I let out a strangled laugh laced with irritation.

"Is that any way to talk to your best friend?"

"That's low even for you," she says.

I jam a hand through my hair in frustration.

"I was hoping you would've worked out some of the tension you've been carrying so you can stop being so short with me. I guess I was wrong."

Silence.

She shuts me out. Again.

"Dom?"

Nothing.

"For God's sake. Are you still on the other end?"

"I am. No need to shout, Rod."

*That's it?*

*I don't get the woman. I swear I don't.*

One minute hot. The other cold as ice.

I didn't think anyone could be worse than my mother, but for the past few months, Dom's erratic moodiness is putting Mom to shame.

I let out an impatient exhale. "Why don't I let you go? I'm sure you have a million things to do. I'll see you at Zoe's party."

"All right," she says.

*Two fucking words?*

"I won't stay too long because the guys will be waiting for me at the Quintus—"

"You mean Dark Compulsion?"

"No, Dom. I mean the Quintus Hotel."

"Surely, you'll stop by the private adult club that caters to Hollywood's Who's Who since it's annexed to the Quintus. After all, membership has its perks. Unless you hook up with a girl on the yacht."

"What kind of statement is that?" Now, I'm pissed off.

"Just sayin'."

I let out a loud exhale. "Are we fighting again, Dom?"

"We aren't fighting," she says. "Why don't you just come out and say it?"

"Say what?"

"After Eddie's party you'll find an eager fuck buddy for the night—like you always do—which is why you'll only pop in and out of Zoe's birthday party."

Her bitter tone jabs at my heart.

"This conversation is heading south. Fast. I called to find out how you were doing after an extended absence from LA"—*and because I missed you*—"I didn't call for us to be at it like cats and dogs. I thought our time apart would cool things off between us. Not that I know why the sight of me—or the sound of my voice—repulses you so much, but it does. I'll catch you later."

With that, I hang up.

*What the fuck?*

## Chapter 2

## *Dominika*

"Wow, this lasagna was amazing, Holly," I say, dropping my knife and fork on the plate. "I can make a mean deluxe grilled cheese sandwich and I'm good friends with the barbecue, but not much more. You, on the other hand, have skills."

Holly Dunham singlehandedly prepared her best friend Zoe's birthday meal. Everything was delicious.

"Being a makeup artist on Food Network has its perks," Holly says, combing her bleach blonde hair behind her ear. "The hours are way more decent than when I used to work on movie sets. And the free cooking lessons are a perk. Waiting around in the dressing room and watching the show as it's being recorded comes in handy. Although right now, I feel a little gypped since I was stationed in LA while you were off to Europe and my bestie here was in the Big Apple."

"It's all about the right connections." Zoe winks at me.

"It was nothing." I shrug.

"Wash your mouth out with soap," Zoe says. "Had you told me a year ago, I'd be the makeup artist to a huge star and I'd travel with her to New York because she was selected—out of God knows how many actresses—to cohost a top-rated daytime talk show, I would've laughed. Without Dominika, I'd still be applying concealer on people's butts to make them appear baby smooth. Working on the set of a porn film isn't all it's cracked up to be. The stuff you see..." Her face twists in a disgusted grimace. "Thanks to you, those days are behind me."

"I overheard Rory and Roark mention they needed a new makeup artist," I say.

Until a year ago, Zoe Hagan was a freelancer. Rod's company has used her on a number of videos I've directed and produced. Her attention to detail sets her apart, which is why I didn't hesitate to recommend her to Rod's brothers. A few interviews later and she'd landed her big break as the makeup artist for then-unknown Adelaide McAdams. The now megastar is leading the award-winning cast of the smash hit political thriller *'Pushing the Distance'* on UTV.com—the subscription-based streaming service co-owned by the two eldest Wolfe brothers.

"If you hear of any more openings at UTV.com, *'Call Me Maybe?'*" Holly jokes. The reference to the iconic hit song is quite funny.

"I thought you loved your job?" I say.

"I do, but New York City? It's high up there on my list. Believe it or not, I've never been. Neither have my parents or my sisters. I'm dying to see the Big Apple."

"Why haven't you been?" I say.

"It's freaking expensive and I'm only a freelancer. I'm still saving," Holly says.

I nod.

"The Big Apple was a dream come true," Zoe says. "Granted, I haven't traveled abroad, I'm pretty sure there's nothing quite like it in the world."

"I can attest to that," I say. "Europe is rich with culture, art, food, and fashion, but cities like New York and Los Angeles are unparalleled."

"Speaking of fashion, I still can't get over how amazing you look." Zoe has been marveling at my new look since I arrived.

"It was time for a little change," I say.

"Little?" Zoe's head jerks back. "Had I not been expecting you, I would never have recognized you."

"Oh, come on," I say.

"You need a new mirror," Holly says.

"See? I'm not the only one," Zoe says. "With the new hair, you could rival any Hollywood starlet. The stunning strapless dress is va-va-voom. The heels are so unexpected for a girl who practically lives in Converse. And the more daring makeup is so sexy."

"Thank you," I say.

"I agree with everything she said." Holly grins. "What brought on the change?"

"There comes a point in life where you have to be willing to let go of your shackles," I say.

Zoe and Holly frown their confusion, their brown eyes staring at me.

"Before I left Europe, I treated my cousin Johanna to a day of pampering at her favorite spa to thank her for allowing me to stay with her and her husband while I was visiting." Thank God I didn't have to stay with my mother. "After six weeks away, I looked like I had jumped out of an eighties music video because my roots were showing big time. Johanna's hairdresser suggested I stop fighting Mother Nature. I did."

"Good call," Holly says.

"What I love the most is your willingness to showcase your ink out in the open," Zoe says reaching out for my arm.

I pull it away, like I always do. It's a knee-jerk reaction I can't seem to help. I'm still not comfortable with the scars.

"I'm sorry. I didn't mean to—"

"It's nothing," I say. Her look of remorse fans my guilt, but I'm in no mood for a long explanation. "Cake?" I veer the conversation. "It's red velvet."

"Yum!" Holly claps. "Did you bake the cake?"

"God, no. I don't want to poison Zoe on the eve of her thirty-fifth birthday," I say with a laugh.

Holly and Zoe join me.

A quick trip to Zoe's kitchen and I'm back.

Holly lifts her glass. "Here's to another milestone."

"Hear, hear," I say.

"Milestone? I feel like day-old bagels marked down for a quick sale," Zoe says, "I'm still sitting on the shelf. People—aka men—like fresh. I'm beyond the sell-by date."

"Oh, stop with your whining," Holly says. "You still have five hours left before the clock strikes midnight. So, you're still *fresh*. Shut up and lift your glass."

I do as I'm told.

She and Zoe follow suit, clinking their glasses to mine.

We each take a long sip of our champagne.

I pull the glass away from my lips and give it an appreciative glance. Zoe and Holly do the same thing.

"This is exceptional. It tastes expensive. I feel so spoiled," Zoe says.

"The French know what they're doing," I say. "I'm glad you like it."

"Speaking of the French," Holly says, "unlike us, those women aren't afraid of aging or delving into their sexuality as the years roll by. Several French actresses I've worked with in the past have confirmed it. Take a page from their book, Zoe.

Your best years are in front of you. You're stepping into sexual exploration years. Let the fun begin."

"All well and good for French women, but I'm struggling with this whole aging thing."

"You need to change the color of your lenses," Holly says. "Work with me. What's left on your sex-bucket list?"

Zoe taps her finger against her chin. "God, I don't know."

"If you're stuck for ideas, I can help," Holly says.

*Let's bypass this conversation.* "Do we need to go there?"

"Oh, don't worry, Dom, you'll be thanking me later," Holly says grabbing her phone.

*I doubt it.*

"Check this out." Holly hands her phone to her best friend.

Zoe's eyes sparkle.

I stretch my neck. "What is it?"

Zoe turns the device to me.

*'FIFTY SEXUAL MUST-DOS PEOPLE SHOULD CONSIDER TRYING DURING THEIR LIFETIME'*

"Got it." I nod, choosing to return my focus to the cake.

"So which ones do you still need to cross off your list?" Holly says.

"Hmmm." Zoe's gaze shifts to the ceiling. "Well, I have no desire to ever French kiss a girl. Group sex is a no for me. Not sure about sex with someone younger. I don't feel like being a teacher."

*She's on a roll.*

"Masturbation? Who doesn't do it daily?"

*I'm raising my hand here.*

"Watch porn alone? For sure."

Holly nods.

I remain quiet.

"Blindfold? Done that. Anal? Roark is into—"

I lift my hand to prevent anymore over-share. "Whoa, I know the guy."

"Well, I guess I should say *was*, since Roark and I are a thing of the past," Zoe says. "Anyway, to finish my list, a quickie in a skirt? Roark would lose his mind if he saw me walk into their studios wearing a skirt—"

"Please, stop." I don't need to know that side of Roark.

She lets out a longing exhale. "Those were the days. Being single at thirty-five sucks."

Roark and Zoe started a heated relationship three months after she joined UTV.com. It was short-lived. At thirty-nine, the middle Wolfe child still isn't quite ready for commitment. Surprise, surprise.

"What about you, Dom? What's on your sex-bucket list?"

I blink at her in surprise at Holly's question. "Why are you picking on me? I'm not the one celebrating a birthday. I'm only twenty-five. I have plenty of time in front of me."

"True, but I'm curious..." Holly's words trail.

I shift in my seat. "What are you curious about?"

"Not that I want to pry, but I'm dying to know something," Holly says.

"Okay."

"How can you be best friends with Roderick Wolfe? The man is dangerously good-looking. We're talking sex on legs here. Five alarm fire. Sex-me-up-every-morning-noon-and-night kind of god. An Adonis. Can-I-have-your-baby-please-hunk—"

"I get the point." It's a struggle not to roll my eyes at her infatuation over my best friend.

"I mean, he's the full package," she keeps talking. "A tattooed, bad boy with a reputation for being a stallion in bed. A badass drummer. A successful exec. A founding member of a multibillion-dollar company." Holly rests her chin against her clamped hands and lets out a long, suffering sigh. "The man is a real catch."

"Yes. He. Is," Zoe says.

Rod has two stellar careers under his belt, on top of being one of the early investors who helped propel StreamTunes—the leader in audio streaming services. The risk paid off. Rod, his former bandmates—Beckett Christensen, Jace Halsey, and Holt Christensen—Lochlan, and Jace's older brother Jagger, along with a few other guys in their inner circle are paper billionaires. Once StreamTunes's founder and CEO, Gage Hollingsworth, buys them out, they'll all be stinking rich. Except for Beckett. He's already a multibillionaire in his own right.

"What's your secret for not throwing yourself at him? God knows I'd make a fool out of myself every time I was near him," Holly says.

"I've known him for so long," I say.

"So?" Holly is staring at me like I have two heads.

"So, we've been practically glued at the hip since we met." I shrug, uncomfortable with the scrutiny.

"And?"

*She's going to be a hard sell.*

"I don't see him like most women do." *Well, that used to be true.*

"Is there something wrong with your eyes?"

"No, Holly. My eyes are perfectly fine."

"In that case, your explanation fails to help me understand how you can keep a guy like Rod in the friend zone."

"I've been dying to know since I found out the two of you have been best friends forever," Zoe says. "I never asked the question because I didn't want to overstep my boundaries since we aren't close friends. But Holly is right, Rod is delicious—"

"So are all the Wolfe brothers," Holly says. "They have

alpha names referring to rulers, warriors and kings. They're gorgeous and they sport their masculinity with pride. Those guys have no idea how to spell the word, metrosexual."

*I couldn't agree with her more.*

"You've never wanted more with Rod?" Zoe frowns.

A stab of guilt slices clean through me as I think of our earlier conversation. I hate myself for having been so short with him. It's just that I have no idea how to share my growing feelings with him without fucking everything up.

Holly and Zoe blink at me, waiting for an answer.

"Dom?" Zoe says.

"Relationships are fragile," I say. "Guys flake out all the time." Thanks, Dad, for the lesson. "There are too many options in LA. Men here suffer from shiny object syndrome."

"They do." Holly nods.

"Tell me about it," Zoe says.

"Rod knows everything about my personal ghosts and demons." I point to my inked arm.

Zoe lowers her eyes. "So, there's more to the intricate tattoos?"

*A lot more.* "It's too heavy to delve into on the eve of your birthday."

"I can respect that," she says.

I'm relieved she drops the subject.

"If he knows everything about you—the good, the bad and the ugly—why not take it all the way? I mean, there aren't any more surprises," Holly says. "I would."

*Wanting more could complicate—or shatter—one of the best things in my life.* "Rod and Dom. Best friends forever. That's who we are," I say, hoping I can convince them, although I can't seem to convince myself lately. "We made a commitment to each other when I was thirteen and he was sixteen—right after he came to my rescue for the first time."

"He rescued you from danger?"

"Yes. Twice, Holly."

"Oh."

"Certain things should remain untouched... like a lifelong friendship," I say.

Rod's been through some heavy shit and his less-than-ideal childhood was as undesirable as mine. I'm an only child with a set of rotten parents. I have no one else but Rod in my corner. I've always been there for him and vice versa. I can't risk losing our friendship. It would break me. I have to find it in me to tame the weird feelings I've been having lately. It's not his fault if I want to move what we share out of the friend zone. It's not like there's any shortage of options for a guy like Roderick. It's so easy for him not to see me as more than his trusted sidekick.

~

I lean into Zoe so I don't have to shout over the music. "What an amazing turnout. You're one popular girl."

"I was dreading this birthday thing, but now, I love it." She grins from ear to ear.

After an hour-long dance marathon, Zoe, Holly and I are taking a short respite by the bar located in the back of the room. I love to dance. There's nothing like moving freely to the sound of the music. I'd still be out there shaking my thing, but my feet hurt. I have yet to get used to these platform heels. Since I've had enough to drink for the evening, I'm nursing a glass of sparkling water with a wedge of lime. My companions opted for red wine. I look them up and down.

Even with these skyscrapers strapped to my feet, I'm still so much shorter than they are.

*Sigh.*

My illusion of being a tall Amazonian in my new heels dies a slow death.

*Oh, well.*

"Nothing beats a milestone birthday like celebrating it in style in a setting like this," I say.

"I know, right? I never thought I'd see the day where I'd set foot in this place," Zoe says.

"Same here," Holly says.

Zoe's older sister, Emma, threw her a party with Holly's help. The upscale venue is a gift from Adelaide McAdams. The Wordsworth is a posh members-only private social club for powerhouses in showbiz. It's reserved for women, but they make exceptions for parties, galas and events. If you have an extra fifteen thousand dollars to burn on initiation fees and a thousand a month, this is the club for you. It's a bit too rich for my blood.

The dance floor is packed. Zoe's guests are moving to the beat of the latest club music. Most of the guests here work with Zoe at UTV.com except for a handful of Zoe's childhood friends and her cousins.

When the DJ drops a chart topper, the crowd goes wild. Zoe, Holly, and I get swept away by the collective energy and raise a hand above our heads, swaying our hips to the catchy tune. It's quite the sight. Gabriel McTillerson pokes his head above the crowd and waves me over. He's been my dance partner for the better part of the evening.

I shake my head. I'm taking a break.

He nods and gives me the thumbs-up before grabbing a co-worker by the waist and forcing her to dance with him.

Gabriel is fit and he has a great sense of humor. He's tall, dark and handsome, but not like Rod. He lacks the badass cock-sureness that characterizes Rod. I've met him at a few of UTV.-com's team events when I've accompanied Rod as his plus one.

Gabriel didn't recognize me at first. I revealed my identity when he started putting the moves on. He was shocked. Since then, he's been all compliments about my new look. In fact, most people who know me are as taken aback as Holly and Zoe.

"Oh, look who showed up," Holly says tugging on Zoe's arm. "Tall, dark, and smoking hot is here."

"Where?" Zoe stretches her neck.

"Near the other bar," Holly says.

Zoe stretches her neck.

So do I.

"*Your* man came for you." Holly points at her friend.

"He's no longer *my* man," Zoe says. "Pity. He looks so fucking delicious. He'd make for a perfect birthday gift." Longing—scratch that—*lust* veils her eyes.

"I believe getting dirty in a public place is part of your sex-bucket list," Holly says.

"You're right," Zoe laughs.

Holly joins in.

I'm unable to laugh, let alone smile. I'm too preoccupied by the erratic beating of my heart. The sight of the gorgeous strapping man standing next to Roark Wolfe is enough to cause me to go into cardiac arrest. His dark brown eyes pierce right into me, taking my breath away and making my pulse hammer.

*Rod.*

# Chapter 3

## *Roderick*

Eddie's party was a departure. I expected topless and naked women, lots of huge silicone tits and a never-ending flow of booze. In other words, I expected raunchiness. Eddie has set a precedent with his trademark over-the-top parties. The last thing I expected was for a bunch of us guys to hang out on a boat, catching up. Other than some of the staff—who were all fully dressed—there were no other women on the yacht. Since we were all confused, Eddie fessed up. He's the lead actor on a blockbuster action series and his short-lived marriage had caused enough talk. His recent divorce exploded in the news. The studio vetoed any possibility of Eddie embarrassing them by putting their foot down late last night when they caught wind of his party. Any inappropriate conduct—on his part or ours—would end his lucrative contract on the next six movies of the series. That's all it took for the notorious bad boy to walk a straight line.

To make up for the lack of pussy, Eddie gave us the next best thing—a guaranteed adrenaline rush. The flying jet skis he rented were a blast. Speed, height, water and daredevil acrobatics. What more can a guy ask for?

By the time Eddie's yacht docked, we had all showered, changed and feasted on a king's meal. For a change, no one got wasted. The rest of the guys made their way to the gentlemen's club while my brother and I hopped in a cab to the Wordsworth. After the security check, Roark and I enter the Hera—the main party room.

"Looks like the team of *'Pushing the Distance'* is here to celebrate Zoe's birthday," I say to my brother, scouring the crowd.

"Emma and Zoe's best friend have—" Roark stops mid-sentence. "Whoa." His eyes grow wide.

"What?"

"Have you seen Dom since she got back?"

"No. Why?"

"Because your best friend came back from Europe a changed woman."

"What are you talking about? Where is she?"

"Over there." My brother points.

*Shit.*

Dom looks stunning. Sexy as hell, even.

Holy smoking-hot bombshell.

What a jaw-dropping transformation.

She was breathtaking before, but now she could stop traffic. I flash her a wide smile, and I'm pleased when she returns it.

"Let me go say hi," I say.

Roark nods. "You better before another guy goes after her."

I frown my confusion.

"What's that face about, little brother?"

"Don't be an idiot," I say. "It's Dom we're talking about here."

He cocks an eyebrow. "*Your* Dom."

I shake my head, shrug, and roll my eyes. "You're crazy."

"And you're blind if you're incapable of seeing what's standing right in front of you."

*Oh, don't worry, I see her.* "Whatever."

He's been on my case for months now about Dom.

I should've never told him about Thanksgiving and I should've kept my mouth shut about the battle shots game.

I take a step forward, when out of nowhere a chesty brunette with glaring fake eyelashes steps in front of me, blocking my way.

"Are you who I think you are?" Her tone is playful.

"Err…" It's not like me to hesitate, but I'm caught off guard. I slide my gaze to my brother's grinning face before focusing on the brunette again. The desperate soul vying for my attention doesn't work for him or else she'd know better. "Sorry, but I'm no mind reader."

"I'd recognize you anywhere. You're the manful and virile drummer from Random Misconception. Aren't you?"

"I don't even know what manful means," I say.

She says drops her eyes to my crotch. "It means I'm a *huge* fan."

Sometimes, stardom can be a curse.

I look up and meet Dom's piercing blue eyes. Her unimpressed gaze tells the whole story.

I have no control over this.

"I'm Clemensia, by the way," the stranger says. Instead of extending her hand, she sticks out her chest.

*Why does Chlamydia come to mind?*

"Clemensia, this evening is to celebrate Zoe's birthday. Now, if you'll excuse me." I brush past her.

"Oh, no you don't." She stops me by placing a hand against my arm. "You're not getting away from me that easily. Since I saw you first, I get first dibs."

I let out an exasperated sigh. "Take your hand off me."

"Fine."

She does as she's told, but I can't quite decipher the expression in her eyes.

*Time to get away from this—*

Clemensia pulls down her super-short red tube dress and flashes a pair of double-enormous tits. Since she has a tiny frame, her tits look like giant inflated balloons.

*What the hell?*

There's a rumble around us. From the look of shock on guests' faces, they're as stunned as I am.

"Can you sign them?" She hands me a Sharpie.

*Where was she hiding it?*

Her question is one I used to get all the time at the height of my rock star career. Since I've retired, I spend my time behind a desk. This is no longer part of my life.

"You're kidding?" My eyes flicker up to Dom.

She's shooting daggers at me now.

*Fuck.*

This is not how I'd envisioned our encounter after not seeing each other for so many weeks.

"I'm not kidding," Clemensia says. "Please sign my boobs. They're big enough, it's not like you can miss them." She shakes her torso, sending her tits swinging from side to side.

"I don't sign body parts." *Well, I don't anymore.*

In our heyday, we used to get crazy requests from groupies. One woman begged our lead singer, Beckett Christensen, to sign the inner walls of her pussy.

"I can beg, if you'd like," Clemensia says.

*Talk about overly aggressive. And delusional.*

"I *said*, I don't sign body parts."

"Oh, come on. Roderick Wolfe is up for all sorts of nastiness."

"Don't you have any decency?" I never thought I'd see the day where I'd say that to a half-naked woman.

"I'll make it worth your while," she says.

Before I can respond, Clemensia pulls her dress over her head and drops it on the floor next to her.

My jaw drops.

The music stops.

The crowd gasps.

A collective round of, *'Holy fucks'*, replaces the latest club hit.

Not only is Clemensia naked, but two silver hoop rings are dangling low from her pussy, staring at me.

*Jesus Christ.*

"I told you it would be worth your while. I'm all yours, big boy."

I used to live for those words. Coming from her, they sound crass.

*No thanks.* "Show a modicum of class."

She looks confused.

"You're at the wrong event, lady," my brother says, "There aren't any strip clubs in this neighborhood. Put your clothes back on."

Clemensia glowers at him. "Who the hell are you?"

"I'll tell you who—"

"You over there, what the hell are you doing?" A large man comes running towards us, wagging his finger. The two bouncers who were manning the door follow him closely. "This isn't that kind of club."

"But—"

"No buts. Chris. Paul. Escort this skank out of here," large man says.

One of the guys picks up her discarded dress and throws it at her.

Clemensia lifts her chin in defiance. "Fuck off."

"You're pathetic." I agree with large man.

One of the bouncers pulls her hands behind her back.

"Get your hands off me, right the fuck now." Clemensia tries to wiggle out of his hold.

"Come on, let's go," he says without giving her a chance to cover up.

"The show is over, folks," large man says. "DJ, please resume the music."

Watching Clemensia's walk of shame with those silver hoop rings clinking between her legs is a sad, sad sight. When she's no longer in view, I shift my attention to where Dom was standing.

*Where the hell did she go?*

*Goddammit.*

# Chapter 4

## *Dominika*

Roderick Wolfe always commands attention when he walks into a room. Even before he hit superstardom, his mere presence would force everyone to stop and stare. It's his smooth, confident swagger. When he was younger, every step he took screamed 'Don't fuck with me or else'. Now, it says, 'I own the place'. And he does.

I knew my dramatic change would get a reaction out of him, but from the sinful sparkle in his eyes, I wasn't prepared for the delicious warm tide rippling all over my body.

*Damn.*

When his eyes meet mine, I gasp under my breath. I smile, blushing when he turns on his trademark bad boy potent charm. I've witnessed him directing that charm at someone else, but when he turns it towards me, it makes me weak in the knees. Rod has this undeniable breathtaking effect on women. And as much as I've lied to myself for years, I'm not immune to it.

Between his former career as a rock star, his devastatingly good looks, intense deep brown eyes, large frame, bulging muscles and inked torso and arms, Rod is every woman's dream. He's so gut-wrenchingly sexy, most other men don't measure up. Yeah, my best friend is so hot, it hurts. And he knows it too.

*I swear, when God was allotting good looks and magnetic personalities, he spent a solid month on Roderick Wolfe.*

Rod never hesitates to use that unfair advantage to disarm —I mean charm—women. Like he is now with the woman who's making a grotesque spectacle out of herself.

"Holy fuck, did you see that?" I'm sure Holly's expression matches my own astonishment.

"How dare she steal the limelight at *my* birthday party," Zoe says.

"Same old, same old," I say. "You'd be surprised how women will degrade themselves to boast they've fucked Rod Wolfe. It was worse at the height of his career. It's sad. Pathetic even. But for some women, it's a milestone to hit." I've witnessed this kind of scenario too many times to count. "Judging by how desperate this one is, she'll get her way." I wouldn't be surprised if Rod ended up fucking her in a random bathroom in this club or taking the action to a hotel.

"Given his godlike status," Holly says, "it's no surprise she'd want to stake her claim on him, but does she have to be such a whore about it?"

"But it's *my* birthday," Zoe says.

"Classless tarts don't care because they don't have an ounce of decency." The words come out harsher than expected.

Both Holly and Zoe turn in my direction and cock an eyebrow.

I attempt to save face. "Like I said, same old, same old."

As the outrageous scene unfolds in front of me, anger billows and blinds me.

I have no right to feel this way about my best friend, but I can't help it.

As the guards escort Miss Classless Tart out of the building, the DJ plays music again. The crowd bounces around to the sound of the beat as if we didn't all witness a travesty a few minutes ago.

Gabriel approaches.

"Wow, that was quite the peepshow," he says.

"I didn't need to know *that* much about her," Holly says.

"But it's *my* birthday," Zoe says again.

"Too much info on *your* birthday." Gabriel laughs.

"My eyes still hurt," I say.

"I can never unsee that. Ever." He grimaces.

*Fuck this.*

*Two can play at this game.*

I hold Gabriel's gaze. "Let's dance."

He flashes me a surprised gaze before grinning wide. "I'd love to." He takes me by the hand and leads me to the dance floor.

Since he's been hitting on me since I arrived and this isn't the first time he's shown interest, maybe it isn't a bad idea to see where things go.

For several long minutes I'm able to pretend I'm unbothered by the disturbing scene and I lose myself in the sultry beat. A tap on my shoulder brings me back to reality. I don't need to turn around to know who it is, so I ignore it. The second tap is more forceful.

I keep dancing.

He comes and stands in front of me. "Can I talk to you for a sec?" Rod is a persistent guy.

I shake my head. "I'm busy."

"The fuck you are!" Rod's voice booms over the music.

"She said, she's busy, bro." Gabriel comes to my defense. "Go find your own dance partner."

Rod pins Gabriel with a deadly stare. "What did you say?" He takes a threatening step forward.

Gabriel flinches and takes several steps back. "I—I need another drink."

"Better," Rod says. "Now, get the fuck out of my face before—"

"Catch you later, Dominika." Gabriel is gone before Rod finishes his sentence.

*That's it?*

*Coward.*

I'm so pissed off, I could spit fire.

"How dare—"

Rod leans into me. "We need to talk, Dom."

His closeness catches me off guard. The dance floor feels crammed. Filled up by this man's intoxicating presence.

His warm breath stirs the tips of hair that's fallen on my face as a result of my crazy dancing. I can't suppress the shiver of awareness that tickles every cell in my body and my nipples tighten uncomfortably. I should be worried, but the sweet sensation pulsing through me is pure, unadulterated bliss.

*Fuck.*

The last time I found myself in this predicament was when I had lost a game of battle shots–to him.

As I'm freefalling and my resistance is freeing, I remember the scene I witnessed. My anger is back, flaming brighter than before.

"Leave me alone, Rod. There's nothing for us to talk about."

I turn on my heel, but I don't get far.

His strong hand clenches around my wrist. His brown eyes narrow in a sliver of determination. It's as if he's daring me to try to get away from him.

*Crap.*

## Chapter 5

### *Roderick*

I thought Dominika had left. Not that I would've blamed her. Six weeks apart and our reunion is marred by some silly slut's train-wreck attempt at making a fool out of herself.

I'm surprised to find my best friend on the dance floor. But to my dismay, she isn't alone. Every muscle in my body tenses when I see her moving so sensually to the beat of the music.

The random prick she's dancing with keeps up with her well. Too well.

My jaw clenches.

*Asshole.*

*Why am I so pissed off?*

She's a grown woman and she's entitled to go out with any man she wants. It's not like she needs my permission to sleep with someone.

The rational part of me accepts that. The alpha, whose eyes are glued to her hips, doesn't.

Every time Dom gyrates and sways those sinful hips of hers, my cock stiffens. It's like she's taunting me. Tormenting me, even.

It's illogical since her back is facing me.

Maybe my filthy fantasies about her are coloring my better judgment. Maybe it's wishful thinking on my part. After all, there hasn't been any crazy surge of electric current between us since the battle shots game.

*I'm sure this is all in my head.*

When she turns around to face me, I can appreciate her new smoking-hot look. Her eyes are closed, so I can take her all in. Her long hair cascades down her back and her dramatic makeup brings out her features. As my eyes travel to her feet, I can't help but shake my head in amazement. Her heels accentuate her perfectly painted toes, which happen to match the same daring shade as her lips.

*Those lips.*

Dom's lips are naturally plumper in the center of the upper and lower. She'll never need to alter her features. No injections for my Dom.

*Damn, those lips.*

I want to drag her off the dance floor, find a secluded place and do debaucherous things to that mouth?

*Fuck.*

And then there's the dress.

Unlike Clemensia's, Dom's form-fitting black tank top dress —that hits her above the knees—is all class. The fabric clings to every perfect inch of her slender curves and does justice to her plump tits.

It's not only the clothes, but she exudes this newfound confidence—something I've never seen before. It's sexy as hell.

*Who is this uninhibited tease threatening to bring me to my knees? And what the hell happened to my best friend?*

The look of utter disappointment I saw on her face as Clemensia was doing her circus act, sliced. Okay, I'm no choirboy, but I've always been careful not to flaunt my conquests in front of Dom. I have too much respect for her.

She left LA with a chip on her shoulder, she was upset with me when we spoke on the phone earlier, and now I'm pretty sure she's spitting mad. I don't care how many times she protests, we need to clear the air between us.

"Let go, Rod," she says, tugging her arm, trying to free herself. "I told you, there's nothing to talk about."

"I disagree," I say. "Whatever's going on between us, we're putting an end to it tonight."

I drag her by the hand off the dance floor, through the entrance doors, down the hallway, past security, out the front door, around the building and into the gardens. I don't stop walking until we reach a wall with three archways.

*This will do in terms of privacy.*

I lead her under the alcove. Well, I should say, I haul her.

She's been throwing a litany of, *'You're a brute'* and a series of, *'Seriously, Rod?'* She even goes for the big guns with, *'Who the hell do you think you are?'* And the classic, *'You're not the boss of me'*. She went for blood with, *'I fucking hate you, Rod Wolfe.'*.

It does little to deter me.

*Sorry, Dom, I'm on a fucking mission.*

"Why aren't you running after your date instead of annoying me? She seemed ready for anything," she says.

*Hell no.*

I place my hands firmly on her bare shoulders.

*Shit.*

From the quick flicker in her eyes, she feels it too.

*I'd forgotten how soft her skin feels.*

I shake my head and force myself to focus.

I pull her toward me so forcefully, she stumbles on her heels and inhales a quick breath.

She gasps, her hands landing on my chest.

Her shock is as great as my own.

No sooner has she regained her balance, than she tries to push away from me.

I won't have it.

I tighten my grip on her shoulders. I want to make damn sure she hears what I'm about to say.

"Is this what our relationship has come to? Because if I annoy you and if you *hate* me, then maybe we shouldn't be friends anymore."

"You refused to let me go."

"With good reason, Dom. For months, you've had a sour attitude towards me. I want to know why. Let's deal with what's bothering you, right here, right now."

"You seemed to enjoy the attention you were getting from that... that... that... *woman*," she says before averting her gaze.

"You don't get to throw something like that in my face and look away."

She's steadfast in her stubbornness.

"Dom," I say.

Still nothing.

"So, you do hate me."

"I thought you had higher standards."

She won't let that go.

"If you're going to insult me, own it. Look me in the fucking face, Dom. Don't be a coward about it."

"I'm not a coward," she says.

"Oh, no? That vase over there is more interesting? Is that why you're staring at it?"

Her mesmerizing blue eyes meet mine. Under the luminosity of the alcove lights shining bright above our heads, it's like staring at the ocean.

*She's so beautiful.*

As I take in her feminine features, my heart does a funny flip thing.

*What the hell?*

Heartburn? Indigestion? Yeah, that must be it. Was the catered feast on Eddie's yacht spoiled? It was a hot afternoon after all. I mean, what else could—

*Focus.*

"You want to jeopardize our friendship over a stranger?"

She doesn't respond.

I let out a long sigh. "Okay, let's do this your way. To answer your question, no, I didn't enjoy the attention. I thought it was disgusting. There was nothing sexy about her. Only a dickless fool would think otherwise. I don't even know who the hell she is. I was on my way to see *you*—because I missed *you*—when she ambushed me."

"You missed me?"

*Oh, now I have your attention.*

I roll my eyes. "Didn't you miss me?"

Silence.

"You didn't?"

"I missed you, Rod."

"I missed you too, Dom."

I take a step forward. She takes one back. I do it again. She mirrors me, but this time her back hits the wall.

"I like knowing that," I say.

Her eyes gleam with amusement. "You do?"

"Yeah. I'd hate for this to be one-sided."

She frowns.

There's such an aura of vulnerability around her right now.

I reach out and stroke her silky hair.

She gives me a shy smile.

"You look so different," I say.

"In a bad way?"

"In the best possible way."

She smiles wide. "Thanks."

"What's up with the transformation?" I twist a strand of her hair around a finger. "You haven't been a blonde since you were seventeen."

She flinches at my words and her face contorts into an expression I can't read.

*What was that about?*

"Did I say something wrong?"

She shakes her head.

"Dom, talk to me."

She clears her throat. "No, you didn't. You know how I never like going down memory lane."

"You lost me."

"It doesn't matter." She shrugs. "Johanna's hairdresser suggested a change. I was ready for something new—I guess something old in my case."

One day, out of the blue, Dom started dying her blonde hair jet-black. It was a dramatic change. It happened during a dark period in her life when she walked around with this gray cloud hovering over her head. She was constantly depressed. She retreated into a shell and I didn't know how to help her. Since the first day I came to her rescue, I've wanted to take care of her. Protect her.

Somehow, in this case, I felt I had failed her.

No matter how many times I asked her what was going on, she never opened up. I thought it was because my career was on fire and I was getting a lot more attention than ever before. She assured me I was wrong. In the end, I chalked off her moodiness to growing pains. God knows I was a handful.

"Good call on the part of the hairdresser. He has a good eye."

"*Her* name is Elka," she says.

"My bad. Elka and I are on the same page." I ponder over my next words for a few long seconds. "Did you plan on leaving with the guy you were dancing with?" *And let him fuck your brains out?* "I mean, it's your decision."

"Why do you care, Rod?" She hooks a closed fist to her waist. "You hook up with random women all the time. Maybe today's flasher was a bit much, but you would've tracked down a willing soul in no time... unless you've had your fill on Eddie's yacht."

*Is that hurt I read in her eyes?*

I haven't told her about Eddie's tame party. And she doesn't know I've been a model citizen over the last few months, other than that unfortunate hookup. I've been too busy playing video production studio CEO. The one time I try, I end up with a drug addict. The studio's packed schedule has kept me at the office past midnight more times than I can count. I'm still not sure I should admit this, but things haven't been the same since Dom left.

"I guess I deserved that. You're right. Your sex life is your business, not mine. If he's expecting to go home with you..." I can't bring myself to finish my sentence.

I'm not sure I'd be able to erase the disturbing images of Dominika and that guy in the throes of passion. That's why I never ask too many questions about the guys she dates. Does that make me a goddamn hypocrite? Maybe.

"Tonight is all about Zoe. I just landed in LA. Inviting a guy back to my place—or going to his—isn't part of the plan."

Relief washes over me.

"All right," I say.

There's something about what she said earlier that still nags at me.

"Are my random hookups the cause of the shit between us?"

She averts her gaze.

*Is that what this is all about?*

I flatten my hands on either side of her head, caging her in.

We're so close our lips are almost touching.

"Don't go shy on me, Dom."

She presses her lips together so tight, they form a thin line.

"If you don't tell me what I did wrong, I can't fix it."

Seconds tick away, and I can't peel my eyes away from her face. The way she keeps working her lower lip, it's driving me fucking insane.

"You're right," I say in a low, rough voice.

Her eyes shift to mine. "About what?"

"I think we're well past talking."

"What do you mean?"

"Maybe we shouldn't have put the brakes on the last time we played battle shots."

She looks baffled. "We were a little tipsy," she says.

"That's often when the truth comes out, Dom."

She folds her lower lip between her teeth and chews on it.

*Please stop doing that.*

My cock twitches at the sight of her teeth nibbling at her plump skin.

Her eyes shift from left to right as if she's looking for a repartee.

Without thinking, I move in close and press my crotch against her stomach. My cock has been on alert since I saw her, but now there's no way of hiding how I respond to being this close to her.

Her eyes widen. "God. Rod, you're... I can feel you."

"Yeah, I'm fucking hard."

"Oh."

Her sexy little body feels damn good against me. Every time she bats her eyelashes at me, a steady stream of adrenaline ramps me up. Still, I coax myself not to rush her. I give her time to decide if she wants this or not.

Her tempting lips part to say something, but she decides against it.

"What's going on in that head of yours, Dom?"

"I can't believe this," she says.

"Why not?"

"Because..." She doesn't finish her sentence.

I let my eyes linger over her and feel a wicked sense of satisfaction when her breathing catches. I'm not the only one who's affected.

*Sweet Dom.*

That's all the encouragement I need.

I cup her face. Her hands come up to my chest as she lets out a low sensual moan.

Her blue eyes fix onto mine. The hunger I read in them is unsettling.

I lean into her and inhale her arousing scent.

*Damn.*

"I've been dying to know if you're really my sweet Dom," I say.

"Rod..." My name comes out in a breathless plea.

*That's so fucking hot.*

A triumphant grin pulls the corners of my mouth.

What's even sexier is how her eyes never leave mine. Those gem-like sapphires have witnessed me at my lowest. She knows all about my closet full of skeletons. Still, she's never turned her back on me.

Heated lust rushes through my veins like a hurricane.

My control is wavering by the second.

I lower my mouth to hers. I wait for her to protest. She doesn't. Instead, she stretches her neck until our lips touch. I kiss the girl who's been the main feature in my wet dreams and filthy fantasies for so long now.

The moment our lips connect, an intoxicating charge shoots straight to my cock, and I can no longer spell the words 'best friends'.

*Goddammit.*

The kiss is soft and tender at first, but in no time, it turns into a depth-smoldering make-out session. I take possession of her lips in the most unwavering way. Our tongues tangle and dance wild. With a feral grunt, I grind my hard cock against Dom's stomach. Her hips tilt forward and she writhes against me.

"Ah, fuck," I say into her mouth.

"God, yes," she says, panting.

Her response catches me off guard. I didn't know she had it in her.

*Jesus Christ.*

The friction of her body against my desperate cock is so overwhelming, I fear I might come in my pants. This is way beyond my dirtiest dreams. I can only imagine how it would feel to slide balls-deep inside her tight warm pussy and fuck her hard until she clenches around my cock, squeezing me tight as she gives in to ecstasy.

*Wait? What?*

*Fuck, fuck, fuck.*

*What am I doing?*

*Get your shit together, Rod.*

Kissing my best friend isn't supposed to feel this good. *Jesus Christ.* I can't fuck her.

Remorse grips me at the idea I may lose the best thing in my life.

I pull away from her.

Despite her protest, I manage to clear my head.

"I'm so sorry, Dom."

"Wh—what?"

"I'm sorry."

"Am I a bad kisser?"

*God, no.*

"I shouldn't have..." *Let my cock do all the thinking.* "That was a bad idea."

Casual pussy I won't remember the next morning, I can handle. This with Dom feels so different. So encompassing. I'm unequipped to navigate this uncharted territory.

"A bad idea?"

The disappointment in her eyes is unmistakable. I'm riddled with guilt.

"I—"

She holds a hand up and cuts me off.

"Save it, Rod. I get it. I'm not your type. Duly noted. Like I said earlier, you should've gone after your skanky date instead of annoying the fuck out of me. Good night," she says and turns on her heel.

"Dom—" I grab her arm.

"Let... go," she says through gritted teeth.

This time I do.

I've fucked things up enough. No need to dig a bigger hole for myself.

"When you see me tomorrow, ignore me. In fact, pretend I don't even exist."

Then, she's gone.

*Fuck. What have I done?*

# Chapter 6

## *Dominika*

It's six a.m. and for the past half hour I've been watching the sun rise over the City of Angels. It's a treat for a night owl like myself. When I stepped out on my deck, dawn had started peeking through the darkness. Now, the sky is washed over by a blanket of warm colors. Soon, the sun will shine bright and LA will be alive with activity.

Being jetlagged has its perks after all.

When my stomach growls for the third time, I decide to feed the hungry beast.

I walk back inside and trail to my kitchen.

I can't tell you how much it fills me with pride to be able to call this beautiful home in Venice mine. It isn't a mansion, but it's nothing like the crammed, dilapidated dump I grew up in. What a departure from where I started soon after landing at LAX. Without Rod, it would still all be a pipe dream. He helped me secure the mortgage on my dream home.

I open the fridge and stick my head inside.

"What to eat? What to eat?"

Since I'm still stuffed from Holly's meal, I decide to keep it light. A fruit salad is the perfect way to start the day. I grab a small papaya, an Ataulfo mango and a few pre-cut slices of pineapple. As I dice the fruits, my mind wanders and I find my face heating up at last night's memory.

*That searing kiss.*

Flashing back to the delicious sensation of our lips touching sets my body ablaze—much like it did when Rod was holding me in his strong arms. A tingle of excitement shoots right through me at the memory, like I've just discovered a secret world. In many ways, I have.

I can't believe I was that bold. It's so unlike me, but there I was squirming into him, wriggling against his mighty erection.

The way he groaned in need...

*God.*

I felt safe in Rod's arms. It's a sensation I'm rarely able to enjoy in a man's proximity. Restlessness and anxiety always rob me of the ability to indulge in an intimate relationship with a man. The agonizing fear is courtesy of a predator. It's different with Rod. He'd never hurt me. Trusting him is as natural as breathing.

I'm making a big deal out of a kiss, but I can't help it. That passionate embrace was the hottest and most pleasurable experience of my life. I can imagine what it'd be like to take things further.

*Wait. No.*

And just like that, the dream crashes into a wall.

I shake my head, snapping myself back to reality.

Things will never go further with Rod.

He's made it crystal clear.

*'That was a bad idea.'*

Thanks for bursting my bubble, Rod.

*I'm such a fool.*

*What did I expect?*

*A man with too many options doesn't have to settle.*

My phone pings, putting an end to my self-pity.

I rinse off my hands and run to the kitchen table. It's Rod's sister-in-law. I grab my phone and shoot off a response.

Dominika: I'm up. You can call.

Isobel: Are you sure?

Dominika: If I were sleeping, I wouldn't be texting you back.

Isobel: I guess you're right. Calling now.

I accept the call on the first ring.

"Hey, Dom," Isobel says.

"It's good to hear your voice."

"Same here. I didn't expect you to be up, but I figured I'd send you a quick text right after my run so we could connect later in the day."

Yeah, Isobel is one of *those* people. She runs eight miles every day before I wake up.

"I'm still on London time and I have a busy day ahead."

"You don't even get a day to recuperate? That's not right," Isobel says.

"One shouldn't require a vacation after coming back from one."

She laughs. "What's on the agenda, Miss Social Butterfly?"

"I'm meeting Zoe for brunch. Later this afternoon, I'm heading to Aaron's parents' place for his going away party."

"Please say hi to him."

"I will."

"Will Rod attend?"

I do my best to keep my voice neutral. "Guess so."

"Alrighty, then. Let's keep this train moving."

Isobel knows me well. It's hard to pull the wool over her eyes.

"How was Zoe's birthday party?"

"Eventful."

"In what sense?"

"A female guest made a fool of herself when Rod showed up. The classless bimbo wanted intimate body parts signed."

"Yikes. Let's not go there."

"Thank you."

"Other than that, how was it?"

"Soon after that incident, I left. I figured, might as well finish unpacking and do a few loads of laundry."

"You left a birthday party because you wanted to be on top of your chores or because you were pissed off at Rod?"

"It'll be crazy when I get back into the swing of things on Monday," I say.

Isobel doesn't answer.

The silence between us speaks volumes.

I'm used to seeing a gaggle of star-struck women flutter around Rod. It never used to bother me much. Something shifted between us last Thanksgiving. I can't put my finger on it, but I just know it. Since then, it's been a constant fight to contain my jealousy when women trip all over themselves. I didn't come home early to do laundry. I sought refuge in my home and lost myself in housecleaning to exorcise the hurt.

"You don't want to talk about it?" she says.

"I'd prefer not to," I say with a weary sigh.

"I thought after that wild incident at Levi Aldridge's wedding, you and Rod would have called it truce. On the contrary, it seems to have deepened the rift between you."

She's talking about one of Rod's buddies, and the incident in question—that happened a few weeks before my training was supposed to kick off—shall remain unspoken.

"Well, it hasn't because Rod will always be Rod." *A skirt-chasing-bad-boy-heartbreaker.*

Isobel lets out an audible sigh.

"I'm sorry, I didn't mean to snap," I say.

"You're right, let's change the subject," she says. "How was Europe?"

"It—"

"I hope a dispute with Rod isn't part of the story, because I'm running out of questions," she says.

"I promise he isn't part of the Euro equation."

"Good. How was it?"

"Unbelievable."

"I loved catching the highlights of your trip on social media."

"I figured it was the easiest way to update everyone since the time difference didn't play in my favor. And the training was so intense, I barely had time to breathe during the first four weeks. The two weeks trekking around Europe were fun. I was even able to stop by Croatia to give my good friend Elsa a hug."

"How is she doing?"

"She's a hairdresser on the most popular fantasy serial drama. Too many wigs, too little time."

"In other words, she's on cloud nine."

"Exactly."

"Good for her," Isobel says. "How was it seeing your mom?"

"Not so amazing. If it weren't for you, I wouldn't have bothered."

For others, seeing their mom after an extended time apart brings feelings of nostalgia, warmth, fuzziness, happy days gone by and excitement. Not for me. Our mother-daughter relationship is a lot more complicated than most. Especially because I still despise my mother for always making me feel like an afterthought. Whenever a new man came into her life, she was always quick to take the shitty boyfriend's side instead of standing up for her own daughter. And the incessant way she's drilled feelings of worthlessness into my psyche for years doesn't swing in her favor. A decade apart, and I still struggle to shake off her venom.

"Nothing's changed between you and your mom?"

"Nope. She's as cheerful and motherly as ever. Not."

"I thought after so many years she'd be more welcoming."

"I knew she wouldn't be. She isn't wired that way, Isobel. Without you and Rory, I would've ended up homeless, in the social system, or I would've been forced to follow my mother back to Europe and live under her miserable cloud."

Isobel and Rod's older brother Rory have been married for two years now, but they've been together forever. With Rod's insistence—he was a fierce advocate to save me from my mother—Isobel and Rory became my legal guardians. Not long after my fifteenth birthday, they helped me petition the courts for emancipation. Living with my mother was a hell I could no longer endure. A year later, Mom decided the American dream wasn't for her after all. She scrounged some money, packed her few belongings, and moved back to Hungary.

"Well, it's her loss. You're my golden child," Isobel says.

"Yeah, yeah." I roll my eyes. "I'm sure you'll change your tune once you and Rory start having babies of your own. Speaking of which..."

She lets out a long sigh. "We're still trying."

"It'll happen."

"I'm doing my best to be patient and remain optimistic. Some days I manage better than others, but it's frustrating and disappointing."

"It *will* happen," I say.

"I hope so. I'm ready." She sighs again. "By the way, love

the new look," she says, changing the subject. "I couldn't remember what you looked like as a blonde."

"I thought maybe the shock of going from jet-black back to being a blonde again would help get a wave in my hair from the over-processing, but no, my hair is still straight as an arrow. I've said it before, but I have hair-envy every time I see you."

"Trust me, this hair can be a curse," she says, "When I'm in Miami, I'm reminded that being mixed race can be a liability when you're dealing with that much humidity. If I don't pull it back tight and gel the hell out of this mass of curls, I look positively crazy."

"Right."

"I do."

She's lying.

Isobel's mom is one hundred percent Californian going back God knows how many generations. She's a stunning blonde with blue eyes. Her dad is as Brit as they come. He's a handsome black man from London. What a mix. As a result, she has perfect hair. It's bouncy and full of volume. Nothing like mine. And she's gorgeous. Her most attractive feature is her confidence. Her inner beauty transcends her looks. She's never needed the approval of anyone. I admire that about her.

"Says the always put together beauty queen."

"You're too kind." She pauses. "I'm glad you're willing to embrace your natural hair color again. It's been so long. Too long."

My heart jumps into my throat. The pain is still there—the constant companion I can't seem to shake off. It's so palatable, for a few agonizing seconds, the memory robs me of my speech.

"Hey, it's over. It's the here and now. You're safe," Isobel says.

"I know."

"The change is good," she says.

"It was time. I was tired of hating my natural hair color."

"Honey, I'm sorry the trauma still weighs on you—"

"It will always haunt me—ingrained in my DNA like a program I can't rewire."

"But at least you're not allowing that painful episode to shackle you forever. After all, your hair color had nothing to do with what happened to you, Dom. Your hair could've been blue—or all the colors of the rainbow—and it would've been enough to trigger the monster."

I shudder at the terrifying memory.

She's repeated this many times throughout the years. Sometimes I believe her. Most times, I don't.

"I hear you. I'm stronger now. That's why I'm taking control back."

"Well said, honey. Don't ever let the pig win."

"Enough about my shitty past. I want to hear all about the latest rights you've acquired at UTV.com for new programming you'll end up turning into blockbusters."

# Chapter 7

## *Roderick*

"What a goddamn awful morning," I say to myself as I step out of the shower.

Even after a rigorous session in my outdoor pool where I swam enough laps to qualify for the US Olympic team, I'm still on edge. I'm pissed off at myself for having crossed the line with Dom.

After she escaped, I went back inside the Wordsworth to find Roark, but he was gone. He sent me a text to let me know he ended up joining the other guys at the gentlemen's club. Normally, I would've headed over there, but there was nothing normal about last night. How the hell was I going to explain to my brother and my boys that scorching burst of passion between Dom and I? For crying out loud, I can't even explain it to myself. Sometimes you have to know when to fold. That's what I did. I ended up retreating home, so troubled, I needed to be alone to ruminate over what happened.

Did I make sense of any of it?

Not at all.

I'm still confused and I'm unable to explain this growing attraction for Dom.

I head to my bedroom to get dressed before making my way downstairs to the kitchen. My doorbell rings as I hit the last step. I receive a text message at the same time.

Roark: Hey, little brother. You up? I'm at your door.

Rod: What do you want?

Roark: Don't play dumb. Open up.

With an exasperated sigh, I march to the door and open it.

Roark steps inside my home. "Morning, little brother. I brought breakfast."

"Did you get laid last night? Is that why you're so happy?"

"Believe it or not, but thanks to Chlamydia—I mean Clemensia," he says, chuckling at his own joke, "I lost my appetite for the evening."

"Why are you here this early?"

"Do I need an excuse to spend some quality time with my brother?"

I roll my eyes. "I'm not in the mood to talk."

"If you think I'm going to let what happened last night slide, you're as high as a kite. Since you kicked your drug habit, that means you're stupid."

"You show up at my door, insult me, and you expect me to welcome you, big brother? You're delusional."

"Rod, you were the center of attention twice last night. I couldn't care less about Clemensia, but I do care about Dom."

I stare him down.

He holds my defiant gaze. "Should I call Dominika to find out what happened?"

The bastard waves his phone in my face.

"Asshole."

"You're the one playing hardball."

"Fine," I say, like a pissed off child.

"Now, now, Roderick. Be a good boy," he says.

I shake my head. "We might as well get it out of the way."

Roark and I are cut from the same cloth. When he wants something, he's like a dog with a bone.

~

"There's nothing like a slut for breakfast." My brother's joke isn't funny.

"You're an idiot, you know that?"

"Maybe, but you're no longer in a foul mood."

I'll give him that.

Roark stopped by EggSlut—some of the best breakfast sandwiches in LA—and grabbed a few of our favorites.

"I was a grouch because I was so hungry," I say.

"You're lying to yourself. You always get this worked up when things are tense—or weird—between Dom and you. Why are you two fighting?"

I shrug. "It's nothing."

"Well, the way you barged out of that party room dragging her behind, spelled anything but. Want to talk about it?"

I study him for a few seconds, unsure if I should fess up or not.

I let out a sigh. "I kissed her."

Roark's eyebrows hit his forehead. "You mean you kissed a woman?"

"No. I mean I kissed Dom."

"You kissed your best friend?"

"Jesus Christ, are you deaf?"

He cocks an eyebrow in that fatherly way I haven't seen in

a while. "Pipe it down, little brother, and keep your attitude under lockdown. My hearing is fine."

Roark is eleven years older than me. Rory is thirteen years my senior. When I step out of line, they're quick to rein me in. A rock star status, several millions in the bank, and being a paper billionaire mean shit to them. I'm still their bratty little brother. After all, they became my surrogate parents and took care of me in a way my own mother and father never could.

"I'm sorry."

"Better. Back to what you said. I thought you didn't kiss women?"

"I don't. I haven't kissed a woman since Sadie Matthews."

"She was your first. You were both sixteen. You dated her for a short while before your career exploded into the stratosphere. You can't compare kissing as a teenager to last night's kiss. Dom is a grown woman."

"Don't I know it."

"Which is why I'm shocked."

*You and me both.*

"Wow. You kissed Dom." Roark shakes his head.

"Yes."

"That's huge."

"Don't remind me."

"You hold Dom on a pedestal. No other woman can touch her pinky toe. You used to warn the guys in your band and in your entourage to steer clear of her. If anyone laid a hand on her, you'd castrate them. Hang around you for more than ten seconds and you knew Dom was off limits."

"You're exaggerating."

"Am I? Rod, you have this invisible protective shield around her."

"Oh, come off it. You make me sound like a caveman."

"The only time you weren't able to hover over her like an

eagle over its chicks is when your career hit big. Your frequent trips across the country and abroad prevented you from being your precious little Dom's shadow. Thank God, she was living with Rory and Isobel by then, so you didn't have to worry too much. She was in good hands."

"You're taking pleasure in this?" I say.

"And now you kissed the untouchable girl." The idiot ignores me.

"You wanted me to open up, and now you're mocking me. Fuck off, Roark."

"You're mad at me or at yourself?"

I consider him. "I'm pissed off at myself. Happy?"

"Was it bad?"

"No. That's the problem. It was incredible. After kissing her, I wanted more. What the fuck is wrong with me?"

"I don't get it." Roark narrows his eyes at me. "Why are you so upset?"

"I shouldn't have kissed Dom. But I wanted to kiss her so damn much. No." I shake my head. "I *needed* to kiss her."

"So you went after what you wanted. What's new?"

"Don't you see it?"

"No."

"I acted on impulse and now I'm petrified I might've ruined something precious. It may be too late to salvage things between us."

"What do you mean?"

"I got cold feet, and I was so weirded out about the whole thing, I might've pushed her away."

"Call her and tell her."

"I've tried. Several times. She's doing a pretty good job at ignoring me. After God knows how many attempts, she texted me back."

"What did she say?"

*"Please pretend I don't exist, Rod."*

"Shit."

I rub the back of my neck. "Exactly."

"There's something I don't understand."

"What?"

"If the kiss was so memorable, why push her away?"

"My attention span is short. I don't fuck the type of women I might develop a connection with that's more than sexual. Things are fleeting in my world and I like it that way. I never lie to those women. I'm always upfront about it. They know the deal before they drop their panties. No expectations. No disappointments."

"What does that have to do with Dom and you?" He scoffs.

"I couldn't bring myself to do a once and done with my best friend."

"Rod, you're letting Rachel screw you up."

"I'm not letting Mom screw me up."

He sticks a finger in my face. "You are. You still keep calling her mom when she's never deserved the title."

"This again."

"She still has the upper hand on you," he says. "You're blind to it. Rachel's been dead for five years. She did enough damage when she was alive. Don't let the woman fuck with your head when she's six feet under. She isn't worth it."

I eye Roark with skepticism. "Hmph."

"What?"

"What's your excuse?"

"What do you mean?"

"With women?"

"I don't have any excuses. I choose to keep it simple," he says.

"I thought Zoe—"

"It was fun with Zoe—"

"But you couldn't commit," I say. "Get off your high horse, big brother, you're no better than I am. Seems like I'm not the only one dear Mom is still screwing over."

The once and done approach sounds superficial, but when you grew up with a mother like ours, it's survival. Rory is the only one who has his shit together.

"I can't commit to a woman who's so high maintenance, it becomes a turnoff. This is LA—the land of the forever young—but Zoe's obsession was tiring."

"What are you saying? You're out there looking for *the one*?" Sarcasm laces my words.

"Rory has set the bar high. The more time I spend with him and Isobel, the more it becomes clear it's about finding the right person. His wife was a friend, lover, partner, and confidant for years. We both know Isobel was an important, integral part of his life long before things turned romantic." He fixes me with a serious stare. "Much like Dom is for you."

## Chapter 8

## *Dominika*

It's eleven o'clock in the morning when I walk into The Griddle Café. The place is packed. My stomach is growling so much, I can hear it over the brouhaha.

"Dominika, over here." Zoe waves.

I weave my way through the tables until I reach the one in the far corner.

"Hey, Zoe."

We do the air kiss thing and sit down.

"Sorry if it seems like we're sitting in Kansas, but I was able to snatch the last table when I got here or else it would've been at least a half hour wait."

"I'd die of hunger by then."

"So would I," she says with a laugh.

"My God, you look so well-rested, your makeup is flawless and you're all dressed up... even on a Saturday." I, on the other hand, look like I spent two minutes on my face before jumping into a pair of shorts, a t-shirt and Converse shoes.

"I had to conceal the fact I partied hard last night," she says.

"It was your day."

"Yeah, but I didn't want to pay for it when I woke up. I needed an intervention when I got home. I splattered a lot of anti-aging serum on my face before going to bed. And, this morning, I applied a generous coat of Prima Golden Elixir—well worth the thousand-dollar price tag."

"That's a lot of money. I hope that buys you a case of the stuff."

"I wish. I can only afford this stuff one bottle at a time. It's LA and I work in the TV and film industry. It's not only actresses who feel the pressure. It trickles down. My job is to make you look incredible. If I look like shit, why would you trust I know what I'm talking about?"

"Point taken."

*I'm glad I don't have that kind of pressure in my profession.*

"Enough about my beauty regime. Let's talk about what's important."

I'm dreading this conversation.

"What's on your mind?"

Zoe tilts her head to the side. "Seriously?"

"I can't read minds."

"Okay, so let's start from the beginning. Guess what?"

"What?"

"The club is going to sue Clemensia."

"Who?"

"The woman who mistook the Wordsworth for a low-class strip club."

"Oh, the classless tart."

"The one and only."

"Her name is Clemensia?"

"Yes."

I grimace. "It sounds like an STD."

"Oh, my God, Holly said the same thing."

We both laugh.

"It kind of sounds like Chlamydia, which I'm sure she has, or must have had in the past," she says.

I have no doubt. "Does she work for UTV.com?"

"No. I thought she was someone's plus one. It turns out, Clemensia crashed my birthday party. She was heading to another party, when she saw Rod heading to mine."

"Another LA wannabe?"

"Yup. I got the lowdown from security before leaving."

"Vulgar whore."

"I couldn't agree more. In any case, she's history." She cocks an eyebrow. "What was that all about between you and Rod after Clemensia was escorted out?"

"He wanted to talk." I shrug.

She frowns and shoots me a side glare.

"What?"

"It looked like a lot more to me."

"You're making too much of it."

"You're bullshitting me."

"Did you end up hooking up with Roark?" I try to change the subject.

"Don't think I don't see right through you." She waves a finger at me.

"I'm curious to find out if you were able to cross off another item from your sex-bucket list." I offer a devious grin.

"No cock on my birthday. Roark came over and wished me a happy birthday. Then, he was walking out the door. Men? At least Rod cares enough to make a fuss. Roark barely acknowledged me. It was clear he was wearing his executive hat. He wasn't there as my former lover." Her lips twist. "So, back to you and Rod." Zoe's eyes are bright and eager for details.

"You're making a mountain out of a molehill."

"Spare me the canned response. You were practically spitting fire at Clemensia—not that I blame you."

I don't respond.

"Even in my semi-drunken stupor, I could tell there was more than met the eye. Everyone at my party saw what was going on between the two of you. There was something caveman-ish about the whole thing. FYI, very sexy. Very possessive. Very *caliente*."

I still remain quiet.

"Listen, Dom, I know we aren't best friends, but if you want to talk, I'm here."

I ponder over her offer.

It's not like I can reveal any of this to Isobel.

I'd welcome a sounding board.

"Let's order some food first," I say.

~

The Griddle Café isn't called LA's king of pancakes for nothing. I couldn't finish more than a third of my frisbee-sized berry-delicious pancake stack. Zoe doesn't fare much better with her Oreo-flavored one.

"Good God, I always forget how huge these are," she says, pushing her plate away. "Who finishes a full portion?"

"You should try coming here with Rod and Roark after they've hit the gym. Not only can they polish off the stack of three enormous pancakes, but they also each order a three-egg omelet with extra sausage and bacon."

"Men. They can eat their faces off. So unfair."

"I'm used to it by now. It was more jaw-dropping when I was traveling on the road with Rod and his bandmates. Some nights, you'd think they were going to eat the restaurant out of business."

"I still can't get over the fact you knew Rod well before he became a sensation. Was he always so hot—and impetuous—even as a teenager?"

I'm unable to contain my smile. Even in my confused mess, a wave of affection washes over me. "The Wolfe brothers are clueless to the awkward teen years the rest of us know intimately. I've seen plenty of photos of Rory and Roark when they were young and they were as handsome back then as they are now."

"What a gene pool," Zoe says.

"Tell me about it. While most of us burnt—or buried—our high school photos for fear of embarrassment, the Wolfe brothers looked supremely confident and self-assured. It hasn't changed much."

"Is their father as handsome?"

"He wasn't in the picture," I say.

"I see. Well, their mom did a great job."

I let that one slide. It's a thorny subject.

You'd never know their mother was a fucked-up mess and their father was a coward.

"Going back to Rod—"

"Sorry," she says.

"He's still the epitome of the bad-guy-slash-good-guy persona. He's the bad-boy-rocker-god who still gets panties thrown at him when he walks into a room. He's cocky, infuriating and a consummate player. But, behind it all, he's also a good man and a fiercely loyal and protective friend."

"You mean overprotective," Zoe says.

I frown my surprise.

"Rod isn't overprotective," I say.

"Everything about the vibe he gives off suggests otherwise when it comes to you, Dom."

I frown harder. "No."

"I guess you don't see it. I have an older brother and I'm

sure he loves me in his own way—when he isn't telling me I annoy the shit out of him—but I doubt he'd take a bullet for me. I can see Rod doing that for you."

Much to my dismay, my cheeks flush.

"Am I right?" Zoe arches a brow.

"He can be fearless for the people who matter most." I pause. "That's how we met."

"Is that what you meant yesterday when you said he rescued you twice?"

I nod. "I can still remember with absolute clarity"—the kind that still makes me shiver—"the day Rod came into my life. I was thirteen years old. A new immigrant who spoke limited English, and I had a huge Eastern European accent. I was awkward, short—well, I still am—and skinny. I had just started at Carter Dyer High and I hated it. It was worse than purgatory. To this day, my old high school is still part of the bottom five percent in the state of California, even if parts of the Fashion District have changed—"

"What? You grew up in the Fashion District?"

"So did Rod."

Zoe's eyes grow round. "I thought he grew up in Van Nuys. That's what I read online. It's far from being Bel Air, but it's not the pit of the barrel."

"It was a complicated story around custody—not mine to tell."

"Oof!" Zoe exhales. "Roark was always tightlipped about his childhood. Since we were casual, I didn't push."

"They had a horrible childhood. I fared better, but not by much."

"I had no clue." Zoe does little to hide her shock. "I mean the Fashion District... skid row is one the worst neighborhoods in LA. It's a hair above the Wholesale District."

"If the violence in the old neighborhood didn't kill you, the agonizing decaying of your soul did."

Don't be fooled by the seemingly sophisticated name. LA's Fashion District isn't the stylish, posh or edgy imagery you might have of cities like New York, Paris, Tokyo or London. It's a shithole. High crime. High unemployment. Low income. Low hope. In other words, hell on earth.

"I'm sorry, I interrupted your story," Zoe says.

"It's okay." Her reaction doesn't surprise me a bit. Rod and I have done a half decent job at putting the past behind us. Going back is never fun. "I met Rod on a Friday, after the morning classes. I was heading to the cafeteria when a bunch of mean girls—led by Connie Washington—circled me. They took turns bumping into me, shoving me around and pulling my hair. They even dumped the contents of my backpack on the ground to humiliate me further. Other kids were gathered around us, snickering and laughing. No one stepped up to help.

"That's horrible."

"It gets worse." I offer a sad smile. "The mean girls started insulting me, *Your foreign food smells like shit. Fart face. Dumb Dom. When are you going to start speaking American? Polish sausage roll—*"

"I thought you were born in Austria?"

"I was. Mom is from Hungary and Dad is Austrian, but mean girls don't care about the facts."

"I can't believe people can be that heartless and stupid. This country was built by people who came with big dreams and big accents, and the willingness to work hard to build a better life for themselves."

I nod. "I agree, but as I said, none of that matters to bullies."

"Idiots. I'm so sorry you had to go through that." Zoe reaches for my hands, wraps hers around mine and squeezes tight.

I wish I had someone like her in my corner back in the days before Rod came along.

"The first month of school, no one noticed me... that's until the math teacher asked the class to solve a challenging equation on the board. After twenty minutes everyone was still stumped. I had solved it in two. Shyly, I raised my hand to give the answer. People heard my accent, ignoring the correct answer. After class, Connie started calling me brown-noser. The bullying started soon after. It was horrible, but on that Friday, it had reached another level of cruelty. As the mean girls kept torturing and tormenting me, I closed my eyes hoping to dull the pain. Against my will, tears started rolling down my face. Then, I heard a voice, *'Leave her the fuck alone, Connie'*. The assertive timbre gave me the courage to open my eyes."

"Rod?"

I nod. "There he was. My savior. He was all attitude and height at the time—the muscles and the ink came later."

"Did the mean girls stop?"

"Connie flew into a fit of rage, insulting and demeaning Rod. She even spat in his face."

"What a fucking bitch."

"I felt so bad for him. He came to my defense and he was getting stoned in the process. But I didn't know who Rod Wolfe was back then."

Zoe frowns. "What do you mean?"

"He never lost his composure. He smirked at Connie before dropping the axe. He shut her up by revealing he had caught her on her knees with her tits out, giving the assistant basketball coach a blowjob in the boys' locker room the previous Thursday. She called him a liar and slapped him. He smirked at her again and proceeded to burst her bubble. He told her he caught everything on camera."

"Was it true?"

"It was. This goes way back, but Rod had found a lost camcorder and always had it with him for fun. He went out of his way to delay the moment he had to go back to his mom's place by hanging out at school. He had found a little hideaway where we could read his superhero cartoon books in peace. He never expected to witness a twenty-four-year-old assistant coach corrupting a thirteen-year-old student. When he started playing footage of the video, Connie went as white as a ghost. She fled like a thief."

"Oh my God. That's amazing. Did she get in trouble?"

"They both did. The assistant coach got fired and Connie was expelled. Nine months later, she became a teen mom."

"Wow."

"Once Connie ran away, Rod turned his attention to me. *'Come, you're with me now'*, he said. I thought my limited English was responsible for me not understanding what he meant, but I ran to him when he extended his hand. He forced a few of Connie's friends to pick up my belongings and apologize."

"What a guy," Zoe says.

"We didn't stop there."

"Why am I not surprised?"

"He then put out a warning, *'Any of you assholes as much as look at her the wrong way, and I'll rain hell on you. Oh, if I hear Dumb Dom ever again, your ass is mine'*."

Zoe fist pumps.

"I was surprised he knew my name, but at least my nightmare was over thanks to this courageous stranger."

"That was badass."

"It's Rod to the core." I smile. "Even at sixteen, he was bad to the bone. He still walks around with the same, *'Don't fuck with me'* attitude."

"What about your arm?" Zoe's eyes drop to my tattoos.

"How did Rod—" Zoe's eyes shift above my head and her jaw drops. "Holy. Jesus."

"What is it?"

"Oh. My. God."

"What is it, Zoe?"

"Did Collin Dennison just walk into the Griddle Café?"

I turn around. "Oh yeah, that's him."

Zoe digs her fingernails into my arm, and my head whips around.

"You're hurting me."

"Sorry. You know Collin Dennison?" Her eyes practically bulge out of her skull.

"Rod and his business partner know him well. So do his former bandmates," I say. "And before I left for Europe, I worked with Collin and his brother. The Dennison brothers partnered up with this guy by the name of Levi Aldridge—"

"Why isn't Collin coming over to say hi?"

"I doubt he recognizes me. He's only seen me with jet-black hair."

"Call him over."

"Zoe, maybe the guy wants to eat alone."

"Point taken." Her eyes are still glued on Collin. "I'd give an organ to be able to oil that man's body in preparation for a photoshoot." She's eyeing the actor-slash-fitness-model with such a sense of longing, you can practically read her dirty thoughts. "Maybe he's in the market for a new makeup artist."

"I think he has that covered."

"Hmmm..."

She taps her finger against her chin and narrows her gaze. The wheels are churning hard.

"Do you need a bib? You're drooling," I say.

"With good reason." Like Rod, Collin Dennison causes a

commotion when he walks into a room. "Can you imagine being kissed and manhandled by a *real* man like him?"

Not sure about the manhandled part, but I can imagine the kissing part.

"Collin is handsome."

"Are you into him?" She almost looks offended.

"God, no. He's a bit much for me," I say.

"Right up my alley."

*Yup. I can see it.*

She leans her elbows on the table and places her hands on each side of her mouth. "Word has it he has a *huge* sexual appetite." She snorts. "That's not the only *huge* thing about him."

"Err... Zoe—"

"If I'm not going to get dicked down by Roark anymore, Collin Dennison is a damn good upgrade."

I'm dumbstruck by her confession.

"I'll be right back."

With that, she's gone.

*Un-freaking-believable.*

# Chapter 9

## *Roderick*

After greeting my buddy Aaron's parents and his sister Claire, I weave my way through their modest home until I reach the gardens. The man of the hour is surrounded by a group of friends.

"Hey, Mr. Bigshot," I say.

Aaron's head whips around. "Holy shit, man, you came."

He steps away from his small circle and walks towards me. A few people huddled together point my way and whisper. I pay them no mind, as my nana used to say. This day is about Aaron.

"I'm proud of you." I take him in a bro hug. "I had to be here."

"I still can't believe it." He pats me a few times on the back before breaking our embrace.

"You didn't even ask me to work my network to help get your foot in the door. You did it on your own like a big boy."

"I don't mooch off of friends. Even celebrities like you, Wolfe." He play-punches me.

"Former celebrity. Now I can go pretty much anywhere incognito."

"You're full of shit. Women still drop their panties when you walk in a room. I don't get the same treatment. That makes you a celebrity in my book."

"You're too easily impressed," I say.

"You just have to flash your perfect smile, and they line up. I have to show my dog tags to get any action these days. The facial scars are a turn off." He points to the side of his face. "They aren't attractive."

I frown at his comments. "Then, those women don't deserve you. Your facial scars are a badge of honor and courage."

"Well, they do make me memorable." He grimaces.

I place a hand on his shoulder. "Stop it, Aaron. You're a war hero. Any woman who can't see that isn't worth your time."

He gives me a small smile. "At least I'm blonde and I have blue eyes. I have that over your pretty ass."

"Haven't you ever heard of tall, *dark*, and handsome?"

"Yeah, yeah, yeah."

We both laugh.

"Seriously, thanks for coming, Rod."

"I wouldn't have missed it for the world," I say. "What an achievement."

"Thanks. When I got back home from service, I never thought I'd be here today. I didn't think I'd make it through the PTSD, but here I am, moving on with my life."

"You mean moving on in a big way. You're Amara Edmonds' head of security. That's a big fucking deal, man."

"Yeah, it's okay. She hired me for my badass looks and the dog tags, but I'm okay with that. I don't mind being exploited by my boss," he says.

"You wish," I say. "Let's face it, you got hired because I taught you how to fight like a man."

"Oh, please. Not that again. There were *only* three of them. I could've taken them on."

I smile.

Aaron and I met while I was staying with Nana Irene after my mother had another relapse. I was thirteen at the time.

The Norris Bradley Recreation Center is where I learned how to play the drums and perfect my craft. Most nights Nana worked until nine, but sometimes her boss asked her to stay until ten. On those longer shifts, she'd always give me a little money to go down to the convenience store to buy a snack.

One night, as I rounded the corner back to the recreation center, three goons were beating the shit out of another kid. I didn't come out of that fight unscathed, but my face looked a hell of a lot better than the three other idiots. The police were called to the scene. Aaron vouched for me. He was a year older and a skinny kid. I was as lanky, but the anger I'd been carrying like a badge of honor and years of self-taught martial arts saved his ass. And mine.

"Well, no one can kick your butt anymore," I say.

"You made sure of it."

The army made Aaron a warrior. For three years, until the courts forced me to move back to the Fashion District, I was his Basic Camp training.

"Look who just got here," Aaron's sister says as she walks into the garden.

My eyes shift to the angelic blonde following her.

My best friend is killing me with her transformation.

I'm still not used to the hair.

She's wearing a little bit more makeup than usual, but it looks good on her. A pair of large Italian 18k yellow gold hoops

I gave her for her twenty-first birthday pierce her ears. The gold bangles on her right arm are also a gift. My chest pumps with pride seeing them on her.

My eyes land on her dainty feet. She doesn't wear heels often, but she's rocking those nude-colored ones.

Her dress is stunning. It showcases her slender body and displays her left sleeve of tattoos. The green and navy lace detail and form-fitting bodice make it super sexy, but still classy. The mid-calf length is such a turn on because it prompts so many dirty thoughts as to what she's hiding underneath.

And those thin straps...

*Damn.*

They suggest she isn't wearing a bra.

My mind had to go there.

My eyes travel back up to her face, landing on her plump lips.

*Why did I have to do that?*

Now I can only think about my best friend's uninhibited response to the hotter-than-hell kiss we shared. My cock twitches inappropriately in my pants. Much like when I was holding her in my arms.

Our gazes lock, and I can't contain my smile.

She chooses to move her attention to Aaron, ignoring me altogether.

*Goddammit.*

"Holy shit, I can't believe my eyes," Aaron says. "What happened to Dom?"

"That's her natural hair color."

"I remember, but it seems like a lifetime ago."

"Yeah," I say.

"It's not only the hair... there's something about her..." He lets his words trail. "Wow. She's all grown up."

"She's twenty-five. She's been grown up a long time now." The defensiveness in my tone is unmistakable.

"Down, boy," he says. "It was meant as a compliment."

"I know that."

"Do you?"

I roll my eyes at him.

# Chapter 10

## *Dominika*

Aaron's going away party is well attended. It's no wonder. So many guests have been there to support him throughout his difficult journey. I'm so proud of him. It's amazing to see him stepping into his new life. Although there are people everywhere, I catch a glimpse of a familiar face in the crowd causing my next step to falter. I knew Rod had arrived because he texted me to find out if I was on my way. So why is my heart beating like thunder? And how the hell do I cool this pulse of heat to my cheeks?

*Dear God, is it possible to have permanent heart palpitations from a simple kiss?*

I wait for an answer, but God is busy elsewhere.

*Figures.*

My teeth dig into my bottom lip as I take him in. Rod lives in jeans and t-shirts. Even dressed down, it's impossible to remain oblivious to his good looks and well-defined body. When he dresses-up, the bad boy takes a back seat to the debonair man. Like now. One can almost forget there's an inked Adonis beneath the elegance. His tall and muscular body is adorned in a pair of slim pants, a fitted suit jacket and a shirt. The head-to-toe black look intensifies his mesmerizing dark brown eyes.

Then there are the shoes.

The classic Gaziano & Girling Cambridge oxfords are straight from 57th Street in New York—a far cry from the poor boy who used to have holes in his cheap shoes.

I force my eyes to pull up to his face, but I get distracted. My gaze is glued to his chest—just hairy enough to make him manly. It's amazing how a few undone buttons can conjure so many improper thoughts. As I continue my inspection, I can't help but approve of the new tight beard.

*God, you're gorgeous.*

I do my best to avoid focusing on his lips because if I do, it'll only bring me back to yesterday's kiss and how his mouth thoroughly claimed mine. I can't allow myself to slip back into that fantasy.

Aaron waves me over.

"You've been summoned," Claire says.

"Looks like it." I do my best to keep it light, praying to God she doesn't hear the tremor in my voice.

"Come on. Let's go see what he wants," Claire says with a hand wave.

I follow her.

"Look at you," Aaron says taking me into his arms. He gives me a bear hug that lifts me off my feet.

"Oh my God, Aaron. Put me down."

He does.

"What the hell do they put in the water in Hungary?" he says. "Gorgeousness serum? You're more beautiful than I've ever seen you, Dom."

"Thank you," I say.

"I begged for her stylist's number. I'm out of luck. I'd have to fly to Europe," Claire says. "It's the same for the killer dress. She got it in the Big Apple. No wonder."

"You guys are making a big deal out of nothing," I say.

Claire swats Rod's arm. "Tell her how amazing she looks."

He flinches.

I blink up at him, and my cheeks flame up.

"Hey," he says.

"Hey," I say.

"I didn't tell you to say hi," Claire says.

"Right." Rod rubs a hand along the back of his neck and clears his throat. Unrushed, he sweeps his eyes up and down the length of my body.

*Good Lord.*

Even though I'm fully dressed, I feel naked.

"I love it all."

Four simple words that have a devasting effect on me.

Rod's eyes bore into mine and for a few seconds, it's as if we're the only two people in the backyard.

"See, I told you. We're so going out later," Claire says. "You're going to be my hunk magnet tonight. You'll have men eating out of the palm of your hand. I'm okay with the left-overs." She laughs.

Aaron chuckles.

Rod isn't amused.

His nostrils flare.

The corners of his lips lifts.

He's displeased.

"It's settled," Aaron says, patting Rod's shoulder. "The girls will hit the town, and you and I will go out in search of desperate souls. The more desperate, the better. Like my little sis, I'm okay with the leftovers."

Aaron and Claire laugh their heads off.

I can't crack a smile.
And from the look of it, neither can Rod.
A lash of hurt stabs at my heart.
*Tonight, he'll be kissing another woman.*

# Chapter 11

## *Roderick*

Aaron and I end up at the Quintus Hotel—one of my favorite hangouts. From there, we weave our way through a more private hallway few are privy to. It leads us to a plush and luxuriant garden. It's a ruse to hide the obvious in plain sight—the black door that leads to more. Behind the prim, proper and respectable façade of the hotel, resides a seedy and lewd underworld—the member's only private adult club. The gentlemen's club, restaurants and bars are all located inside the hotel. No one would ever bat an eyelash. The black door and covered passageway leads to Dark Compulsion. That's where the rich and famous come to play. The owner spared no expense to ensure the outside matches the majestic design you find inside. It goes without saying security is tight.

Aaron is my guest for tonight. He was in the mood for something edgier. I wasn't. We settled on the first floor of the building. The action is pretty vanilla down here compared to the other floors, but there are still plenty of great options for an illicit hookup with no strings attached.

As I scour the room, I can't stop thinking of Dom and how

stunning she looked. Maybe Aaron is right. Maybe it's in the water. I chuckle internally. I wish it were that simple. Dom was always pretty, but now her striking beauty is almost blinding. I don't know what to do with myself when I'm around her.

No sooner has her angelic face popped into my mind than my hand curls up in a fist. As lovely as she is, Claire can be a bit of a wildcard. I can't help but wonder what kind of trouble she'll push my best friend into tonight... especially since she enlisted her reckless best friend Kelley as her wingman. Three beautiful single women out on the town in LA. What could possibly go wrong?

*Fuck.*

I shake my head, hoping to dissipate the millions of possible scenarios. It's in vain.

*What the hell is this stupid fluttering sensation in the pit of my stomach?*

Dom's return is turning my world upside down.

I take in a deep breath hoping to settle my stomach.

It's to no avail.

The unfamiliar stir is still as present as the erratic beat of my heart.

*Shit.*

I have to find a way to shut down my undeniable—scratch that—unreasonable desire for Dom. I'm too screwed up, and she deserves better. She needs someone who's been loved and who knows how to love. And that isn't me.

*Jesus Christ.*

I need to get a fucking grip.

I need to get laid.

"Rod?" Aaron shakes me out of my mental rumination.

"Sorry. What were you saying?"

He knits his eyebrows. "We're in a room surrounded by

some of the most gorgeous women in LA, and your mind is in Iceland. What gives?"

"No. I'm still here." *Lies.* "I was checking out... the options."

"Sure, and I'm the Pope."

"Don't break my balls."

"Glad to hear you still have a pair. I want to make sure you're with me, Rod."

"I'm with you."

"Good because I'm leaving first thing Monday morning for Tokyo," he says. "I have tonight and all of tomorrow to get some action and there's no way I'm not dipping my dick in an inviting pussy."

Everything about this place guarantees a home run.

Rhythmic music thumps in the background, low enough not to drown our voices. Soft lights bathe the room in a luminous sheen, casting a seductive glow against bare feminine skin. A long slab of black stone stretches wall-to-wall in the back. Four bartenders mix, pour and serve your poison of choice. Several high, round tables surrounded by small groupings and conversation nooks are dispersed around the room to elicit foreplay. This is where connections are made.

"Stop worrying. Remember, you're okay with my leftovers," I say.

"Fucker."

We both laugh.

"Do you want another drink?" He raises his empty tumbler.

"No, I'm good. Thanks."

"I'm going for another tequila on the rocks. I'll be back."

"All right."

Aaron strides across the richly appointed lounge, evaluating every woman on his way to the bar. Since he keeps walking, I can only assume he's still looking.

The place is starting to fill up. Women are clad in appropriate club wear—tight dresses that don't cover much. My eyes bounce around the room, hoping they'll land on a tempting distraction—a cute little thing sure to stir my interest and my cock. The beauties abound, but from my less than excited cock, you'd never know.

*Great. My best friend is cock-blocking me.*

A few long minutes go by and there's no sign of Aaron.

I pull my phone out and text Dom.

Rod: How's it going? Breaking hearts?

I stand there like an idiot with my phone in my hand staring at it, willing her to respond.

No answer.

*Fuck.*

With a huff of frustration, I tuck my phone back into the inner pocket of my suit jacket.

Small fingers tap my back.

I turn around to find curvy redheaded twins staring up at me.

"Hi," they say in unison before flashing me an inviting smile.

"Hi," I smile back.

"I'm Julka."

"And I'm Violina."

"Ladies." I nod. "I'm Rebel."

Dark Compulsion is a place where real identities are undisclosed. Privacy is key here. Random names are assigned to each member when they join. It's uncanny how mine fits.

"Gorgeous and dangerous Rebel," Violina says, and licks her bottom lip.

I smile.

The twins are wearing identical light-gray dresses. *How original.* Their tops are so low, their fake tits are a breath away from popping out. Their silicone jugs look like pumped projectiles. Their nipples are so erect, it's obscene. At least the duck lips are somewhat under control.

"Your friend is also pretty cute," Violina says.

"He's a handsome guy, for sure," I say, playing along. "And a war hero."

Julka's eyes widen. "Ohhhh."

"Impressive," Violina says.

"Don't tell him I told you, but he can be a little reckless and wild."

"Thank God we came over," Julka says.

"You two look lonely," Violina says.

"In all fairness, we just got here. We haven't had time to make... friends."

"Maybe we can be your friends," Violina says.

"Yeah. Fast friends," Julka says.

They giggle.

It takes everything in me not to roll my eyes.

"My sister and I are members," Julka says, flashing me her ring.

"We have a room upstairs. Maybe you and your friend would like to join us?" Violina says.

I search the room.

Aaron has a huge grin on his face. He's leaning against the bar, working a brunette. She's pretty and from her flirty demeanor, I'd say she's into him. The large ring on her index finger—identical to mine and the twins'—indicates she's a club member.

*He's in good hands.*

"I think my friend found his match for the evening." My chin jerks in his direction.

"Boo hoo," Julka says.

"Well, I guess it's just the three of us. It'll still be fun," Violina says.

"Yeah, we like to play dirty games with each other and with guys." Julka cups her sister's tits.

Violina closes her eyes and moans.

*Un-fucking-believable.*

Julka and Violina look like pleasure dolls.

I've had my fair share of threesomes and foursomes in this club, but these two tip the scale of plastic perfection. So unappealing. And sister play? I'll pass.

I open my mouth to respond, but my phone vibrates.

"I'm sorry, ladies," I say, pulling it out.

*It's Dom.*

Dominika: Breaking hearts? Hardly. I bailed out on Claire and Kelley. We ended up at Ransack, and I couldn't handle it. Not my scene. I'm home. I just got out of the shower.

I will myself not to visualize beads of water running freely down her sexy naked body, but I fail miserably.

Rod: What's the plan for the rest of the evening?

Dominika: My couch and UTV.com Prime. Lame, right?

Rod: Not at all.

Dominika: You must be breaking hearts? Were the paramedics called in yet?

I smile.

Rod: Not even close.

Dominika: You're lying, Wolfe. They must be fighting all over you.

I cut to the chase.

Rod: Can I come over?

Dominika: Why?

Rod: We need to talk.

Seconds tick away.

Dominika: Okay.

And if I don't grin like a fool.

Rod: I'm on my way.

Dominika: Okay. See you soon.

I tuck my phone into my pocket. "I'm sorry, ladies, but I have somewhere else to be."

"Oh no." Julka pouts.

"So soon?" Violina pulls down her lips and frowns.

They're disappointed.

Too bad.

With that, I leave the twins behind, shoot off a quick text to Aaron and head to the door.

# Chapter 12

## *Dominika*

Everything was too much at Ransack—the loud music, the crowded space and the eager men. I can handle the first two, but I struggle with the last one. With good reason.

I should feel guilty for pulling the *'Jetlag is such a bitch'* card, but I don't. After bidding Claire and Kelley goodbye, I'd hopped in the back of a cab.

Surprise, surprise, I could only think of one person during the ride back to my place. In an attempt to distract my thoughts from who Rod was doing, I jumped in the shower and turned the knob to the coldest setting, praying the iciness of the water would help me regain my composure. Everything was going great until I noticed his text message.

I may never have wanted to set foot in Dark Compulsion, but I'm aware of what goes on there. I was certain Rod would be balls deep inside a willing pussy by now. My mind was on overdrive—conjuring all sorts of filthy scenarios. Turns out I was wrong. I'm unwilling to admit I was relieved.

My phone chimes, pulling me away from my thoughts.

Rod: You're still home?

Dominika: Where else would I be?

Rod: Just checking. The cab is close.

Dominika: All right.

Rod: I can't wait to see you.

I type and delete my message three times before I have the courage to send it.

Dominika: Same here.

My anticipation climbs with every passing second—along with a feeling of longing I've come to make peace with over the last few months.

"Damn battle shots game."

My body ignores my scolding. It hums with excitement, yet my heart beats with trepidation. It's as if my senses are at polar opposites of the spectrum. Like everything else surrounding my best friend lately.

As I pace my home, Rod's words ring in my ears.

*'That was a bad idea.'*

Is there anything more for us to talk about?

The humiliation from the rejection hasn't subsided. Still, I'm curious and apprehensive of what he has to say.

The doorbell rings, forcing me to stop ruminating.

*Oh, God.*

As my emergency person, Rod has a spare set of keys to my house and studio, but he won't use them unless he has to. I hurry to the door, get on my tippytoes and glance through the peephole to buy myself some time. I suck in a hasty breath when I see him standing on the other side.

*Like I wasn't expecting him.*

I unlock the door and open it.

He flashes me a languorous smile and when he winks at me, every cell in my body comes alive.

*Calm down, Dominika.*

"Hey." I wave him in.

Like earlier, my nipples approve of his perfectly tailored suit, but my brain still can't comprehend how the hell he has this kind of power over my body.

"Hey," he says, stepping into my home.

I'm still holding onto the door like a protective shield.

Rod turns around and lifts his right hand. Two bags obstruct my view of his gorgeous face. When I read the name of one of my favorite dessert spots in LA, my eyes light up.

"You stopped by Small Batches?"

He peeks between the bags. "I figured I needed a little ammo to seduce you into listening to me."

*Honey, you don't need any ammo whatsoever.*

"What did you get?"

"Everything we need to make ice cream sandwiches."

I arch a brow. "I'm listening."

"I got two flavors of cookies—chocolate peanut butter and birthday. And two pints of ice cream—cookie monster and popcorn. I even bought wine, and an assortment of cheese and those British crackers you like," he says. "It would be a crime to watch UTV.com Prime without the perfect set of snacks." He glances down at the canvas bag he's holding in his other hand.

"You're a good man." I smile.

He frowns. "Are you going to hang out behind the door the whole evening?"

I roll my eyes at him. "Funny."

"You seem attached to it," he says.

"Let's put the ice cream in the freezer before it melts," I say.

He nods and heads toward the kitchen.

The view from behind is sinful.

Some men walk. Others stride. Rod takes ownership of the space.

I close the door, lock it and follow him.

Rod's expensive shoes scuff the wooden floor, and my pulse thumps with every scrape.

When we get to the kitchen, I don't even have to say a word. He knows where everything is. I lean against the kitchen island and watch him in action. He drops the bag of cookies and crackers on the granite counter, stores the ice cream and cheese, and places the bottles of wine near the fridge.

"Done," he says turning to face me. "We can start with—"

Rod glances down at my chest.

His lips break into a huge smile.

"What?" I lower my head.

"Does it mean you still like me?" He points to my new London-purchased *'I Like Cute Boys In Bands'* tank top.

"You're no longer in a band. And you're no longer a boy." You're a man... a smoking hot man.

"Point taken. At least you didn't say I'm no longer cute."

"You're incorrigible, Wolfe."

"But do you still like me?"

"Don't be ridiculous, Rod. I'll always like you. You're my best friend. Stop asking silly questions."

"Fair enough."

His eyes are still glued to my chest. It takes me a second to understand why. I didn't think twice of my wardrobe selection when he said he'd drop by. The loose-fitting gray tank top with open sides and cut-off jeans shorts were the perfect choice when I was alone, but a pretty bad one when I have company, especially considering I'm bra-less. Rod's dark brown eyes are veiled with a predatory glint I've never seen before. The fact my treacherous nipples are poking hard against the thin fabric of my top makes this moment even more awkward than it already is.

He tilts his head to the side, a dangerous smile tugs at the corner of his mouth when he meets my gaze again.

"I—I should go change," I say, pushing myself off the island.

Rod stalks forward.

I back up and gasp when my ass hits the counter behind me.

Those coffee-colored eyes heat up, and the expression on his face is unreadable. Two more steps and his expensive shoes halt only a few inches from my bare feet.

My breathing speeds up as my mind desperately tries to comprehend what's unfolding.

He leans into me until his nose is practically touching mine. "Don't."

He extends his hand and drags a finger down the length of my tattooed sleeve. My breath hitches. I shiver and close my eyes.

"It doesn't hurt anymore, Dom." His voice is as soothing as a warm blanket.

I nod.

"The past is behind you."

I nod again.

"Look at me," he says.

I open my eyes and meet his caring gaze.

"You've turned the pain into your power," he says tracing one of my tattoos.

"I know. I'm always a little uncomfortable when people touch me."

Bad memories stay with you for a lifetime. Ditto for scars.

"It's me that's touching you. You shouldn't be uncomfortable."

"I'm not."

"Sure about that?"

He steps closer, crowding me as he presses his palms against the counter on either side of my hips.

"Rod."

Any other man, and I'd run terrified. I no longer allow anyone to cage me. But it's different with him. No part of me feels the urge to flee. Instead, my nipples tighten into sensitive peaks.

*What's going on with me?*

He leans into me, leaving only a couple of inches between us.

God, the man smells so good.

"Rod, what?"

I'm stumped.

He pulls back and with his eyes locked onto mine, he reaches out and brushes his knuckles against my protruding nipples.

I swallow a moan.

*Jesus Christ.*

"I like this top on you," he says.

"I—I—"

"I'm listening." His seductive smile is disarming. I can't even remember what I was going to say. "Those are fucking gorgeous," he says before lowering his eyes to my nipples.

"I—"

"You, what, Dom?"

This time he strokes the tips of my peaks with his middle fingers in a slow circle. His tempo is agonizing.

My eyes fixed on his hands. "Good Lord."

"And they feel fucking amazing."

I'm at a disadvantage here. Grasping at straws, I go for a low blow.

"Is your game off? You didn't score tonight? That's why you're here?"

He doesn't answer.

The silence is killing me.

"You're wrong," he says. "I turned down a few offers. Because I'd rather be here... with you."

"Oh."

"Wanna know why?" His face is a raw mix of tenderness and wickedness. How is that even possible?

"Why?"

"I can't stop thinking about you, Dom. And not as my best friend. It's like your soft, warm mouth put a spell on me. I didn't get enough of you last night."

A relieved breath escapes my lips.

*He wasn't hunting for prey.*

The thought sends a thrill through me and threatens to melt my body into a pool of heat. A warning voice rings an alarm bell.

"I bet you say that to all your conquests," I say.

"Other than the girl I lost my virginity to and maybe a few girls here and there when I was still a teenager, I never kiss the women I'm with," he says.

"You don't?"

We talk about everything, except our sex lives, so this comes as a shock.

He shakes his head. "It's too intimate."

"And it isn't with me?"

"No." His answer is so definite. So steadfast. So unwavering. I don't even know how to respond. "As far as you being a conquest, it'll never happen."

"What makes you so sure?"

"Short-lived relationships don't allow me time to care. You

and me, we've been going strong for over a decade. We're solid. And I care about you."

"As a friend."

"As my *best* friend," he says.

I'm not so easily swayed. "What happened to *'This is a bad idea'*?"

"I freaked out."

I scoff. "Rod Wolfe loses his cool? That'll be the day."

"I didn't expect to like kissing you so much."

*Oh, my God.*

His words fan the fire raging inside me. "You... liked it?"

He lowers his head and skims his lips along my forehead to my ear. "A lot. I jerked off thinking of your mouth, Dom."

"You did what?" *I shouldn't be this excited.*

"Last night when I got back to my place, and a couple times today. What can I say? That kiss had quite an effect on me."

I can't believe his confession.

Power fills me at the thought I could do that to a guy like Rod.

"But nothing made me come harder than thinking of all the other things I want to do to you—dirty, filthy, lewd things."

I heave a shaky breath.

His revelation renders me speechless.

"Did I shock you... or turn you on?"

*Both.*

Heat travels from my nipples to my clit in a flash at the hunger I read in his gaze.

*God, all these years, I thought my clit was broken.*

I blink up at him. "You're pulling my leg, Wolfe."

Rod brushes his body against mine. There's no hiding what's going on here. "Feel that?"

"Mother of God."

"That's right." He's sporting a devilish grin as he grinds against me with more resolve.

This is the moment when I enter fight-or-flight mode, but instead of panicking, I tilt my hips forward, pressing close against him and feeling the hard ridge of his impressive erection against my stomach. "You're so incredibly hard." I don't recognize the raspy voice that escapes my lips.

Rod grabs my chin, forcing our eyes to lock. "It's all for you, baby."

*That's a lot to handle.*

I lower my gaze in an attempt to break the bewitching trance he has me under. "God, Rod."

"The way you say my name is sexy as fuck, Dom."

"You shouldn't say that."

"Why not?"

"Because..." *I might get addicted to your words.* "What are we doing?"

"Just one more kiss," he says.

"One more kiss?"

"Let's get it out of the way—flush it out of our systems. Maybe last night was a fluke. Maybe this thing between us is a passing infatuation."

"What if one more kiss isn't enough?" The words fly out of my mouth before I can catch them.

Goosebumps pebble my skin as he studies me, his searing gaze traveling down to my breasts before returning to my face. One corner of his mouth lifts, and triumph morphs his gorgeous features. "Then you tell me what you want and I'll give it to you, sweet Dom." He holds my stare hostage. "But I warn you, this time, I'll want more than one kiss. Are you up for the challenge?"

My mind is spinning so fast.

Can I handle more? Can I handle a demigod like Roderick Wolfe?

I'd be lying to myself if I didn't admit I'd give up an organ to feel as safe as I did yesterday in his strong arms.

"One night," I say. "I don't want to become your fuck buddy."

*God save me if I want more after tonight.*

"Agreed, but for the record, you'd never be a fuck buddy."

I laugh quietly, shaking my head. "You don't date, Rod. You fuck," I say.

He opens his mouth to say something, but changes his mind.

It's not like he can deny it. That's who he is.

A few beats pass and we're still staring at each other.

"One night and we can go back to being best friends," he says.

I nod.

I don't know if either of us believe the lie, but when he lowers his head and captures my lips in a blazing kiss, all thoughts escape me.

Rod pushes my lips apart and when I taste his tongue, my pussy clenches so hard I dig my fingernails in his forearm for fear I might come. He doesn't just kiss me. He takes full ownership of my mouth. Of my soul. To my astonishment, I match his passionate fervor. Our tongues dance, and I let out a litany of small mewls of pleasure in response. I thought I was greedy last night, but now I'm unleashed. I drink him up like a woman who hasn't had a sip of water in weeks. Nothing so far in my life compares to this.

As soon as he cups my head between his large hands and lets out a deep growl, all my worries fade away.

*I'm in a safe place.*

I want this.

No.

I *need* this.

I need *him*.

With this blazing kiss, Roderick Wolfe relinquishes his role as my best friend.

He's no longer the loyal guardian who watches over me and protects me.

Gone is the man I've placed on a pedestal because he's the only one who's never betrayed or hurt me.

He's now the smoking hot guy who's devouring the hell out of me. And I'm not afraid to say, I'm relishing every second of it.

# Chapter 13

## *Roderick*

Dom is giving me one night.

She could've refused, but she didn't.

She wants this as much as I do.

We've been skirting around our attraction for far too long. It's time we did something about it before I go fucking crazy.

I lean into her and press a soft kiss to her lips. Unrushed, I linger, taunt, tease, but never deepening the kiss. I want to give her time. Heck, I need time. This is combustive and my mind has yet to catch up. She melts into my kiss, allowing my tongue to flirt with hers. I welcome her taste when her sweetness floods my tongue. I cup her face and draw her into me.

*Jesus Christ, those little mewls of hers will be the end of me.*

I press my body against hers until her hard nipples are scratching my chest through my shirt.

She gasps at the contact. "Dear, God."

"Fuck," I say.

Our kiss grows more urgent with every tongue stroke.

It's scorching.

It's laced with pent-up lust.

For six months we've been pretending. Choosing to be oblivious rather than to give in to what we both needed.

Dom can live in her shell, sometimes. I didn't expect this from her.

She matches my voraciousness with unwavering passion.

*Damn, she responds beautifully.*

Kissing Dom shouldn't feel this fucking good the second time around.

I should feel guilty for ravishing my best friend's mouth.

I should repent for wanting to dominate every part of her.

And God knows, I shouldn't want to take possession of her sexy little body.

But I don't feel an ounce of guilt.

I twist her blonde hair around my hand to control the slant of her mouth beneath mine and I deepen the kiss.

"You taste so fucking amazing, Dom. Tell me I can kiss you hard enough to bruise," I say.

"Kiss me hard, Rod."

My cock swells in approval.

She's no longer my best friend. She's the woman I want more than my next breath.

*Damn.*

"Feel me, baby," I say.

"What?"

"I want you to know what you do to me." I don't wait for an answer. I let go of her hair, grab her hand and slide it down the ridge of my stomach, past my belt until her fingers curl around my bulge.

"Oh, God," she says.

I squeeze both our hands tight and nearly black out from the sharp pulse tugging my balls.

"Fuck me." I breathe those words like a solemn prayer.

When I inhale her arousing scent, my appetite for her kicks

into overdrive. Claiming her mouth is no longer enough. I need more. A hell of a lot more.

With one last tongue stroke, I pull away from her and drop a soft kiss against her forehead.

"You stopped," she says, breathless.

"I need a second to allow my heart to stop beating so fast."

She glides her hand up my torso and places it against my chest. "Mine is beating fast too."

I mirror her gesture, but the result is vastly different.

I intended on feeling the thumping rhythm of her heart against my palm, but unable to restrain myself, I grope her left breast. When I do, the fabric of her tank top shifts, revealing her naked right breast.

*Shit.*

I'm unprepared for this moment.

I'm going to hell for wanting to defile my best friend.

So be it.

"I don't think you need this anymore," I say, tugging at her top.

I stare at her, waiting for her to protest. But she offers a shy smile.

Grabbing the hem of her tank top, I pull the thin cotton fabric over her head. Dom's exposed full breasts are a work of art.

"Fuck, I'm delirious just looking at you. Tell me you want me to put an end to this madness."

"Don't."

"You sure?"

"I am."

"I'm warning you, once we start this, I won't be able to put the brakes on."

"I'm okay with that." She smiles wide. "I've never been more certain of anything in my life."

"Neither have I." My grin matches hers.

Unable to contain myself, I run a finger from the tip of her chin down between her tits. She follows my trailing finger and when our gaze meets, the lust I read in her sapphire eyes consumes me. The intensity between us is combustive.

I fill up my palms with her plump tits and knead them greedily, giving her as much pleasure as I rob from her. Her natural breasts jiggle and mold under my touch and she moans for me so beautifully.

"Goddammit, Dom. You're so beautiful." I can't stop devouring her with my eyes.

"You do this to me," she says.

"No, it's always been in you. You're just allowing me to pull it out of you, baby,"

She smiles shyly.

When I let her tits fall against her chest, they hang beautifully. They aren't Hollywood-huge. They're fucking perfect.

"I bet your tits taste amazing," I say, lowering my head.

Her response catches me off guard.

The second she weaves her fingers into my hair and pushes her gorgeous breasts into my face like an offering, it's game over. This is an invitation I can't refuse.

I flick my tongue across the ridges of her taut nipple and she moans for me again.

"Your tits are exquisite, Dom."

I nip at her tits, then suck her deep into my mouth.

My sweet Dom arches her back, demanding more.

*Good girl.*

I give her what she needs in spades. I suck on her left breast with fervor while my thumb circles the hard nipple of her right breast. Her body trembles under my touch. I heighten my pleasure by groping her in my large palm, relishing the suppleness and bounce of her breasts.

"God that feels so, so good," she says, clutching more hair until my scalp burns.

*Oh, yeah, baby.*

After a few long minutes of sinful play, I release her nipples, ignoring the sound of her protest. Impatient to discover every part of her, I let my hand roam down her stomach until I reach her ripped jean shorts.

She places her hand against mine to stop me.

"It's okay," she says.

I frown my confusion. "What's okay?"

"You—you don't have to try. It doesn't work."

"You lost me. What doesn't work?"

"You can't make me come with your fingers."

My eyebrows hit my forehead.

It takes me a second to recover from the shock. "The hell I can't."

"Rod, don't be stubborn."

"I'm at a loss."

Her eyes lift to the ceiling.

"Talk to me, Dom."

Still no answer.

"Are you a virgin?"

She shakes her head.

"Answer me."

"I'm not."

"Okay, now we're getting somewhere. You can't have an orgasm because of a medical condition, or you've only been with shitheads who needed a map and a flashlight... and even with those, they couldn't find their way around?"

She shakes her head again, but she does a pretty poor job at hiding her smile.

"What? It's a legitimate question."

She purses her lips and blinks up to the ceiling. She always does that when she's uncomfortable about something.

"Dom." I place my fingers around her chin and lower her head so our eyes meet. "I'm your best friend. Talk to me."

"I've never allowed myself to... you know..."

"No, I don't know. Tell me."

"It's hard for me to get into it. To block everything out and let my body do the thinking. My mind is constantly... active."

*What a crying shame.*

"What happened to cause that?"

"Nothing. It's me." Her answer is lighting quick.

I frown.

I don't buy it, but I don't push her. We can talk about it another time.

I try a different approach. "I know everything about you, except for what drives you over the edge. What do I have to do to make you scream out my name when you come?"

She laughs.

"What's so funny?"

"I've never been able to have an orgasm with a guy, so I wouldn't know."

"But you've had them?"

She blushes. "I have."

"What's your vice?"

She blinks.

"Porn? Toys? Fingers? Tell me. You can't shock me."

"I'm not... comfortable with those."

*Fair enough.* "What's your trick?"

"Humping my pillow always does it for me... in a big way." Her cheeks flush in the most seductive shade of pink.

And if the imagery of my sweet Dom chasing after her orgasm, rocking back and forth on a pillow doesn't make me harder than I already am.

"We'll have to try the pillow another time."

"I thought this was only one night, Wolfe," she says.

"If you think I'm going to let that bombshell slide, you're wrong, Dom. That kind of explosive revelation warrants a second night. And a third. And a fourth. And a fifth."

"Really?"

"I have to make up for all those losers who've let you down."

She giggles.

*But she hasn't said no.*

"You trust me?"

I get a small nod.

"I asked you a question, Dom."

"I trust you," she says.

"I'm not convinced."

"Don't be silly, Rod. You know I trust you."

*A little better, but I want more.*

"Implicitly?"

"I do."

"If you trust me, let me make it good for you."

She readies herself to say something, but I cock an eyebrow in warning.

"Okay."

I resume my mission.

I undo the button of her shorts, unzip them and glide my fingers underneath the denim fabric. With an eager hand, I push her underwear aside and travel to her pussy.

"What's that, baby?" I stroke the top of her pussy.

"This is so embarrassing," she says, blushing. She even hides her face against my chest.

"There's nothing to be embarrassed about. As your lover, I'll know every part of you."

She looks up at me with those giant eyes. "My lover?"

"Yeah. I can be your best friend and your lover."

"I like how you make up these random rules along the way."

I grin in response.

I trace the contour of her pubic hair and I swear I'm a breath away from coming in my pants when realization sets in.

"Is that a heart?"

"I'm mortified. No one was supposed to find out."

*But here we are.*

"I think it's sexy."

"It's the new thing in Budapest. My cousin dared me to try it," she says.

"I like your cousin even more now."

She laughs.

"I can't wait to come smack in the middle of your little heart."

Her laughter subsides.

"I told you there were a lot of dirty things I wanted to do with you, Dom. I just added another one to the to-do list," I say in a matter-of-fact way.

"You're a pervert, Wolfe."

"Thanks for the compliment," I say without a trace of humor.

Her jaw drops. "You're serious?"

"I'm as serious as the erection I've been sporting since it became clear you were braless and I had an effect on you."

"I might not survive this night."

"You'll do fine."

Impatient to feel her slickness, my fingers continue their exploration.

"Dear God," she says when my finger glides between her pussy lips.

I probe her wetness. "Is that for me?"

She shakes her head and rolls her eyes.

"No? It's for another guy?"

"You know it's for you."

"Good answer."

I plunge two fingers so deep inside her, her breath hitches. That does little to tame me. I use my fingers as an extension of my desperate cock and finger-fuck the hell out of her.

"Oh, my God, Rod, what are you doing to me?"

Her agonizing plea threatens to make me lose my shit.

"You want me to stop?"

"No, I don't."

I can't help but chuckle at the tremor of panic in her voice.

"We're on the same page, then. You keep riding my fingers."

"God, that sounded positively obscene."

"Yeah, but your body is singing a different tune, baby. You're drenched. I fucking love knowing I'm responsible for this little flood."

Her cheeks flame up.

"You're dangerous, Wolfe."

*You don't know the half of it.*

"So, the guys you've been with so far haven't got a clue what to do with this?" My eyes locked onto hers as I caress her clit.

She shakes her head. "No. I guess it's my own fault—"

"Tsk. If you aren't melting in a guy's arms, it's *his* fault."

"Like my parents, I guess life has dealt me a pretty mediocre hand when it comes to men," she says.

"We can change that tonight."

"I'd like that."

I drop a soft kiss against her lips.

I'm starting to think the reason I haven't kissed too many women in my life is because I was waiting for her tempting lips.

I skate over her hard clit over and over again.

She squirms. "Rod."

"I love taking care of you, Dom."

Her juices travel down my hand.

"Baby, you're going to come so hard."

A flicker of worry flashes in her eyes.

She places her hands on my chest and drags them down the tight muscles of my stomach.

"What about you?" She plays with the metal buckle of my leather belt.

"This isn't about me, Dom. It's about you. If you think you're going to distract me, think again."

She averts her gaze. "I don't want to disappoint you."

It pains me to hear the insecurity in her voice.

*Who did this to her?*

"Look at me."

She still avoids my gaze.

"Look at me," I say again.

She obeys.

"Rod, I—"

Framing her face in one hand, I tip her head up to mine and devour her mouth. She moans, but she's still tense.

She leaves me no choice.

I pull out the big guns.

"Wanna hear about a recurring fantasy of mine since we almost made out when we played battle shots?" I don't wait for an answer. "You climb on top of my face and graze your succulent clit across my tongue like a greedy little slut. You fuck my face until you're so wet, the only way I can prevent you from sliding off my tongue is by clenching your beautiful ass in my hands."

"The things that come out of your mouth," she says.

She glides an arm around my shoulders, pulling me closer. I drop my forehead against hers.

*Her walls are coming down.*

"I'd make you lose your head by wiggling my tongue against your little ball of nerves, leaving you no choice but to chase after your climax until you come gushing in my mouth."

My fingers never stop working her pussy.

She rocks her hips back and forth.

I have her where I want her.

*Good girl.*

"I'd struggle to lap up every last drop of your delectable juices, Dom."

Her body trembles and her eyes roll to the back of her head. "This is too much."

"That's exactly how I'd feel, but I'd manage to clean up your sweet release real nice."

"Ha— I—"

"I can't wait for you to feed me, baby."

The pace of her breathing nears hyperventilation.

"Stop fighting it," I say.

She rocks at a frenetic pace against my hand.

*She's there.*

She digs her fingernails into my forearms so hard, I jolt. "Dear God."

"I bet you're so fucking beautiful when you come. Give me that gift. Let go, baby."

"No. No. This can't be happening again."

*The fuck it can't.*

I push against her clit, trapping all the blood there.

"Oh, Rod—"

She goes off like a rocket, chants my name so many times, I lose count after eight.

There's nothing like hearing your name on a woman's lips

as she tips over the edge, but knowing what I know about Dom, this moment fills me with pride.

*God help me.*

One night might not be enough and I haven't even buried my throbbing cock inside her pussy. Yet, every cell in my body is humming to claim her as fucking mine.

*What's wrong with you, Wolfe?*

Her body slumps against me. *She's spent.* I'm sure she's still floating on a cloud.

I pull my hand away from her pussy and lift it to eye level.

"You did good, baby."

I only get a faint moan from her.

"I wonder what you taste like."

I stick my glistening fingers into my mouth and lick them in a chorus of raunchy noises.

A wide-eyed Dom is too stunned to speak.

I wink at her.

"Damn, you're sweet, baby. I can't wait to turn my fantasy into reality. It'll be a privilege and honor to have you sit on my face."

Her breath catches in the back of her throat.

She's still staring at me with those huge eyes.

I eat pussy, but I never grant any woman the permission to sit on my face.

I drop a kiss on top of her head and stroke her hair. "Too much?"

She holds onto me so tight, it's like she's afraid I might run away. "There are no words to describe how dirty that was."

"I shouldn't do it again?"

"It's only one night, Rod."

"We can talk about it later."

"I don't know why you insist. It's not like I can keep up with you."

"I beg to differ. You thought you couldn't have an orgasm and I proved you wrong. And you fucking looked like a goddess coming apart in my arms."

She blushes.

"How did you do it? What's your superhuman power?"

"You're funny."

"No, seriously, Rod. That was earth-shattering. I've never experienced anything close to that. You have amazing fingers."

"Your pussy is intoxicating."

"So, my clit isn't broken?"

"Nah." I trace her lips with my finger. "Your body was waiting for me."

Her eyes bore into mine.

For a few seconds, neither of us says a word.

"I think you're right," she says.

My cock throbs at her response.

*I know I'm right.*

# Chapter 14

## *Dominika*

I could stay wrapped in Rod's arms forever.

His masculine scent washes over me as my body comes down from one helluva high pinnacle. Orgasms from humping my pillow are pretty amazing, but Rod's precise touch set me off like a rocket.

*Finally.*

Even in this whirlwind of near euphoria caused by my first heart-stopping orgasm at the hand of a man, my mind is screaming at me to proceed with caution. I'm fully aware this is to be short-lived. But my body is begging me to stop over-thinking and allow him—my lover—to do with me as he wishes. The heat emanating from his muscular body floods through me like the sun on a perfect summer day. It's so hot, it's scorching. I decide for once to quiet my mind. Yeah, my pussy wins.

Rod caresses his palms down my bare back and over the curves of my ass until he's squeezing my ass cheeks, pressing my body against his raging erection.

*God.*

His lips are a mere inch from my ear, each hot breath fanning my desire.

"We're done with the warmup. Let's go upstairs. I need to devote a few hours wringing every ounce of pleasure from your delicious body as I can."

"I don't even know what that means," I say, looking up at him.

"You'll soon find out." The uncompromising tone of his voice ricochets through me. "How do you like it, Dom?" His question startles me.

"Like what?"

"Sex."

*Oh.*

"You want it fast and furious or hard and deep?"

*Those are my options?*

*I only know pain or predictable.*

*I've been missing out.*

"Tell me how I can rock your world, Dom."

"I wouldn't know. No one's ever rocked my world before."

"Do you need nice and soft?"

His face contorts into an agonized expression.

I laugh. "Do you even know what that means?"

"Fuck no, but for you, I'd figure it out quick."

"You'd do that?"

"How many times do I have to tell you, this is about you, baby?"

"I'm a blank canvas." I give him a one-shoulder shrug. "Turn me into *your* masterpiece."

The searing flames in his brown eyes turn them dark, almost black.

"Did I just make a deal with the devil?" I bit my lower lip.

"Close."

"Please don't taint my soul," I say.

"When I'm done with you, there'll be no doubt who owns you… and that includes your soul."

"That sounded so primitive, Wolfe." *But, I can't tell you how sexy it was.*

"It's a promise I intend on keeping, Dom."

A delightful ribbon of pleasure twines through me, tingling my senses.

"Possessive much? After all, it's only for one night." It's good to keep things in perspective or else I might lose my head.

He pins me with his stare. "That's all I need to ruin it for all the others, Dom." The depth of his expression lets me know he's dead serious.

His words cause my pussy to throb like crazy.

"Asshole."

"You can throw that in my face the next time you come your head off."

I blink.

"And you will come again." He's been repeating that, but I thought he was joking.

It's a miracle he made me come once. I doubt it will happen twice in one night. I don't share my thoughts with him for fear they'll only fuel him.

His overconfidence might be misconstrued as arrogance, but then again, we're talking about Rod Wolfe. He's raised the bar so high for the next guy, I doubt anyone else will dethrone him. Ever.

"Come on, I need to get started on *my* masterpiece," he says before crushing my lips.

He lifts me in his arms. I wrap mine around his neck and nestle my head in the crook of his neck. He climbs the stairs, enters my bedroom and drops me to my feet with care. He walks to the nightstand to turn on the light. I cock an eyebrow. He responds with a dazzling smile. He does it again with the second lamp. I scan the room, adjusting to the new scenario.

*I'm half naked and I have a gorgeous man standing in my bedroom. What's wrong with this picture?*

Rod has been up here countless times, but this is different. Something transcendent is about to take place and there's no going back.

I'm still in a daze when it becomes clear his eyes are on me.

"I want to see your beautiful face when you come," he says.

"That's a lot of pressure. What happens if I suffer from performance anxiety?"

He chuckles. "You kill me, Dom." He closes the gap between us. "Let me lay your concerns to rest. It won't happen."

"And you can guarantee that, Wolfe?"

"Damn right I can. I'd be a piss poor lover if I allowed that to happen." He drops a soft kiss on the lips.

Things heat up, and our kiss turns ravenous. I get on my toes and wrap one arm around his neck, pulling him closer until my chest touches his. He grabs my free hand and slides it between us, cupping his mighty erection. He feels much bigger than he did earlier. I was so overwhelmed, I didn't feel the full weight of his cock when he was pressing against me, but now, I do.

"I can't wait for your hungry pussy to choke my cock, Dom."

*Jesus.*

The more he rubs my hand over his erection, the more my whole body heats up.

I look up and meet his lustful gaze. "I don't know if I can handle you. I mean it."

His beautiful mouth breaks into a wide smile.

"We don't have to rush things. One inch at a time is all it takes. Before you know it, you'll have swallowed me whole."

*Mother of God and all the Saints above.*

While he still holds my gaze hostage, he pushes me to the edge of my king size bed.

"I want you on your back."

I do as I'm told.

Rod slides his suit jacket off his wide shoulders and flings it across the room. It lands on the chair near the window.

He sits next to me on the mattress before lying on his side. "I can smell your headiness, baby. You're ready for more."

I'm unable to speak.

His impatient hands grope my breasts and he squeezes them before lowering his mouth. I bring my hands down to his head and weave my fingers in his thick silky hair.

"I could shoot my load just playing with these," he says, his hot breath caressing my nipples. "But, I'd rather fill you up instead."

My breath quickens as my excitement heightens to unprecedented levels. Just when I think I'm about to lose my mind from all his dirty, filthy talk, Rod releases my breasts. He sits up, slides off the bed and kneels in front of me.

"These are in the way of my creative process," he says, waving his finger over my pussy. "Time for them to go. Lift your hips for me, Dom."

I do.

Rod reaches out and tugs my jean shorts and panties down my legs. My slickness slides down with my underwear. Feeling the unmistakable proof of my arousal is surreal.

I gasp, my heart drums faster with every inch.

I'm naked. And wet again.

*Dear God.*

My first reaction is to cover myself, but I refrain when I read the disapproval in his eyes.

"Good girl," he says, eating me up with hungry eyes. "You're fucking gorgeous. Don't ever try to hide your body from me, Dom. It's blasphemy. Got it?"

His words bring a huge smile to my face. "I do."

"I'm going to take a lot of pleasure painting your pussy with my cum."

I'm astounded by his bold promise.

"No one's ever done that before," I say.

If he doesn't grin like a fool.

*Crap.*

That was supposed to be my inner voice.

"No one's ever marked you?"

I shoot him a sly smile, but don't answer.

"I like knowing I'll be your first."

"Why are you still dressed, Wolfe? I feel incredibly vulnerable here." I move the spotlight away from me.

"You want me naked, baby?"

"You've seen every part—"

"And now you want to see what you'll be getting?"

*Yes, I'm dying to cast my eyes on your sexy body.* "It's only fair. What happens if I have buyer's remorse?"

Rod cracks up.

"You're doing this to throw me off my game."

"I'm doing this because I'm nervous as hell."

"Don't be. You're in good hands."

"So you say."

We both smile at each other.

Rod gets off the bed, toes off his expensive shoes and peels his socks off before stripping out of his tailored black pants. His shirt receives the same treatment. In a flash, he goes from sophisticated businessman to inked bad boy. He has this uncanny ability to move fluidly between both worlds.

*Damn him.*

This isn't the first time I've seen him shirtless or in his boxer briefs. Back in the day, I toured with him and his bandmates across the country. I'm no ingénue to Rod's body, but I was always a spectator. Now, I'm a willing participant.

He bends down, pulling his boxer briefs with him. When he straightens back up, his magnificent cock stands proud. I suck in a breath, mesmerized by his impressive length and generous girth. His striking physique and his size put the few guys I've been with to shame.

He fists his cock, and looks down at me in all his naked gorgeousness, stroking his veiny mightiness in his hand.

*So many firsts tonight.*

I stare, unable to peel my eyes away. His well-defined V muscle looks like a master artist sculptured it with precision. The line of dark hair that extends like a path from his belly-button down to his cock is so inviting to ogle at his cock. I'm transfixed by the dark purple head. It screams of raw, feral hunger.

*Is there any part of him that's imperfect?*

"Now you're the one making me feel vulnerable."

His voice puts an end to my lustful inspection. "Like that's even possible."

"Should I assume you're okay with what you see?"

*Very much so.*

I force indifference into my voice. "Looks can be so deceiving. A pretty package doesn't mean much." I struggle to keep a straight face. "I might need a good test run to validate what I'm getting."

I can't believe I had the guts to say that.

"Fair enough." He nods, pursing his lips. "Let's make sure you give everything a *thorough* test... multiple times."

"It's wise. You can never be too sure nowadays."

He chuckles.

I grin.

He picks up his pants, rummages through the pocket until he pulls out his wallet. With a condom in hand, he steps up to the bed.

"Help me out, baby," he says extending the packet to my lips. I sit up and rip open the packet with my teeth. "Good girl."

Rod sheaths his cock without ever leaving my gaze.

"Watching you put on a condom is one of the sexiest things I've ever seen."

"Wait until we both look down as your pussy swallows my cock."

*I'm so out of my league here.*

Rod strides to the foot of the bed and drops one knee against it. "I need you right here," he says before grabbing my ankles and pulling me down until my ass is hovering at the edge of the mattress. He hoists my right leg up and places it over his shoulder. His hand clasps my ankle before dragging his fingers down my inner thigh.

I giggle. "That tickles."

"Really?"

I nod.

"There's so much I have yet to discover about you, baby."

"Same here."

"Let me make it better," he says.

He drops soft kisses against my skin, and I moan.

"Oh, yeah." My back bows off the bed.

He reaches out and skims a finger over my pussy.

"Hmmm," he says.

He continues his tease by tracing the seam of my pussy lips.

*Fuck.*

I bite down on my lip.

I'm shocked—and delighted—when he does the same.

He glides the tip of his fat cock up and down my slickness. It's a tease at first, but soon he picks up the pace. The sound of him skating through my juices is so raunchy, it sets off little spasms inside me. He's on a mission for a few long pleasurable minutes. It's so delicious, I roll my eyes to the back of my head, savoring each revolution. When he slows down his cadence, I want to beg him not to, but what he has in store for me is so much better. Rod focuses all his attention on my clit. A few more strokes and I feel the same heart-stopping sensation as I did earlier build up in my core.

*God.*

"Who does this gorgeous little clit belong to?"

"Huh?"

"Who does this little clit belong to?"

"You." The word slips so effortlessly from my lips.

"Who?"

"You, Rod."

"Better. I want this little clit that belongs to me to fucking explode."

"Jesus, Rod. I can't."

"No, Dom. The answer is, 'Yes, Rod', or, 'I will, Rod'. If you're so inclined, 'Your wish is my command, Rod' works too. Try again."

"I'm—"

"Tsk." He puts even more pressure against my clit as he rubs his cock hard against it.

I grunt.

"Give me what I want, Dom."

My body obeys and before I know it, I'm freefalling.

"Rod, this feels so fucking good..."

"That's it, baby." And he rubs his cock faster.

"I'm coming again." My pussy contracts in mind-blowing pulses as I ride my second toe-curling orgasm.

*Dear God.*

"My cock is for your pleasure. Remember that."

No sooner have the words escaped his lips than he drives into me with force.

*Shit.*

*He's huge.*

My pussy convulses widely, clenching around his intrusion as I relish in the aftermath of my climax. His sheer size and the way his fingers rub against my pussy as he drives into me elicit another orgasm.

*What is this guy doing to me?*

"Oh, Rod, I'm coming." *I'm so loud.*

His hungry cock plows through me with determination, pounding hard, and filling me. His thrusts are so assertive, they disarm me.

He's merciless.

Unrepentant.

Relentless.

"Fuck, Dom."

My desperate pussy weeps with pleasure.

"Baby, I'm close, but I come when you come."

"I already did. Twice."

"Three times, but who's counting. I want one more," he says.

"You're crazy, Wolfe." Perhaps not very convincing, but it's all I can manage.

"Give this to me, Dom. Force my load out of me," he says, driving into me.

I lower my eyes to where our bodies meet.

*He's right.*

Watching his cock disappear between my lips is freaking hot. I've avoided this intimate position in the name of self-preservation, but now I see the error of my ways.

He angles his body so each stroke is even deeper. In this position, he brushes against my clit each time he pumps in and out of me. Feeling his balls thud against my ass is an indescribable jolt.

*Mother of God.*

Getting my ass and clit stimulated at the same time is more than I can bear. Beyond my control, my body starts to convulse. I tremble underneath him as another orgasmic wave washes over me.

"You're going to give me another one, baby."

It isn't a question. It's a statement.

"I can't—"

He wins.

I lose my mind in the most toe-curling climax of the evening.

That says a lot because he's already been so generous.

I come so hard, I forget my own name until he calls it out.

"Look at me, Dom," he says. "I want to stare in your blue eyes when I pour my cum inside your warm pussy."

It's a struggle, but I obey his command and lock eyes with the gorgeous man who's rocking my world.

"Ah, shit, baby," Rod says. "You're choking my— Oh, Dom..." He growls as he releases himself between my legs.

# Chapter 15

## *Roderick*

Rays of sunlight spilling through the large windows wake me up.

I guess we were so out of it, we forgot to draw the curtains.

Dom's naked body is wrapped around mine and her silky blonde hair is fanned out across my chest.

This sensual image will be seared in my brain for the rest of my life.

I lift my head to look at the time.

*Eight o'clock.*

I let my head drop against the pillow and circle my arms around her.

*It's Sunday morning. There's no rush.*

When I negotiated the terms of our steamy night, it never occurred to me I'd be desperate for more.

*Fuck.*

I push the thought aside and focus on the now.

*I'm still in her bed and that's all that matters.*

I drop a flurry of kisses on the top of her head, relishing her warmth.

"Morning," I say.

"No, not yet," she says and nuzzles her face against the roughness of my stubbled cheek.

"Hey, where's my morning kiss?"

"You're such a demanding tyrant," she says. Still, she extends her neck. It's a soft and gentle kiss, but enough to stir my cock.

"Better. Morning, Dom."

"Morning, Rod." Her voice is so groggy.

"Come on. Wake up, sleeping beauty."

I pull her closer to me.

"Hmmm, your beard feels so manly," she says, her eyes still closed.

"You like it?"

"I like it a lot. It's well-trimmed and well-groomed. You were a pretty boy before. Now, you're ruggedly handsome."

"You know where my beard would feel even manlier?"

That gets her attention.

She lifts her body and pins those ocean-blue eyes on me. "I'm afraid to ask."

Her pillow-rumpled hair makes me smile.

"You're right. Talk is cheap," I say, sliding from underneath her.

"Where you going, Wolfe?"

I don't answer.

She narrows her gaze.

"You look suspicious. You don't trust me?"

"Everything about your demeanor suggests I shouldn't."

I lower my head and press my mouth against her stomach.

"So, back to my question."

"Which one again?" The mockery in her voice doesn't go unnoticed.

"You know, where my beard would feel even manlier?"

"My tummy?" She giggles.

"Uh-uh," I say, traveling down to her pussy, nibbling and kissing her smooth skin.

She weaves her fingers into my hair and pulls gently, forcing me to halt all movement. "Wh—what are you doing?"

I look up at her. "I want you to come on my face, baby."

"Y—you don't have to—"

I let out a long sigh. "I let that silliness slide last night because being inside you was so fucking amazing, but I need to know how it feels to have your juices gushing into my mouth, Dom."

She stares at me, stunned.

I continue. "After four core-shaking orgasms, I didn't want to push you further, but this is a new day."

"Isn't your time up, Wolfe? It was supposed to only be one—"

*Oh no she doesn't.*

I bury my face between her legs, lashing her with my tongue. "You taste so fucking good, Dom."

"Oh, shit."

"You're so wet."

"It's— It's— Oh, Rod."

I bite off a smile.

"No one's ever done this to me," she says.

My eyebrows climb to my hairline. "What? No one's ever gone down on you before?"

"The few guys I've been with made oral sex seem like a chore. Most times, it was so bad, I went numb down there and it was more pain than pleasure. But not with you. You're so passionate about it."

"I fucking love eating pussy."

She laughs. "I can see that."

"But you know what?"

"What?"

"You're my favorite pussy."

"Is that one of your standard lines, Wolfe?"

"No." One word, but that's all she needs.

She looks flabbergasted. "You're serious?"

"Very."

"Wow."

"Here's something else you might not know about me. I've never woken up with a woman in my arms. I never sleep over. Ever. There could be a tornado raging outside and I'd find a way to make it home."

Dom's eyes grow so wide, she's at a loss for words.

"Can I go back to ravishing my favorite pussy now?"

"By all means. Don't let me stop you."

I chuckle. "Open wide for me."

She does.

I slip my hands beneath her ass, hauling her body towards me.

I look up and practically lose my shit when I see her beautiful face. Her pupils dilate as her teeth dig into her lower lip.

*What a sexy sight.*

"Christ," I say. "Dom, I'm going to tongue-fuck your pretty little pussy until you beg me to stop, and even then, I'll keep sucking on your clit until you lose your fucking mind."

"Rod, enough with the raunchy talk. I can't handle it anymore," she says, trying to push her pussy into my face. "Please..."

Hearing her plead arouses me more.

I answer by slipping my tongue deep inside her pussy.

"Holy Jesus," she says, raising her hips off the bed.

*You're going nowhere, baby.*

My hands close around her thighs, holding her in place, as I circle her clit in punishing flicks.

She moans so beautifully and I'm insatiable.

I devour her juicy pussy like a starved beast. I slide my hands up her body until I cup her tits. I knead, squeeze and taunt them, taking my pleasure from feeling her erect nipples scratch my palm.

*Damn.*

The tempo matches my sensual tongue licks. When Dom wraps a leg around my neck, I go fucking nuts.

"Oh, God, yes."

As I lap at her wetness, my erection grows hard as steel.

I slide two fingers in and out of her, pumping her pussy like a greedy bastard, fucking her real good, wishing it was my cock instead.

"Ah, Rod. Rod. God, Rod."

I lift my head.

*Fuck, I love hearing the way she chants my name.*

She looks down between her legs. She's in a daze.

"Are you a virgin here?" I pull my fingers from her pussy and skim over her tight hole. "Has anyone claimed your ass?"

She squirms under my touch.

"Good try, but I want an answer. Yes or no?"

I've never felt this possessive about a woman before. I may not have been her first, but I want to make damn sure I mark every part of her. She'll never be with another guy ever again without remembering how she melted like butter under my touch. I'll make sure of it.

"No," she says in a low voice.

"I'd be the first to fuck you there."

"You're impossible," she says.

"You didn't say no, Dom. That leaves the *back* door wide open."

She laughs.

I join her.

"You stopped," she says, dropping her eyes to her pussy.

"Forgive me. Let me get right back to it."

"Yes, please."

I scoop slickness from her pussy and spread it between her ass cheeks.

Her body tenses.

"I'm not going to do anything crazy, Dom."

"And if I don't like it—"

"Everything stops."

She nods her approval.

I put my mouth on her pussy to distract her as I venture my thumb into her ass.

*Jesus Christ.*

"Oh, oh, oh." She wiggles underneath me, trying to pull away.

I meet her gaze. "It hurts?"

"I don't know how it feels. I'm a little freaked out by the whole thing."

"Relax and trust me."

"Okay."

I resume my mission.

I suck her clit and tease her asshole.

"Don't stop, Rod," she says in little hard breaths.

"Hmmm," I moan against her.

"Fuck, I love your mouth," she says as her body starts to tremble.

She's there.

I grip her hips with both hands and close my mouth over her clit, sucking hard in frenzied circular motions.

I could eat her sweet pussy every hour on the hour and still not get enough.

"I— Rod— Mother of—" Her body convulses and her hips

jerk up. She clamps her legs around my head, squeezing so hard I'm certain she'll suffocate me. "Oh, God, Rod."

*That's it, baby.*

A few minutes go by before I climb up next to her on the bed. I don't rush her. I stroke her face as she comes back to life. I bury my triumphant grin into her beautiful long hair. "You're still with me?"

"Nngh."

"What language was that?"

She opens her eyes, a shy smile teasing her lips. "Barely."

I pull her up to me and kiss her.

"Oh, God," she says.

"What?"

"Is that me I taste on your lips?"

"It is. Didn't you taste yourself last night after I'd licked my fingers clean and kissed you?"

"There's too much going on for me to keep track."

"Don't worry, we can take it slower today."

"One time, Wolfe." She lifts her finger. "You're tricking me into a second."

"You're right. My fault. I shouldn't have made you come again. I should've stopped after the clock stroked midnight. Bad Rod."

She rolls her eyes.

"What about you? I feel like I'm floating on air. I should return the favor."

"No rush. Like I said, we have all day." I wink. "Since I kept you busy all night, we still have all the ice cream and cheese to eat. And I'm pretty sure I'll need another serving of your pussy in a few hours. I'm not due in the studio until eight tomorrow morning and I know it's the same for you, which leaves me with plenty of hours to fuck you, or for you to suck my cock."

She hides her face in my chest and laughs.

She has me so turned on, I could fuck her for the next eleven hours without taking a break.

"So, do you have any buyer's remorse, blondie?"

"Not even close. What about you?" Expectant eyes blink up at me.

"Are you kidding me? My sweet Dom is a hot a little thing."

"You don't have to say that, Rod. I'm sure the women you've been with are maneaters in bed. I lack experience—"

"That has nothing to do with how much I wanted you, Dom."

"You wanted me that much?"

*More than you'll ever know.* "That was a genuine connection between us. Tell me you felt it."

"I did. I felt a sense of vulnerability I don't typically allow myself to experience with guys."

Nagging thoughts I managed to push aside creep to the forefront.

I weigh what I'm about to say next. "You didn't want to talk about it last night, but now that I'm your lover, I need you to open up to me. What happened? Who's the asshole who robbed you of your confidence?"

I swear I detect a glint of panic in her eyes.

"Did someone hurt you, Dom?"

"It's... it's..." She sighs. "It's water under the bridge."

"The fuck it is."

She extracts herself from my arms, sits up and pulls the sheet up to her neck, hiding her tits.

"Fuck the past. That's what you always say," she says.

"This isn't about our shitty parents or our soul-crushing childhood neighborhood. This is about something that happened to you. Something you're dead set on hiding from me. How the hell am I supposed to protect you?"

"You can't protect me twenty-four-seven, Rod," she says.

*What the fuck?*

"That's what I do. That's what I've done since you were thirteen."

"Let it go, Rod."

There's such defeat in her comment.

"Dom," I say.

"We've made something of ourselves by slamming the door in the face of adversity. We keep moving forward without ever looking back. No matter how hard life hits, we hit back, Rod. Dwelling on shit is a waste of energy."

I narrow my gaze at her, studying her.

"What are you not telling me?"

"All you need to know is that with you, I feel cared for and cherished like I never have before. I know you'd never hurt me."

"Who—"

"This is now, Rod, and it trumps everything else. For the last time, drop it. Let. It. Go."

Her tone doesn't bode for a retort.

It's a good thing because I'm so stunned, I don't even know how to respond.

*How did a perfect morning take such a bad turn?*

# Chapter 16

## *Dominika*

I look forward to starting my day because I love what I do so much. Not today. I've been away for a month and a half, it's not like I can wiggle my way out of my commitment and responsibilities. The shoot for Joel Banner's video was booked two months ago. Not showing up at the studio wasn't an option. Although I have my own small company, Rod and Loki are my most prominent clients. It would not only make me look bad, but it would also reflect negatively on them. I couldn't allow that to happen. I had to put on my big girl panties. I've been coaxing myself since Rod stormed out of my place yesterday.

*I can tough it out. I got this.*

*I think.*

After a moody breakfast yesterday morning, the tension between us weighed so heavy, Rod decided it would be best for him to go back to his place. He was so upset. I was crushed to see him leave, but at the same time, I was relieved my secret would remain locked up.

This morning, I woke up feeling miserable and alone in my king size bed, his absence agonizing. It's my fault things took a nosedive. Rod meant well—he's always been a protector—but before I knew it, my guard was up like an impenetrable fortress. It's self-preservation. I've sealed the tragic parts of my past in a dungeon and I have no intention of opening that door ever again.

*Especially not to Rod.*

One look at him this morning, when I enter the main studio of his building with my small crew in tow, pretty much negates all my pep talk.

*Crap.*

With my heart somewhere in the vicinity of my throat, I take a semi-confident step forward and keep walking. I try not to stare as I get the equipment set up, but it's impossible.

*He's freaking gorgeous.*

The broad-shouldered piece of hunk with tattoos who gave my preconceived notions about sex a good kick in the ass slid back into his CEO role. I have no preference for either persona. Today, I do. I can't even put into words how it feels to have his muscular inked arms wrapped around me, embracing me, making me feel safe. Now, we're back to being friends... if I can call it that.

Rod's brow arches as his appreciative gaze sweeps the length of my body. When our eyes meet, he offers a dazzling smile. That's all it takes. A sea of sinful memories washes over me as I flash back to our smoking hot encounter. I pull my lips up in a shy smile and avert my gaze. I don't want him to see how much he affects me.

*You got this.*

"Dominika, is that you, love?" Joel's question forces me back into professional mode.

"Oh, hi, Joel."

"What happened to your hair?"

One look at him and I can tell he spent hours in the makeup and hair chair. He's ready for his big day.

"It was time for a change," I say.

"A change?" He cocks an eyebrow. "Miss Jacek, you went from beautiful to supermodel-worthy in the blink of an eye. You're absolutely gorgeous, love."

A few people standing around us nod their approval and offer wide smiles.

I blush.

Don't ask me why, but my gaze shifts to Rod.

His brown eyes are nothing more than a sliver of dark fierceness. His pursed lips suggest he isn't amused.

I focus on Joel again. "Thanks so much."

"And I love the smashing new look." His eyes sweep up and down the length of my body.

Joel Banner is a British rocker and lead singer of Brawn Impulse. He's signed under Holt Christensen's—one of Rod's former bandmates—record label. I've been entrusted with the responsibility of creating an attention-grabbing video to kick off his band's North American tour. He has the voice and the look to make a successful crossover. Joel's crafted style stands out thanks to his tall, lanky frame, piercing blue eyes and blue-black dyed hair. The British accent helps a lot.

"I did a little shopping while I was in New York and Europe," I say.

I balked at Pepperdine University's hefty price tag for the month-long training. Rod told me to ignore it. I told him I couldn't afford to take a month off. He refused to accept my excuse—I run a tiny studio with a small, but dedicated team. I can't close shop and take off. Rod assured me I could rely on him for money. I had every intention of turning him down, but out of three hundred plus applicants, I got a spot. In fact, I was selected in the first round. I'm glad I listened to him. My time in the Big Apple and Europe is unforgettable. The shopping and makeover are a bonus.

"It's recherché. I approve ten times over," Joel says with a wide smile.

Wow.

"Thanks."

"And the shoes... a touch of good girl, but the daring print says otherwise." Joel pauses. "I approve."

Zoe is right. I have an impressive collection of Converse shoes. In my line of work, they're practical. I can move around with ease and still look cute. Along with the hair, my cousin Johanna was instrumental in nudging me into embracing a makeover. So today, instead of jeans and a t-shirt, I opted for a fitted cap-sleeved top, a maxi skirt that ties at the waist with a long belt. Both in black. I completed the look with a pair of leopard print flats. To make life easier for myself, I brushed my hair up in a high ponytail. I also dabbed on a little bit more makeup than usual. Why not?

"Oh, stop it, Joel." I wave a hand at him, dismissing the compliment.

"No, love, you're—"

"Maybe the two of you might want to press the pause button on the heavy flirting for a minute or two." Rod's comment stings.

"I'm paying the lady a compliment," Joel says.

Rod takes several steps forward. His threatening vibe rolls off his shoulders. I've witnessed it many times before. At six-one, Rod stands four inches taller than Joel. In other words, he has an unfair advantage. "You've only met her a couple of times." He shrugs. "She doesn't need your approval on the way she looks."

*Holy shit.*

My gaze shifts as fast as a ping pong match, back and forth between the two men butting heads.

"I've been told," Joel says.

"You have," Rod says, his nostrils flaring. His gaze meets mine. His eyes are as cold as ice. "Time is money. We should get started. We have a full crew waiting."

My jaw drops in shock.

I'm so upset, the only thing I can do is shoot daggers at him.

How dare he cut me at the knee in front of everybody.

Loki claps. "All right, boys and girls, let's shoot a kick ass video, make the client happy and turn Brawn Impulse into a sensation."

Everyone around us cheers.

Joel's mood seems to lighten instantly.

But not mine.

And not Rod's.

My best friend and I stare at each other like bulls in a ring.

# Chapter 17

## *Roderick*

Dom and I spent the better part of the day ignoring each other. The tension between us when we're near is ridiculous. I guess it's easier to pretend we didn't have a major blow up after our blazing weekend. Right. Best to sweep the memories under the rug. As if yesterday's fight wasn't detrimental enough, I had to act like an alpha silverback gorilla, pissing around who I deem belongs to me to ward off a bastard—I mean an adversary—who thinks he can charm her with some sweet talk.

*Fucking pompous accent.*

I intended on approaching the whole thing with finesse, but the way Dom was blushing like a schoolgirl from Joel's compliments, set me off. Maybe if she didn't look so damn good in her sexy black outfit, I might not have chewed up Joel like I did. Now, I feel like a fucking idiot and I don't know how to patch things up since she won't even look at me.

*Way to go, Wolfe.*

I don't spend this much time on the set when Dom is working her magic, but I can't help it. I've been going back and forth between important calls, urgent emails, pressing staff inquiries and the set. Every time I pass Loki's office, he looks at me as if I've lost my marbles.

Maybe I have.

I'm compelled to loom over her. It's like if I don't keep a vigilant eye on Dom, the British rocker might think he has a chance.

*Dream on, buddy.*

I shake my head.

All this is absurd.

*Who the hell do you think you are, Wolfe?*

Not only is Dominika a grown woman—and she can be with whomever she wants—we agreed to one night. I knew the terms going in. For God's sake, I set them. A taste wasn't enough. I want more of Dom's hot body. After yesterday, I know it's wishful thinking. Now, I need to make sure my cock understands releasing myself between her legs is a thing of the past.

*Shit.*

"Let's try this one last time before we call it a wrap, people," Dom says waving her finger above her head in a circular motion.

She's totally immersed in her role.

I love watching her work.

She's so passionate about her craft.

She's an incredible artist.

Regardless of all the misery I had to endure when I was forced by the courts to move back with my mother and the numerous crushing setbacks of trying to crawl out of the shit-hole known as the Fashion District, Dom wouldn't allow me to give up. She pushed me to never let go of my dream to become a professional drummer. God knows all the odds were stacked against me, but she never lost faith in me. I returned the favor and pushed her to become a video producer/director even when she thought it was an unreachable dream. I even forked out the money for her education. That's how much I believed in her.

"*And* action!" Morgan, Dom's blue-eyed blond 1st Assistant Director who is as passionate about his surfboard as he is about his camera, waves a hand over his head.

For the next hour, I observe Dom and her team in their elements.

"One second." Dom lifts her hand up and looks up from behind her camera. "Joel, I need you to pull Nina closer to you and stare into her eyes. We have three cameras on you capturing every blink. So go for it. I want passion. I feel you're holding back."

"Got it," Joel says.

"Nina, he's the man you've been waiting for your whole life. I want to feel it. Right now, I don't. I need you to lean into him more," Dom says.

"Like this?" Nina presses her chest against Joel's. He responds by placing his hand on her lower back, inches away from her ass.

Nina Frey is a Victoria's Secret model. Joel insisted on casting her for the shoot.

Dom gives the blonde model a thumbs-up.

"Dominika you should be my leading lady for this video. I should be embracing you in my arms," Joel says.

My eyebrows shoot to my forehead.

"Well, thanks, Joel. I guess I showed up for nothing," Sarcasm laces Nina's words.

"No offense, doll," Joel says. And if the asshole doesn't pin me with a challenging gaze.

"You requested Nina. We gave you Nina," Dom says.

"You weren't a blonde back then," Joel says. "Had I known..."

"Maybe I should go home?" Now, Nina is pissed off.

I feel her pain.

"Nonsense. It's just a little banter with Dom," Joel says. He shifts his attention back to my best friend. "You're always hiding behind the camera when you should be front and center."

I avoid looking at Dom. If I do, I'm likely to run my mouth. I know how well that went yesterday morning.

As much as I hate to agree with the idiot, Dom would've done a much better job. Nina might be a gorgeous supermodel, but acting isn't her forte. The beauty is as stiff as a board.

"Joel, focus," Dom says.

At least my girl isn't falling for his bullshit.

"I quite like being disciplined by a forceful *Domme*—I mean, Dom," Joel says in a pointed accident.

*Seriously?*

His fake slip of the tongue is so obvious, it's grotesque.

It takes everything in me not to punch the stupid grin off his face.

"Joel, we don't have time for this," Dom says.

"Yes, *madam*."

Exasperated, I step away from the set before I cause another scene.

*Fucker.*

~

After the shoot, I corner Dom as she's packing up her equipment.

"Hey," I say.

"Hey." She glances up at me, her gaze guarded.

"Your vision for the video came to life. I love the concept."

"Thanks. Since the band is using their love song to enter the American market, I thought I'd give it an edge so it's not too sappy. I wanted to adapt their smash hit UK video for the American audience."

"Great call."

"Thanks," she says before averting her gaze.

"Kudos for forcing some passion out of Nina."

"It took a little coaxing."

"Yeah, but you did it."

We're all business.

Such bullshit.

She lets out a heavy sigh. A frown creases her brow. "What do you want, Rod?"

What a loaded question.

*You underneath me.*

"Do you want to grab drinks and dinner? We can go out to a restaurant or we can crash at your place, or mine. I'd love to hang out."

"I can't."

"You have plans?"

*I shouldn't insist.*

"I do."

*Could you be more vague?*

"Going out with girlfriends?"

"No."

*Jesus, woman, give me an inch.*

"What's on the agenda?"

"I—"

"Dominika, I'm off to the hotel to shower and change. I'll see you at the restaurant, love," Joel says.

*What?* My eyebrows knit together.

Joel moves his attention to me, staring at me, almost daring me to say something. I'm so stunned, my brain hasn't caught up yet. "I'd ask you to join us, but three's a crowd. Have a great evening, Rod."

*Smug, condescending fuck.*

The idiot has the audacity to wave at me.

It feels like a slap in the face. I'm this close to reverting to a Neanderthal and roaring my disapproval, but I remember the look on Dom's face when I went all fucking caveman earlier.

*Calm down.*

I turn to face my best friend. "You're seeing him?"

"Joel and I are going out for dinner."

*I don't need a road map to figure that one out.*

"You're spending the evening with him?"

"I am. We planned this while I was in Europe."

*Well, I'll be damned.*

"You guys are friends now?"

I sound like a five-year-old.

"Rod, grow up."

*Okay, I deserved that.*

I will my boiling anger to settle down.

"What about after you're done with him? Maybe we can connect?"

"It might be late."

"Are you kidding me right now?"

"No, I'm not," she says.

"You're interested in him?"

The question churns my stomach.

"Do you see me asking who you're going to spend the evening with?"

I take a step closer so my voice doesn't carry. "For God's sake, I'm trying to spend the evening with you, Dom."

"Call one of the girls in your little black book. I'm tied up."

*Fuck, I hate it when she's like this.*

I try a different approach. "Maybe we can talk when you get back home. It doesn't matter how late, you can call me." I'm a goddamn liar. The last thing I need is a timestamp reminding me of how many hours she spent with the British asshole, doing God knows what with him.

The thought annoys the hell out of me, but there's something else. A pull at my heart I've never felt before, catches me off guard.

"Let's leave it for another day," she says.

"I don't want what transpired between us yesterday to hang over our heads like a dark cloud. Let's talk about it."

"Rod, lately, when we *talk about it*, it ends up in a disaster. Why bother?" She punctuates her stinging remark with a one-shoulder shrug.

"Why bother?" I say. "Because it fucking matters, Dom."

"You're fishing for something I can't give you. Talking won't change a thing. You, me, nobody can change the past." Her lips pull up into a tight smile. "Not to mention the way you humiliated me today doesn't make me want to spend any time with you or talk to you. Now, if you'll excuse me." With that, she walks right past me and out the door. She doesn't even look back.

*Shit, I screwed up in a big way.*

# Chapter 18

## *Dominika*

My heart bleeds at how I left things off with Rod. *Fuck.* But, how do I open up to him without tripping all over the ugly past? This is the kind of truth that would bring his world crashing. His axis would flip upside down and God knows how he'd react if he ever found out. It's not like he trusts easily to start off with.

After leaving the set, I made my way back to my studio—which is adjacent to Rod's—dropped my equipment and left. I drove back to my place to shower and change before meeting Joel. As I was slipping behind the wheel of my car, Joel texted me. He's no longer in the mood for Mexican. Instead of meeting at Cantina Zaragoza, he wants to have dinner at Matcha Flip. Fine Japanese dining, he says. It doesn't make me hate sushi any less. Tempura it is.

I pull my Porsche Cayenne into a vacant parking spot right in front of the restaurant. I had to negotiate with Joel before we came to an agreement. First, he wanted us to meet in his hotel room. That was a hard no. Second, he wanted to send a car to pick me up. Not happening. I want to have the freedom to leave when I want. He thought I was being so North American about it. I'm being practical. There was no way I was going to tell Rod any of this, he'd have a heart attack. Pushing thoughts of my best friend from my mind, I step into the restaurant.

Joel is already waiting. He gets up when he sees me and welcomes me with a warm smile. He's changed into a gray suit and a crisp white shirt—no tie. We exchange a euro kiss before locking eyes again.

"I know I said it earlier, but the transformation is remarkable. You look even more spectacular now than you did earlier. I'm not even sure how that's possible."

I opted for a long-sleeved white lace dress, which I paired with nude patent-leather shoes with a buckle-fastening ankle strap. It has a two-inch heel and the color complements the lining of the dress. The ponytail still worked, so I didn't bother with my hair. I toned down my makeup and added a few large gold hoops and I was set. The look is chic and professional.

"Flattery will get you everywhere," I say.

"Good, because I have my work cut out for me. Please sit down," he says, pulling out my chair.

"Thank you," I say, taking a seat.

Rod thinks this is a date, but it isn't. While I was in Europe, Joel insisted he had the opportunity of a lifetime to present to me. When I hesitated, he buttered it up, claiming it would be a crying shame if I refused to at least listen. Rod likes to quote, *'You miss every shot you don't take'*. So, this is me, stepping into something that could be epic.

Joel leans into the table. "Shall we start with sake or wine?"

"No, I'm fine. Thank you so much, but I'm driving."

"One glass won't put you on the wrong side of the law."

"I'll stick to Perrier if that's okay with you."

"Whatever the lady desires." He smiles. "I took the liberty of asking the waitress what she recommends since you're not a fan of sushi. She suggested the pan fried gyoza and the steamed edamame for appetizers."

"I can handle dumplings and soybeans," I say.

"Good. Wait until you hear about the mains."

"I'm all ears."

"The *pièce de résistance* is their eighteen different types of tempura dishes."

My eyes grow wide.

"Seriously?"

He leans into the table. "I'm having the sushi, but you're more than welcome to sample all eighteen dishes," he says in a low voice as he's sharing a secret.

"I might take you up on your offer."

"A woman with an appetite is a woman after my own heart."

"Let's not get carried away, it's only Japanese food," I say.

We both laugh.

~

As usual, my eyes are bigger than my stomach. I gave it a valiant effort, but in the end, the tempura won. I'm so taking the rest home. Joel polished off his massive tray of sushi. The food was delicious—far better than I expected. Despite this being a business meeting, Joel couldn't resist putting on the charm. He gave me the whole, *'I can't believe a stunning and smart woman like you goes to bed alone at night. What a crying shame'*, spiel and the, *'It so happens, I'm also single and I'll be posted in the US more now. Maybe we can hang out'*. I smiled and explained I was happy with my singleton status and waking up alone in a king size bed has its advantages. All arguments I wholeheartedly believed until yesterday morning. Nothing compares to waking up pressed against Roderick Wolfe's hard body.

*Damn him.*

I clear my throat. "So, what's this opportunity of a lifetime you wanted to talk about?"

He refills his beer glass. "Straight to business?" His eyes shift up to mine as he drops the bottle back on the table.

"I disagree. We've been chatting for the past hour. You know everything there is to know about me."

He shoots me an incredulous gaze. "Good try, but I don't buy it. I doubt we've even scratched the surface. There's so much more to know about you, Dominika. So, now that you're stuffed silly, you can't wait to get the hell out of here?"

*He almost sounds offended.*

"I have a long day of complicated editing work tomorrow. I could've opted for drinks, but I agreed to dinner. Getting to know me, isn't part of our agreement. I direct and produce your videos. You know the essentials. You have something to share? I'm listening."

The longer we drag this out, the easier he might misconstrue this for a date.

"Fair enough," he says. "I want *you*."

"Don't they all. Take a number, mate," I say.

"Your sense of humor is contagious. Can you blame me for liking you so much?"

"Joel," I say.

"All right, all right, you win." He lifts his hands up in capitulation. "Let's get down to business. As you know, in four months, the band are embarking on our first US tour."

"Yes."

"I want to capture every moment of it."

"That's a great idea. I'm sure you aren't looking for my blessing or a step-by-step strategy on how to fill arenas. How do I fit in?"

Joel meets my gaze. "I want you to come on tour with us."

"Joel, I'm not a musician," I say.

"That's why we're sitting here today. I want to put your incredible talent to work."

"I'm sorry, but I don't follow."

"I'm thinking of a behind the scenes music documentary. Something memorable. Something award-worthy. I want to prove there's more to us than sex, drugs, and rock 'n roll. America loves woe to whoa stories. It fazes no one anymore in the UK, but we're four lads who rose from the pits of hell to where we are today. I want people to know about that."

"I didn't know you had a hard childhood."

"Hard is putting it mildly."

"I can relate."

He cocks an eyebrow.

"Yeah, let's not get into it. That might require me to drink."

"It seems we have a lot more in common than we thought," he says.

"It sounds like it."

"Let's write a new story... for both of us. I want you to film behind the scenes of our Ripped Incognito tour. Once done, we'll shoot for the stars—the Oscars."

*What?*

"If we miss, we'll shop the documentary around to content-on-demand channels like UTV.com for a chance at an Emmy. Who knows? If we go deep enough—which means opening up candidly about our fucked-up childhood—we might have a chance at Sundance. The thought is terrifying, but it might be worth it. In the end, your name would be on the credits, therefore, your name would be on the ballots."

"Me?" I'm dumbfounded.

"Yes, you. Give me a sec," he says reaching for his phone. He taps and swipes and hands me his phone. "See this?"

The headline from indiewire.com jumps off the screen. *'THE 25 BEST MUSIC DOCUMENTARIES OF THE 21ST CENTURY'*

*Wow.*

"I do."

"I want our documentary to be on that list."

"That's ambitious."

"It's doable. In preparation for this tour, we've been interviewing talent in the UK and via Holt's contacts, we've also been in touch with people here in LA. I'll be honest, you put them to shame."

"I'm flattered—"

"You're the best, Dominika. Intuitive. Creative. Edgy. Brilliant. I'm impressed as hell by your keen eye."

I glance down at my folded hands, my face flushing.

"I don't know what to say." A million thoughts collide in my head... and my heart. "I'm already established here."

"You're still an independent contractor, right?"

"I am, but I owe Rod and Loki a lot."

"It's not like Pending Inference Productions owns you. If you give them advance notice, it's fair game."

"It doesn't sit right with me, Joel."

"You're not an employee of theirs. You're a free agent," he says.

"I can't throw loyalty out the door."

I cut my teeth at UTV.com. Thanks to Rod's persuasion, Rory and Roark allowed me to shadow some of the best directors and producers in the industry. When it was time to fly on my own, Rod didn't waste any time in hiring me as a contractor.

"This isn't forever. You can always go back to *Rod* and Loki once the tour is done."

*There's something about the way he said that.*

"And there's my crew—"

"Part of the offer."

I tilt my head to the side. "You've put a lot of thought into this."

"I have. It's become an obsession. If you agree, I'll have no problem selling it to Holt. He has big dreams for us on this side of the pond. I have even bigger ones. I don't want to be another rock star, I want to become a legend."

This is a whole new side to Joel. He comes across as fleeting. I never suspected a deeper, more complex person was hiding beneath the surface.

"It's a six-month tour," he says.

"I—"

"I'll double whatever Pending Inference Productions pays you. We'll foot the bill for all your expenses. And I'll even offer a percentage of box office sales and royalties from TV stations."

*Whoa.*

"Are you serious?"

"I'm bloody serious."

"That's potentially a lot of money, Joel."

"I know." He grins. "Like I said, you're the best. Why would I settle for less?"

"Oh."

Now, I'm at a loss for words.

"Think about it. This elevates you from a director-slash-producer to potentially an award-winning director-slash-producer. A subtle nuance that will get you noticed."

More like a big fucking huge nuance that kicks doors wide open.

"It's only a few months in your life. The outcome could be very interesting."

*You mean epic.*

"You're young. This would put your career in overdrive." Several beats tick away as we stare at each other. "What do you have to lose?"

*Being away from Rod.*

# Chapter 19

## *Roderick*

I *can't believe she's on a date with Joel.*

It's like a slap in the face. I guess what we shared meant nothing to her.

After I took care of her Saturday night, we lingered lazily, wrapped into each other in her deep bathtub before going back to her bedroom and crashing. No way was I going home. I swear that was the best sleep of my life. Waking up with my mouth on her pussy first thing Sunday morning was fucking hot. What happened after that is still a puzzle to me. And now, I'm the last one to find out about fucking Joel.

*Why the hell didn't she tell me she was interested in him?*

Had I known, I would've gone home and jerked off in the shower instead of losing myself between her legs on Saturday night.

*Fuck.*

I'm staring at the screen of my iMac, but everything is a blur. I'm engrossed in all sorts of bad scenarios involving my best friend and a certain pushy British rocker. The troubling thought makes me want to plant my fist into a window. It took herculean strength not to ask her where she was meeting the bastard. It's not like I intended on dropping by. There's a difference between being her best friend and a stalker. I've never crossed the line so far. Joel Banner makes me want to change my mind. Now that I know how good it feels to have Dom's sexy body wrapped around mine while she swallows my cock, it changes everything.

"It's been a long day," Loki says walking into my office. His entrance catches me off guard and I jolt. "Am I interrupting your evil plan to kill Joel and dispose of his body in the Pacific Ocean?"

I look up at him and frown. "What are you talking about?"

"Word has it Dom is out on a date with Joel—"

"Good for her."

"You're full of shit, Wolfe."

"Jesus Christ, Loki. She can do whatever she wants. With whomever she wants."

*Good one. Too bad you don't believe any of it.*

"Right," he says, a half smile hanging from the corner of his lips.

*Damn, I hate when he does that.*

"In any case, I have a corner booth reserved for us at the back of Vego's Lounge. Let's head over there for drinks and dinner."

"Thanks, I'll pass. I'm not in the mood. I'm going home." *Where I can wallow in my self-pity alone.*

"I don't care what fucking mood you're in, Rod. You're coming."

"What the hell is your problem?"

"No, the question is, what's up your ass?"

I jump to my feet, circle my desk and stand in his face.

I'm six one and Loki towers over me by three inches, but

right now he's giving off a don't-fuck-with-me vibe that makes him appear ten feet tall.

I tilt my head to the side and challenge him. "What did you just say to me?"

"Let me answer the question for you," he says. "Your head is up your ass, Rod. You can come to Vego's Lounge willingly or I'll haul your ass over my shoulder and carry you there kicking and screaming if I have to. Roark is there waiting for us."

"What?"

"I need backup. The only reason Rory isn't also there is because he's in Miami."

"You organized an intervention?" Betrayal burns a hole in my gut. "I've been off drugs for a while now so you're wasting your fucking time, Loki."

"Rod, your ridiculous caveman attitude towards your best friend is affecting your judgment *and* team morale. The shit you pulled today is unacceptable. Not only were you unprofessional, but you were rude. Your mother might have been a poor excuse for a parent, but I know your brothers and your nana instilled better manners in you. I didn't recognize the guy who was running his mouth. He looked like you, but he didn't sound like you. And what was it with all that back and forth to the set? Dom is a grown woman. You don't own her."

"I—"

"We've worked too damn hard to lose everything to your inability to control your temper. Not to mention, Joel is signed under Holt's label. Holt is not only a long-time and loyal friend, but he's paying us a lot of money. How do you thank him? By pissing all over one of his top artists. That's why we're fucking meeting at Vego's Lounge."

I consider him long and hard.

We stare at each other, neither of us is willing to back down or compromise. His eyes are burning in anger.

I can't remember the last time I saw Loki this upset.

*You're just collecting trophies today, Wolfe.*

I wouldn't even know where to start when it comes to justifying my reprehensible actions other than the fact I hated the attention Joel was showering Dom with.

*Fuck, am I jealous?*

*What's happening to me?*

"Rod, you're a great friend, a kick ass businessman and partner, but I won't—"

"Okay, I'll come."

Roark is laughing his head off at something Victor Bakhmeteva —the Slovenian former hockey superstar of the Los Angeles Kings turned upscale sports bar owner—says when we make our way to our table.

"Ha, the drummer and roadie," Victor says when he sees us approaching.

"Hey, Victor," I say taking him into a bro hug.

"Rod," he says patting my back. He pulls away from our embrace and turns his attention to Loki. "Are you keeping him out of trouble?" He jerks a thumb in my direction.

"I wasn't gifted with such superpowers," Loki says.

Victor's brows lift. "That bad?"

"You know when they say God works in mysterious ways?"

"Yes."

Loki shifts his gaze towards me. "This one is a lost cause."

My brother chuckles. "Good one."

*Thanks a lot for the vote of confidence.*

"Har, har, har." I'm not as amused as my brother.

"I'm not trying to be funny," Loki says. "After today, I'm sure even God has washed his hands of him."

"Sounds like the three of you need a few stiff drinks and a lot of good food," Victor says.

"Well, it would be a start," Loki says with feigned affliction.

As the two commiserate, I slide into the seat across from Roark.

He greets me with a cocked eyebrow.

I shoot him a, '*What?*' look.

"In that case, you're in luck," Victor says. "I just received a shipment of limited edition Belvedere vodka. Only three hundred bottles are produced each year and I snatched ten of them."

"That sounds expensive," Loki says.

Victor nods. "Worth every penny. I'll also get your waitress to bring over a platter of smoked salmon—straight from Finland."

"Polish vodka it is," Roark says.

"Done deal," Victor says.

"You're a good man." Loki pats Victor on the shoulder.

"My pleasure. I have to go, but enjoy." He walks away from our table.

Roark leans into Loki. "What'd he do this time?"

"Let me sit down first," Loki says.

And he does.

Both of them are facing me.

*Great.*

Over the next fifteen minutes, I listen as my business partner recounts the day. He even talks about how tense things were between Dom and I, well before she left for her training. By the time Loki is done, our waitress shows up with our drinks and appetizer.

We thank her.

"I thought you were going to pacify things with Dom? Sounds like you've made things worse," my brother says.

*Fuck this.*

I lift my glass.

Both Loki and Roark are thrown off, but follow my lead.

We clink our tumblers and take a long sip of our drinks.

The vodka is cold, clean, crisp and smooth.

*Damn.*

This is perfection.

Maybe Loki's idea isn't so bad after all.

I move my attention from my tumbler to my brother and business partner. "Here's to a *fun* evening out with the boys. Cheers!"

Roark drops his glass on the table. "Sarcasm won't get you out of this."

"What do you expect me to do? The two of you are ganging up on me," I say.

"Let me help you," Roark says. "Why don't you and Dom talk it out once and for all?"

Loki mods. "It would make life a hell of a lot easier for everyone around you."

I don't respond.

"You can sit there and stare at us as much as you want, but we aren't going anywhere until we get to the bottom of this," Loki says.

I let out a long sigh and rake my fingers through my hair in frustration.

*How much do I tell them?* "We did talk it out."

Roark frowns. "It didn't go well?"

"It went *really* well."

"Huh?" Roark scrunches his nose.

"Your definition of really well differs from mine," Loki says.

I lean into the table. "Things got... intimate."

Both men frown.

"As in..." Loki lets his words trail.

"You mean..." my brother says.

"Yeah." I offer a small nod.

Loki and Roark look at each other before allowing their backs to collapse against their seats.

Their expression is unreadable.

"Finally," Loki says at the same time as Roark says, "It's about fucking time."

I don't understand. "What am I missing?"

A smile curves Roark's lips. "The prize that's been staring at you for years, Rod. That's what you've been missing."

"Dom is something else," Loki says. "I never dared to go after her for fear you'd castrate me—"

"Damn right he would've," Roark says.

"Oh, fuck off." I shake my head.

Roark smirks.

"There's another reason why Dom was never a consideration... why most of us in your entourage never bothered going after her."

Loki's revelation surprises me. "Why?"

"She's had eyes for one guy for a long time... although he's blind." Loki gives me a pointed look. "The tension between Dom and you has been intense for months. I guess you two getting together was the logical outcome. I'm glad you see more in her than just your sidekick or a little sister figure."

"Or an untouchable saint," my brother says.

"I never saw her that way—"

"Please," Roark says.

"Okay, maybe I have." No point in arguing. "I didn't want to fuck up a good thing. Women come and go in my life. Dom is my pillar."

"She isn't going anywhere, Rod."

"And you know that for certain, Roark?"

"Dom has been with you through thick and thin. She

accepts every part of you—the good, the bad, the ugly and even the nasty. She knows what hell you crawled out of. She knew you before you could afford three-thousand-dollar shoes. Not even your addiction days scared her."

Unpleasant memories flood my brain.

"At your worst, Rory and I thought we'd lose you to drugs," Roark says. "Dom wouldn't hear of it. She forced you to fight and get your act together. She slept in on the floor near your bed to be at arm's length when you needed comfort all those nights you were shivering from the symptoms of withdrawal."

I had no desire to go to rehab no matter how many times my brothers and Dom begged me, so I duped myself into believing I could kick my habit on my own. I was so arrogant and so full of it. After the third nightmarish day, I willingly checked myself in.

"She refused to *quit* on you, Rod," Roark says, making air quotes. "She's this tiny little thing with a mighty will."

"She is." I can't help but smile.

"She'd die for you, and I suspect it's mutual," Roark says as he runs a finger along the rim of his glass.

"It is," I say without a shred of hesitation.

"And let's be honest, without Dom, you'd never be Rod Wolfe, the kickass drummer of Random Misconception—one of the edgiest rock bands of our era. You'd never have this extraordinary career, nor would you be recognized as one of the Top 100 Greatest Drummers Of All Time. Without her unwavering belief, you'd never have been inducted into the Modern Drummer Hall of Fame."

John Bonham from Led Zeppelin was my idol. I lived to emulate him. Thank you, Dom. "I know what she's done for me."

"Do you really?" Roark doesn't allow me to answer. "She shot the videos of your killer renditions of '*Kashmir*' and '*Black*

*Dog'*, figured out how to edit them like an Oscar winning visual effects editor and uploaded them on different social media platforms. And she was only fourteen at the time. Gideon Wilding would have never discovered you without them. That video gave you your big break."

I hold his gaze.

"You've been best friends forever, but what she's done for you goes above and beyond the call of duty. And you kept your promise to watch over her no matter where you were in the country or the world. I think it's been more than mere friendship between the two of you for a long time. Neither of you were willing to see it."

I'm speechless.

"At least with Dom, you know it's about you."

My gaze drifts to Loki.

"It's not about what you can do for her. She doesn't care about who you can connect her to. She isn't waiting for you to push her career to the next level. It's not about your money. Even though you're a bigshot, it's still about you, the person. Few people will ever experience that kind of unconditional friendship."

Loki's words further silence me.

After a few short minutes, I find my voice again. "I recognize what we share runs deep."

*And now things are different between us.*

*Maybe I never should've touched her.*

We sit there in silence. It's as if Loki and Roark are giving me time to process it all.

"So how did things go from pretty fucking amazing to the colossal mess I witnessed today?"

I shift my attention to Loki. "We had an argument yesterday morning."

His head jerks back. "What happened?"

"She's hiding something from me. I just know it."

Roark leans forward. "What do you mean?"

I share with them the highlights of the discussion that led to our fight.

"I think someone hurt her, but she won't open up to me."

"Maybe she's had a few asshole boyfriends. It doesn't mean she wants to revisit the past," Loki says. "Heck, I've had my fair share of crazy flings I'd prefer to forget."

My brother nods. "Same here."

"I think it's a lot more," I say.

Roark pats me on the shoulder. "You're making a whole lot out of nothing."

I narrow my gaze at him. "Are you saying my suspicions are unjustified?"

"What I'm saying is, you took a big step in your relationship with her, and all of a sudden, you're demanding to know everything about every guy she's ever been with," he says. "How would you feel if she came poking into your past?"

"I wasn't poking. I care." I comb my fingers through my hair, irritated as hell at his accusation.

"Rod, it's true sometimes Dom retreats into her own little world, but give her time. Have you even defined what's going on between the two of you?"

Roark's question throws me.

"What do you mean?"

"Are you seeing her casually or is this more?"

"We haven't gone there yet. We blurred the lines of our friendship—"

"More like you stomped all over them," Roark says.

"Thanks for stating the obvious." I roll my eyes at him.

"Just being helpful," he says.

"As I was saying, everything happened so fast and it was far more intense than I expected. And now things are awkward.

Not to mention, she's out on a date tonight with another guy and it's driving me to drink hard liquor."

Loki and Roark drop their eyes to my tumbler at the same time.

We all laugh.

"Who's the guy?"

I give Roark the lowdown.

"Fuck awkward and fuck Joel," Roark says. He's never been one to mince words. "One evening isn't enough for him to seduce her—"

"They've been text buddies since she was in Europe."

"That doesn't mean a damn thing, Rod," Roark says.

"Decide what you want with Dom and go after it," Loki says. "The Rod I know doesn't hesitate nor does he second-guess himself."

"I agree," Roark says.

*The Rod you know is tripping all over himself because of a girl.*

"What if I'm not enough or what if I'm incapable of giving more?" Old insecurities creep to the surface. "Dom seems like the kind of woman who would want—no, need—more. I don't know if I can go there. Heck, I don't even know how to love or how to be loved."

"Rod, it's called baby steps," Loki says. "I doubt she'd expect a marriage proposal on day one."

"I've never dated before." I blow out a breath. "I'm likely to disappoint her. I'm not sure I want to risk jeopardizing our friendship because I'm not boyfriend material. If I lose her, I might lose myself."

Roark slams his hand on the table causing a few patrons to turn in our direction. "For fuck's sake, stop letting Rachel fuck you up. I told you that the last time we talked about Dom. And for the record, you're dead wrong."

"About what?"

"You do know what love is."

"I—"

"I love you, little brother. I'd like to think it's mutual."

Roark's comment surprises me. He isn't one for sappy talk.

"Stop being an idiot," I say. "You know it is. Although right now I hate you for busting my balls."

"Just doing my brotherly duties," he says. "Rory loves the hell out of you, even though you made it a point to butt heads with him as often as you could growing up. We stepped in when Rachel checked out and River left our asses dry. Fucking losers."

You don't choose your parents.

So many nights I cried myself to sleep begging God to give us a better mother because Rachel Chalmers was a pretty shitty one. River Wolfe is our father, but our parents were never married. Dad kept drifting in and out of Mom's life. Around the time Roark turned six, Dad disappeared for a long stretch. According to Nana Irene, he was involved in some pretty shady shit—always flirting with the wrong side of the law, but never getting caught. Then one day, he popped by again. Nine months later I was born.

A year after my birth, Dad was still around. Since Mom thought he was ready to grow some roots, she started campaigning. She wanted Dad to man up and build a safe home for his boys. Mom worked menial jobs her whole life, but her obsession with self-help daytime TV shows paid off. She had saved enough for the down payment on a tiny no-frills house in a not-so-great neighborhood. Rory was there when Mom flashed a wad of cash in front of Dad. She didn't trust banks. She hid her money under her mattress. Dad agreed to Mom's request. She was thrilled.

Ten months later, we were all packed and ready to move

out of the Fashion District, except the movers never came. By midnight, it was obvious Dad wasn't going to show up either. He was gone. So was Mom's life savings. She hit rock bottom and started drinking again. One day, Rory told her she needed to act like a mother. In response, she handed him a duffle bag stuffed with clothing for me, a few baby bottles, and fifty dollars. She told him she needed space, and then pushed us out the door and slammed it shut in our faces.

Rory was fifteen.

Roark was thirteen.

I was a few months shy of turning two.

On that night, my brothers slept outside of the front door—with me curled up in Rory's arms—hoping Mom would come to her senses. She didn't leave her rented house the next day, nor did she open the door. Starved and afraid, my brothers sought refuge at a neighbor's house. Linda had small children. She taught them how to take care of a toddler. A week later, Mom still kept shouting for us to get lost every time we knocked on her door. Desperate and under Linda's guidance, Rory called Nana Irene—Dad's mom—to ward off Child Protective Services. For the better part of my childhood, I bounced from Mom's to Nana Irene's place whenever Mom checked out—which was often. With few career options, my brothers enlisted as soon as they could. In time, Mom grew more verbally abusive, predicting I'd turn into a thief like my asshole of a father. At twelve, she declared she was done being a mother. Nana could have me. She changed her mind a few months before my sixteenth birthday.

Thanks to music, I turned my rage and rebellion towards my drums. Aaron's parents bought me a secondhand set of drums when I was forced to move back with Mom. I kept them in the small shed in the backyard. Without their generosity, I would've had to watch my dream vanish.

Living with Mom was toxic. The only reason I stayed under her roof longer than I should've, was Dom. The minute I was able to get her away from her own dysfunctional mother and her lineup of douchebag boyfriends, I was out.

"And there's Nana Irene," Roark says cutting through my gloomy thoughts. "She fought the courts—and Mom—to the grave to save you from going back to The Fashion District. She may have lost the fight in the end, but it's not for lack of determination. If that isn't love, I don't know what is."

Mom hated Nana with a vengeance. A judge who doesn't know anything about how fucked up my mother was made a decision that was like a prison sentence. Nana retaliated. Mom made it her life mission to spew as much venom as she could towards my grandmother, accusing her of knowing where my father was hiding and protecting the lowlife. Mom was wrong. Nana hadn't heard from her son since he skipped town.

I stare at my brother harder. "Those are family ties. And why are we rehashing things I already know? It's not as if I don't remember where I come from."

Roark shoots me a crooked smile. "Because you seem to believe there's only one shade of love."

"Says the guy who's never been in a relationship in his life." I roll my eyes. "Rich, big brother."

"I get why you don't let women close enough to develop feelings," he says. "I'm the same way. You and I choose flings who don't want anything beyond a quick fuck because being abandoned creates trust issues. I'm thirty-nine and still trying to get my act together—"

"Then spare me the lecture."

"You know what differentiates us, Rod?"

I press my lips in a thin line. "No, but I'm sure you're going to tell me."

"You're right. I'm a lost cause. I'm getting up there in age and with each passing year, I'm more and more jaded. Maybe if I had rescued a pretty girl in high school, there would still be hope for me. All I'm saying, is you're in a different boat. You have someone like Dom in your life. You trust her—implicitly. And you love her—"

"As a—"

"I know, I know, as a friend." He holds my gaze. "I don't even have that with a woman. Never have." Another pause. "Dom is determined, smart, gorgeous, and loyal to a fault. And she's always been yours, Rod."

I open my mouth to retort, but the expression on his face convinces me otherwise.

"So now, the question is—especially after Saturday night—do you think she's worth going after? It's that simple, little brother."

"I couldn't have said it better. Decide," Loki says. "Once you do, everything else will fall into place."

*They make it sound so easy.*

# Chapter 20

## *Dominika*

I swear to God I'm going to end up cross-eyed.

I rotate my head in an effort to dislodge the kink in my neck from hours of pouring myself into my work. It's to no avail. My whole upper body aches.

Thanks a lot, Auburn Sorrel, for being clueless.

Loki accosted me yesterday morning in between takes to beg me to fix Auburn's mistakes. Given the complexity of the video, I knew I would have my work cut out for me. I didn't expect it to be this bad. Auburn's screw ups are proof he's all talk and zero talent. It'll take me a couple of weeks before I present the band with a kick ass music video. I guess I can't complain too much because Loki promised me a generous bonus. Since Joel and his band will be bouncing around from one interview to another for the next two days, the timing couldn't be better.

*I need a break.*

I look at the time and decide I need to put something in my stomach before I pass out.

One of the advantages of having my head wrapped in my work like this is there's no room for Rod Wolfe. This consuming busyness allows me to cast him from my thoughts. It also prevents me from replaying my conversation with Joel. On one hand, his offer is tempting, on the other, it's so life changing, I don't know if I have the guts to take him up on it. And of course, the idea of being away from Rod for six months doesn't weigh into my indecision.

*Right.*

I ready myself to get up from my chair, when my phone rings. It's Marissa Feiffer, Rod's executive assistant.

I accept the call. "Hey, Marissa."

"Hi, Dominika. I hope I'm not catching you at a bad time."

"You're preventing me from jumping behind the wheel of my car to track down Auburn and strangle him with my bare hands. He's a poor excuse for a video editor. Even his skills as a director are lamentable."

"That bad?"

"I had better skills at fourteen."

"Yikes."

"I may even have to reshoot parts of it. Thank God there are hours and hours of footage I can salvage something from, or else it would cost Rod and Loki a fortune in production."

"Well, that's why the bosses keep raving about you. You're their secret weapon."

"Thanks for the vote of confidence."

"Oh, please, you don't need it. You have mad skills and talent coming out of your yin yang."

I blush, even though she can't see me. "Is your boss asking you to do his dirty laundry?"

"What do you mean?"

"Are you calling me because Rod has a request, but instead of picking up the phone, he's going through you?"

I haven't heard from him since I left him standing there at the studio yesterday afternoon. It's weird. We've talked or texted each other every day since we became best friends. Even when he was traveling, we'd still be in touch.

"Nah. The boss was at an offsite meeting until half an hour ago. I'm calling because someone has a not-so-secret admirer."

"You lost me."

"As Rod was walking into the office, this delivery guy holding the biggest bouquet of flowers I've ever seen in my life was also entering the building. Said bouquet, had your name on it."

"Flowers for me?"

"Not just any flowers. We're talking top of the line. Primo. The best of the best. And the sender is pretty cute, if you ask my opinion."

*I guess they aren't from Rod.*

"Are you going to enlighten me?"

"So it's true?"

I expect her to elaborate, but she doesn't.

"What's true?"

"You're seeing, Joel. I guess last night's date went well."

"It was dinner. It wasn't a date."

"Those stunning flowers say otherwise," she says. "So... you guys are dating."

The woman is relentless.

"This is LA... the land of smoke and mirrors. I shared a meal with a guy. It doesn't mean anything more."

"Oh, come on, you can tell me. I won't tell a soul."

"My lips are sealed."

"You're no fun. In any case, your maybe-boyfriend—"

"You're impossible."

"What? You're not giving me much of a choice than to

come to my own conclusions and we all know how dangerous that can be."

I laugh.

"As I was saying, Joel sent you a spectacular arrangement from Eric Buterbaugh on Melrose Ave. He's been voted—five years in a row—top florist in the city by voop.com. I don't care much about Gail Voopowski, but her blog is pretty addicting. In any case, your maybe-boyfriend selected the Parisian Flair arrangement—all white flowers with a few anemones here and there. The monochromatic color schematic is stylish—like you."

She sounds like a professional commentator.

"I'm grateful, but Joel knows my studio is next door. Why would he have the flowers delivered at Pending Inference's studio?"

"I think your maybe-boyfriend is sending a not-so-subtle message to your best friend."

I didn't see that coming.

I'm so taken aback, I don't even dare to ask what prompted her comment.

*Best to move on.*

"I'm sorry about that," I say. "Let me get Morgan or Felicity to drop by and pick up the bouquet—"

"Oh, it's more than flowers."

"Really?"

"Uh-huh. There are also two boxes. One is heavy, and they both have your name on them."

"Wow." Joel went all out. He's selling me hard on this idea.

"Don't worry, Rod took care of everything."

"As in, he threw everything in the garbage?"

"You're hilarious. No, my boss is a gentleman. He took everything to your studio and placed them in your office. FYI, the crystal vase weighs a ton. Joel certainly didn't skimp."

"Rod did that?"

"He did. I called to give you the heads-up."

"Thank you," I say.

"Alright, got to go. I'll let you at it. Have a great afternoon, Dom. You're in tomorrow?"

"Yes, in the afternoon. Thanks for the call, Marissa. See you tomorrow."

I hang up and stare at my phone in shock.

From Marissa's description, the bouquet is stunning. I have no doubt something dazzling is hiding in the heavy box. Ditto for the second one. But none of those things are a source of consternation. Rod's attitude is. From what I witnessed yesterday, I would've never expected him to react that way. I guess there is a gentleman hiding behind the gruff wolf.

My stomach growls, reminding me I need food.

Twenty minutes later, I'm sitting in front of an enormous homemade Cobb salad. I devour my food in a few forkfuls. Once satiated, and after washing my plate, I head upstairs to my office.

I drop my butt into my seat. "Back to work." I wake up my iMac.

My phone rings.

My eyes drop to the screen.

*Elsa.*

I accept the call. "Did they unshackle you?" I laugh.

"We've wrapped for the day," she says. "It's eleven at night here in Croatia. I'm enjoying a fabulous glass of wine and I thought I'd touch base. How's LA?"

"Perfect weather, as always. That's one thing I'll never miss about London. I loved the British experience and culture, the weather, not so much. I'm spoiled here in California. However, Croatia's weather is pretty dreamy."

"You won't hear me complaining about the sun or the sea... or the hot men. How was it getting back into the swing of things?"

"Jetlag is a bitch."

"There's no escaping it."

"It's been back to the grind since yesterday. I'm only now starting to feel human again."

"It takes a few days," Elsa says.

"How are things on the set of the most popular fantasy serial drama in TV land?"

Elsa is a hairdresser on the set of Risen Slayers. They film all over Europe. For the past few months, they've been posted in Croatia. I was able to visit her for three days while I was in Europe.

"It's good to be me," she says. "Seriously, it was another grueling fifteen-hour day—I had to be on set at seven o'clock this morning. I've been working in the movie and TV industry for too long to complain. And as you know, I love what I do."

"You do."

Our passion for our chosen professions is something we have in common. Being violated by a predator is another.

Elsa Dewsbury and I are good friends. She's two years older than me. I doubt we would've become friends had it not been for the fact we sought counseling at the same sexual trauma support group for women.

"I was calling to check up on you."

I frown at the phone. "Why?"

"How quickly she forgets."

"Are you going to give me more than that to go by?"

"All the weird tension between Rod and you," she says. "Did you talk to him?"

Overwhelmed by my colliding feelings for my best friend, I

opened up to Elsa when I visited her. With everything that's happened since I got back, my promise to her slipped my mind.

"Sort of."

"Sort of?"

I let out a long exhale. "We did more than talk."

"That's good, right?"

"Well..."

"Well what?"

"I don't know how to say this. I'm still trying to wrap my head around everything that's transpired between Rod and I since I got back to LA."

"Oh, God, did you have a fight?"

"We had two, but that's after..." I let my words trail.

"After what?"

I don't answer.

"Dom, do I have to fly to LA overnight to shake it out of you?"

I can't help but laugh.

"Things got intimate between Rod and I on Saturday night—"

"You slept with each other?"

"Yes."

To my bewilderment, a roaring laughter echoes on the other side of the phone.

"It's about time," Elsa says when she finds her composure.

"I didn't expect that kind of reaction."

"I'm not sure why you're surprised. You had confessed your feelings for him had changed, but you didn't know if it was mutual. You saw him as more than a friend, but didn't want to compromise a pretty amazing friendship by telling him you were falling for him... which, I'm certain happened way before you were willing to admit it to yourself."

She's right.

"In any case, it was killing you because you were living in no man's land—too chicken to tell him, yet, tormented by the fact you felt compelled to keep it bottled up. I guess Rod made the decision for both of you."

"He did, but now things are awkward between us."

I can't lose this friendship. I'm an only child. I'm distant from my family in Europe. My dad never looked back after leaving us. I'm estranged from my mother. Rod is all I have.

"Do you want to start from the beginning?"

Over the next half hour, I spill my guts, keeping the more salacious parts of the story to myself.

"It's like a volcano waiting to erupt," she says. "Talk about combustive. So why did you end up fighting?"

Leave it to Elsa not to miss a beat.

"You know how uncomfortable I can get—more like weirded out—about sex. It's not as bad as it once was, but there's always that underlying fear—"

"Even with Rod?"

"No, not with him. Some of his questions were potential landmines and I guess he sensed my unease. Rod being Rod, he started scratching the surface. My defenses went up and I pushed him away. The second fight happened yesterday before I went for dinner with Joel Banner—"

"Wait. What? You had dinner with the lead singer of Brawn Impulse?" Elsa's voice goes up several octaves. "After you made out with your best friend, the ex-rocker turned badass CEO? Holy shit, girlfriend, you're my new hero."

"You make it sound so sordid."

"How many women make out with two rock stars within the span of twenty hours?"

"I wouldn't know because my dinner with Joel was purely business."

"Oh." The disappointment in her voice in unmistakable. "Nothing happened?"

"Other than a mind-bending proposal that could alter my life forever, no."

I tell her all about Joel's offer.

"You have big decisions to make."

"I do."

We both remain silent for a few short seconds.

"I'm glad Rod is the one who helped you move forward. At least you felt safe with him."

"I always feel safe with him. Everything was amplified when we were together. I not only felt safe, but I also felt cherished beyond belief. He was patient, caring, and considerate. Those adjectives don't come to mind when you think about sex with a bad boy like Rod, but for some incredible reason he managed to make it kinky and loving."

"Sometimes, you need a good man to wipe the slate clean," Elsa says.

I sneer. "Can you ever forget a predator?"

"I didn't say forget, Dom. I doubt people like us can ever forget the monsters who robbed something from us, but we can't let them prevent us from enjoying intimacy. I know where you're coming from. Last summer, I had to call in reinforcements."

"What do you mean?"

"I was stuck. Every time I started dating a guy, I would stress out to the point of being sick, dreading when he'd want to have sex. My anxiety was so high, it was a self-sabotaging exercise. The guy would break things off because I was a mess. Jason had moved back to my parents' house after his latest company had failed."

Her brother is determined to become the next dot-com king.

"Alex was hanging out with him for the evening. Jason drank a little too much and fell asleep. Alex and I started talking, and one thing led to another—"

"Alex? Your older brother's best friend?"

"Yes. I had a long-time crush on him and it turns out it was mutual. I told him what had happened to me and how I desperately wanted to get past my trauma—or at least not freak out like I always did when it came to sex. So, last summer, Alex taught me how to trust again."

"Wow. You never said anything."

"I felt weird sharing because he's my brother's best friend."

"You didn't want more than a summer fling?"

"Alex was chasing after his own dreams. He had his sights set on Tokyo. It was right at the time I found out I got the job on Risen Slayers. It was perfect in many ways. What we shared was meant to only last a season. It was never supposed to be forever. We didn't have the deep connection you and your best friend share." She pauses. "From your question, should I assume you want more with Rod?"

I bite my lower lip.

A beat of silence passes.

I sigh. "I'm not sure of anything right now."

"You're not sure or you're unwilling to be honest with yourself?"

*Damn her for asking the right questions.*

Another beat of silence stretches between us.

"You need to tell him, Dom. He deserves to know. It's been too long."

"That's part of the problem. I'm not sure how he'll react when he finds out I waited eight long years to drop a bomb-like revelation I've worked hard at hiding from him."

"It wasn't your fault," Elsa says. "Someone broke your trust... and his."

"But I never told him. What if he hates me for it?"

"Rod hating you is like saying the earth is flat. Both are impossibilities. You were young, and someone with a black heart manipulated you to silence you. Only a dickless coward without balls would do that to a seventeen-year-old girl. No way Rod would hold that against you."

*Maybe not, but he'd kill the guy who hurt me with his bare hands.*

# Chapter 21

## *Roderick*

I came back from my morning meeting ready to call Dom so we could meet up at the end of the day. I didn't expect the delivery guy entering the building at the same time as me was here for her—flowers and gifts from fucking Joel Banner.

*Great.*

When I told Marissa I would take the gigantic bouquet to Dom's studio, my first instinct was to dump it in the garbage at the back of the building and dispose of the two boxes. I didn't. Not because I'm not that kind of bastard, but because I don't want to give Dom any more reasons to distance herself from me. So, like a good boy, I placed the crystal vase on her desk along with the boxes. Not sure what's in them, but from the delicate packaging and weight, I suspect it's expensive. Then I went back to my desk and ruminated on how amazing a date it must've been for Joel to go out of his way like that. I could've been stuck in that headspace forever, but replaying the conversation I had with Loki and my brother was the catalyst I needed. I put my CEO cap on and put in an honest day's work. I didn't stay longer than I had to. At seven, I waved the remainder of the staff good night and drove to Dom's favorite Nashville-style hot chicken restaurant.

As I approach her house, I pull over and text her.

Rod: Do you hate Auburn yet?

Dominika: More than words can ever express. He has an inflated ego, but he doesn't even master the basics.

Rod: Did you make any headway?

Dominika: What a waste of time. I scrapped everything. I went back to the raw footage. I might have to get some scenes reshot. In other words, I have to redo the video from scratch.

Rod: Shit.

Dominika: Yeah.

Rod: So, you're still home?

Dominika: I've been at it since seven this morning.

Rod: Thirteen hours. Wow.

Dominika: It's eight? No wonder I'm famished.

Rod: I'm here to the rescue.

Dominika: You're doubling as a knight in shining armor now?

Rod: Almost. I stopped by Flaming Hot Chicken and my Maserati smells so good right now.

Dominika: Shut up. You're lying.

Rod: I got all your favorites, including chicken leg quarters and wings. I made sure to select two levels of heat for the sauce—mild and medium—for you, and Nashville Hawt for me. I got a serving of your three favorite side dishes—I doubled up on the seasoned fries. And for dessert, I scooped up a dozen of their mini lemon sour cream pound cakes.

Dominika: Shut up. You're lying.

Rod: It must've been a long day because you're repeating yourself.

Dominika: You're pulling my leg.

I bite off a smile. She takes food very seriously.

Rod: I can drive back to Manhattan Beach and stuff my face in the comfort of my home or I can come by your place and you can help me eat all this food.

Dominika: Bastard. You're playing hardball.

I can only think of being inside her again.

*Focus.*

I push aside the thought of how badly I want her.

Rod: Speak up now, blondie, or forever hold your peace.

The three little balls bounce around a few times because she sends her response.

Dominika: I'll be waiting with fork and knife in hand.

*That's my girl.*

Rod: See you in five.

Dominika: See you soon.

"What took you so long?"

That's how she greets me when I pull up to her driveway.

She's waiting outside in this cute floral dress with thin-straps. She's so tempting, I'm blinded by lust. Her little fists are pinned to her waist. She's even tapping her foot on the asphalt. Her impatient gaze tells the whole story. She means business. I force myself not to focus on how her bare legs look a mile long.

"I said five minutes. I made it in three. What more do you want, woman?" I say as I slide from behind the wheel.

"Hurry, I'm hungry." She waves me in.

I can't help but laugh.

I was worried there might be some awkward tension between us, but I'm glad to see I was wrong. We're back to being Dom and Rod.

~

As Dom cleans her plate, I wonder—not for the first time—how such a petite woman can eat so much food.

"I was hoping to have some leftovers for tomorrow," I say, pointing to her plate.

When she lifts her blue eyes to mine, there's an unmistakable shadow of guilt in them.

"Oh, sorry."

"I was joking. I always love watching you eat."

"Thanks for feeding me," she says.

"My pleasure."

"All this focus and concentration burns a lot of calories."

I reach out and place my hand over hers before squeezing.

She doesn't pull away. It's only been two days, but I miss feeling her skin under my touch. "We're lucky to have you." I smile. "I guess I should speak for myself. Loki is a big boy."

"Are we still talking about video editing?" Her gaze holds mine.

"What do you think, Dom?"

She blushes.

I groan internally when she folds her lower lip between her teeth.

*Damn.*

I want nothing more than to devour her lips, but there's the matter of Joel's gifts.

"It slipped my mind, but you received a special delivery today."

"Yeah, Marissa called me earlier."

"It's a nice bouquet." I can't believe I managed that.

"That's what Marissa said. And there's more stuff. Thanks so much for taking care of it all," she says.

"Not a problem."

"I'm surprised you didn't find a clever way to dump the flowers somewhere."

"What kind of animal do you take me for?"

*She doesn't need to know it crossed my mind a dozen times.*

"It was pretty clear from your macho-alpha-standoff yesterday with Joel, you two will never be best friends."

"I have a best friend. I don't need another one," I say.

There's a flicker of surprise that crosses her eyes.

I take in a deep breath before allowing it to escape through my flared nostrils. "Listen, Dom, you're a grown woman. If you and Joel are seeing each other, I'll respect—"

"It wasn't a date."

"Those flowers tell a different story."

The words fly out of my mouth before I can catch them.

"Wow. They must be something else because Marissa made the same comment."

"They look expensive. Someone put a lot of thought into selecting them. A guy doesn't go to the trouble unless he's intent on seducing a girl." *And then fucking her.*

"You speak from experience?"

"Nah. Never met a girl who was worth it... well, not until now anyway." I exhale. "Joel beat me to the punch."

She tilts her head to the side. "Jealous, Wolfe?"

"What if I was?"

Her jaw drops.

"It was a business meeting," she says.

"It was?"

She nods. "Yes."

*I guess I got it all wrong.*

"Nothing romantic?"

"Only if you consider eighteen varieties of tempura sexy."

I laugh.

"What kind of business?"

"He wants me to help him make his mark in the US," she says.

"I thought we had that covered."

Over another glass of wine, she tells me all about Joel's proposal.

"Like us, Joel had a troubled childhood," she says.

His current stardom betrays his less-than-perfect beginnings. I guess a lot of people could say the same about me. I never thought I'd have anything in common with Joel.

"Are you thinking of going for it?" As much as I hate to admit it, it's a phenomenal opportunity for someone with Dom's incredible skills.

"It's a big decision."

"It's a big opportunity."

"It comes at a price."

"Like everything else worthwhile," I say.

"I'd be away for six months."

*That's a fucking long time.* "It's a problem?"

She twists her lips. "It worries me."

"Why?"

"Out of sight, out of mind." She glances up at me from under her lashes.

"Once you're back, everyone in the industry will know your name. It'll put you on the map."

"Yeah, I have no doubt it'll do wonders for my career, but..."

"But what?"

She sighs. "Will the distance widen the rift between the two of us?"

I hate the insecurity in her voice.

I reach for her beautiful face and stroke it with the back of my hand. "You and I are solid, Dom."

"Even after last weekend?" Her huge blue eyes are so expectant.

*I see.*

"About last weekend... I should've never been such a demanding bastard. I'm sorry if my questions made you uncomfortable."

"I know you care."

"I care a lot. Always have. Always will. It's just sometimes I'm a little territorial when it comes to you."

"A little?" She giggles.

"Shut up. You knew it was part of the contract when we became best friends."

She returns my warm smile.

I study her for a few beats. "There's something else I regret about last weekend."

"Oh, no." Her brows furrow. "You regret what happened between us?"

"Did you hear me say that?"

"Don't sugarcoat it, Rod."

She looks positively terrified now.

"Come here." I extend my hand to her. When she gets up, I pull her towards me, lift her up and straddle her on my lap.

The flash of her thighs makes me hard.

*Not now, Wolfe.*

I will myself to stay on track.

I caress her inked arm.

She doesn't shiver under my touch this time.

"On Sunday, I noticed some new ink on your upper back while you were still sleeping in my arms. I meant to bring it up..."

"But we had a fight." She finishes my sentence.

"That's behind us."

She nods and rewards me with a brilliant smile. "I got it done right before leaving for Europe. I also asked my tattoo artist to saturate the color on my old flowers. It pops like it did when I first got them done."

Dom's tattoo is like an eye-catching garden of orange lilies running from her shoulder to her wrist. When she decided to go for it, she didn't do it half measure. Her tattoo is a striking kaleidoscope of vibrant colors.

"How come I missed that?"

"You were in Miami."

"That explains it. I love the new ink on you." My fingers caress her back in slow rotations.

"Thanks." She flashes me an anxious look. "Are you changing the subject because you don't want to hurt my feelings? I'll never be able to match your experience. I'm terrible in bed, right? Just tell me, Rod."

I press two fingers to her lips. "Hey, don't you dare talk about *my* girl like that. I told you, you're a hot little lover in bed. Next stage for you? Maneater status."

"Huh?"

I bore my eyes into hers and open up my soul to a woman like I've never done before.

"I regret asking for only one night."

She pushes my hand away from her mouth. "Wait. What? Your girl? I'm not terrible in bed? You want more?"

"Very much so."

"Have I entered a parallel universe?"

"Why is it so hard to believe?"

"Everything happened so fast—"

"We've been pining for each other for months."

"There's something unspoken in your admission," she says.

"What do you mean?"

"It wasn't only me?"

"No. It wasn't one-sided, Dom."

"Oh."

"I was hoping there might be more nights between the two of us. Many more."

"Oh," she says again.

"I liked being with you—"

"You mean being inside me."

"Yeah, I'm quite partial to that as well."

She laughs.

"I love spending time with you. We hang out all the time, but the intimacy over the weekend made things... different."

"I was overwhelmed," she says.

"Same here."

"Really?"

"Really, baby," I say before dropping a chaste kiss on her lips. "I know hookups aren't your thing—"

"I—I need time to feel comfortable with a guy," she says in a near whisper.

As much as it kills me, I let her troubling comment slide. I'm here to make amends, not to be all up in her business.

"I figured. I think we should take a leap of faith."

Her eyebrows knit together. "I don't follow."

"We should make it official and start dating."

Her head jerks back and she fixes those piercing blue eyes on me.

She opens her mouth, then shuts it. She does that a few times.

"Huh?"

"I said we should start dating."

"Dating?" She's blinking so fast, you'd think she's trying to take flight.

I nod. "Obviously, it has to be mutual."

"You... us..." She ping-pongs her finger between her chest and mine. "Dating? As in girlfriend-boyfriend? That kind of dating?"

"Yeah, that kind of dating, silly."

"Whoa."

*This isn't going quite as planned.*

"You don't want this to go any further?"

"Did you hear me say that?" She borrows my words from earlier.

I chuckle.

"Rod, you don't know how to date. You're a consummate bachelor."

"You'll be my tutor like you were all those years back."

Bouncing around between two homes didn't bode well for a kid who already struggled in school. As a result of my mother's inability to be a decent parent, I ended up straggling by one year. It was embarrassing. Without Dom's unwillingness to give up on me, I would've never graduated. She saw intelligence where I—and all my teachers—saw inadequacies.

"We're no longer in high school, Rod. We're adults, and this is a big decision."

"One I've thoroughly thought through."

She considers me for several long seconds.

"I may have a little bit more experience, but it doesn't mean I'm any good at it. My relationships don't tend to last long."

"Maybe because you were with the wrong guys," I say.

"And you're the right one?"

"I am."

Loki and Roark's intervention got me thinking hard. I woke up this morning with an unwavering sense of urgency. I'm here to stake a claim on my girl.

"Wow. You're pretty confident."

"I'm feeding off what happened between us." I pause. "Why don't we learn together?"

Her gaze intensifies. "You understand you'll have to become a one-woman-kind-of-guy? No more chasing skirt."

"I wouldn't dream of it."

"What about Dark Compulsion?"

"We can have a lot of kinky fun at the club as a couple. We can rent a private room for the night. Maybe a little role-playing…? You can be my naughty secretary, or I can be your daddy. I'd love nothing more than to corrupt you there."

"You're impossible, Rod."

"I said dating, not sainthood."

"Can you even spell monogamy?"

Will I screw up a few times? Yes. Yes, I will. But the one thing I know for certain is I can't stand the thought of another man touching her. I want her all to myself. It makes sense I return the favor.

"I gave you my word, Dom. What more do you want? A signed oath in blood?"

She draws in a long, slow breath and releases it.

"Not to mention, I haven't been with anyone since before you left for Europe. I almost hooked up with a woman a few days before you came back, but it never happened."

Her eyebrows hit her forehead.

"See, I'm already a pro at monogamy." I chuckle.

She stares at me.

"Dom, talk to me. I have no idea what you're thinking."

"You... mean it?"

"You know me well enough to know I don't say things I don't mean."

"There I was thinking you came over to save me from starvation and going cross-eyed, but instead you turned my world upside down."

"In a good way?"

"Absolutely," she says with a smile.

"So, we're doing this or what?"

"I'm in, if you're in." She grins wide.

"I'm one-hundred percent in, baby."

# Chapter 22

## *Dominika*

I'm still bewildered by Rod's words.

If I wasn't staring into his beautiful dark eyes, I'd think this was a dream.

We're grinning at each other like fools.

I'm elated, scared and eager all at the same time.

I trust Rod.

He accepts every part of me because he knows everything there is to know about me. He's the guy who helped me break the horrible spell I was under. Without him, I would still be freaked out about sex. And now, he's my boyfriend.

What a difference a few days make.

His stare rakes over me and I can't help but feel the rising heat between my legs.

"Can I show my girlfriend how much I've missed her? Holy shit, I can't believe I just said that to a woman for the very first time in my life."

A rush of excitement zips through me.

*I'm his girlfriend. I'm his girlfriend. I'm his girlfriend.*

*Freaking mind-blowing.*

"If you must," I say.

"Oh, okay. So, you don't care one way or the other if I take good care of you like I did over the weekend?"

"I wouldn't go that far."

"You want me to show you or not?"

"Yes, please."

"Good answer, baby."

Rod slides a hand into my hair, leans in close enough for my breasts to brush against his shirt. The sensation is sublime. My nipples tighten, nearing the pain point as a blissful shiver runs over me.

He tilts his hips up, and I gasp when I feel the solid length of his thick cock.

I press against his erection.

"Fuck," he says. "Greedy Dom."

"You're so hard."

He raises a brow. "Are you using my cock for your own pleasure?"

I laugh. "You'd be offended if I did?"

"It would be a crying shame if you didn't," he says before taking my mouth in a smoldering kiss. After a few long steamy seconds, he pulls away. "I'll wine and dine you to celebrate our first official date in style, but for tonight I thought I'd sixty-nine you."

"You're a big ol' romantic, aren't you?"

He flashes me a worried glance as if he's afraid he said the wrong thing.

*Oh, no.*

"Not that I know from experience, but I've been told a girl can never have too many sixty-nines."

"Oof," he says. "I thought you were going to ask for violins, red roses, heart-shaped balloons, and chocolate-covered cherries."

"Nah, you're more than enough, Rod," I say.

"Fuck, you're perfect, Dom." His eyes drop to my mouth, his gaze turning dark.

The intense lust I read in his eyes is unsettling. Will I ever get used to how one glance disarms me to the point where I can't remember my own name?

"Wanna take it upstairs or are you okay with me pushing you out of your comfort zone?"

"I trust you implicitly. You decide where you want to corrupt me."

I think the last part surprises us both.

He growls before ravishing my lips again. I'm lost in a dizzying and passionate kiss. The more he deepens the kiss, the more I rub my impatient pussy against him.

"Baby, I want you so much," he says.

"I want you too."

He grabs hold of the hem of my dress, pulls it over my head and lets it drop to the floor.

"Wow. That's one hell of a bra," he says.

"It matches the flowers on my dress."

"And your ink," he says before unhooking my lacy orange bra, allowing my erect nipples some relief. "Holy fuck, Dom, your tits are fucking amazing."

I can't help but pull my lower lip between my teeth. I'm not used to being praised like this.

"Your rosy nipples are small enough to cover with my fingertip."

And he does. His sensual touch ignites me.

"But large enough so I can draw them into my mouth. I couldn't ask for more."

His mouth closes over my breast, and I whimper.

"You know what I've been fantasizing about since Sunday?"

"I'm afraid to ask." My voice comes out shaky.

"I can't wait for both of us to watch as my cock slides between your tits until I jet my cum all over them."

"Your words are going to set me on fire," I say.

"I'd hold back just enough of my release to mark your heart."

I should be wary of his wicked grin.

"This one, baby," he says, running his fingers up my legs. In a flash, they find my aching clit. He rubs my clit through my panties, forcing my body to cave to his arousing touch.

"Oh, God."

I press my face into the crook of his neck and wrap my arms around him. When he gets up, I wrap my legs around his waist. He palms my ass in his large hands and holds me steady as he crosses my kitchen. He places me on the granite counter like a delicate and rare museum artifact.

He waves his finger at my panties. "Off, before I rip them off."

"I'm not wearing much. Aren't you going to join me?"

"Ladies first."

I mean to follow his orders, but I can't seem to pull my eyes away.

In his dark wash jeans—designer I'm sure—that hug his thighs in all the right places, and his black shirt, Rod is as devastatingly handsome as he is when he sports a suit. His body is all muscle, but he isn't built like a fridge. Every inch of his six-one physique was crafted with care by God.

*Yup, Rod Wolfe is striking.*

"Dom?"

"Sorry, I got distracted."

"Now you know how I feel when I look at you."

I blush so fast, I bet there isn't a part of me that isn't red.

I return his smile.

I wiggle my way out of my matching lace thong, push it down my legs, and pull it free before dropping it to the floor. Rod's eyes are on me as he toes off his Italian blue suede ankle boots before removing his shirt and jeans. He rises to his feet before me and without wasting time, he pulls down his boxer briefs.

I shake my head in disbelief at the sight of his massive erection.

This gorgeous man is finally mine.

"I know this is only the second time, but I still wonder how the hell it'll fit," I say, with my eyes riveted to his cock.

He closes the gap between us. "Are you complaining about my size?"

"It's a lot to handle."

"You proved yourself up to the challenge on Saturday."

"It might take a few tries before I adjust."

"I'm more than happy to sacrifice my body until it happens... even if it takes a couple hundred tries over the coming week before you get there."

"Sounds like I won't be doing much other than having sex."

"Don't worry, I'll be right there by your side... or inside you... or on top of you. Regardless, it's all semantics. All that to say, you're not alone."

I laugh. "I'm touched by your concern and your generosity."

"What are best friends for?" He grins.

"Indeed," I say reaching out to stroke his six pack. My fingers run down his abs, relishing the feel of his defined V muscle. I'll have to muster up the courage to trace those lines with my tongue one day.

*God, the man brings down my inhibitions.*

"This is all yours, Dom."

"So is this?" I run a finger across his hard cock.

He nods. "Every inch of me." Rod comes to stand between my parted legs, spreading them further apart. He cups my face in his hands and covers my mouth with hot kisses as he pushes my body down. I'm so turned on, it's ridiculous. "Fuck, I love the way you smell. Your heady scent tells me your tight little pussy needs my cock."

I blush.

"Am I wrong?"

I shake my head.

He cocks an eyebrow and stares at me.

It takes me a second to pick up on his unspoken words.

"No, you're right."

"Better. For the record, I like words."

"Duly noted."

"Cocky, Dom. I like it."

He reaches behind me, places his hands against my ass and pulls me down, scooching me right up to the edge of the counter.

My eyes widen in surprise. "Oh, shit."

"What?"

I laugh.

"What is it, Dom?"

"Nothing."

"Tell me."

I avert my gaze. "I left a trail of wetness behind."

Rod tilts his head back and roars.

Once I get over my embarrassment, I allow my laughter to spill free.

"My sweet Dom," he says, tapping the tip of my nose with his finger. "I'm going to enjoy corrupting you." He presses his body against mine, his cock nestled against my dripping pussy, and I can't help the moan that escapes me.

"Fuck," he says. "It's so hot to feel your pussy without anything between us."

"Is it different without a condom?"

"I wouldn't know from firsthand experience, but I've been told it's like comparing Japanese Kobe strip steak to cheap fatty ground beef."

"Would you like to know how it feels? I mean..." I let my words trail.

Rod's eyes are as wide as saucers. "Are you saying what I think you're saying?"

"I've always used a condom with guys," I say.

By a miracle of God, my rapist had spared me from getting pregnant with his baby and God knows what nasty diseases.

"So have I," Rod says.

"With guys?" I can't resist.

Rod laughs. "I'll rephrase. I've always used a condom... with girls."

"Do you want to try... without a condom?"

"My girlfriend wants all of me?"

"I want you to be the first." My answer comes before I even have time to think.

"Fuck, those are some powerful words, baby."

"Too much to handle?"

"Since this will be my first time, it's likely you'll have to call 911, or else one of us might be seeing God tonight."

I laugh.

He joins me.

Rod leans over me until his chest hair is teasing my taut nipples. "You'll be all mine after this, baby," he says boring his eyes into mine. "No other man in the world will ever be able to mark you like I will."

I nod breathlessly as a wave of emotions engulfs me.

"Words, Dom."

"I want that." I bite down a sob as I avert my gaze.

I can't go back and change the past, but this is my second chance with the boy I've loved for over a decade and the man I've fallen in love with recently.

"Hey, look at me."

I do.

"What's wrong, baby?" He gives me an agonized expression.

*Shit.*

I'm about to say nothing, but don't. It would only fan his concerns.

I let out a shuddering exhale. "I'm a little overwhelmed, that's all."

"But you're okay?"

"I'm more than okay." I offer a small smile.

"Sure?"

"What I'm sure of, is I can't wait to feel your lips against mine again."

"Well, damn. I've been told." He chuckles.

With a blazing kiss, he shuts out the past.

His mouth is greedy, demanding, unapologetic.

He devours me with such fervor, I practically whimper from the kiss. He says he's only kissed one girl before, but like so many things in his life, he masters this.

He presses the head of his cock against my clit, skating around my slick pussy. I gasp when he brushes down past the entrance to my ass.

"Mother of God."

"Jesus fucking Christ," he says. "This is also mine to take."

"What?"

"Not today."

I don't even find it in me to protest.

After a few more teasing seconds, Rod touches his forehead against mine.

"My first girlfriend and the first woman I take bareback. It had to be you, Dom."

I blink several times in rapid succession as my brain struggles to soak up his words. They're as warm as an armful of sunshine.

*My first mind-blowing sexual experience. It could only be you, Rod.*

Myriad emotions constrict my heart.

He slides into me.

We both look down at where his cock disappears into my pussy.

All of a sudden, he halts all movement.

"Why did you stop?"

"Shit. I should've asked before dipping my cock inside your warmth. Are you on birth control?"

"I am."

"Thank the fuck God. There's no way I'm putting the brakes on now." Rod resumes his mission.

"How does it feel?" *It's hot having you inside me like this.*

"Oh, fuck, I'm never getting out."

"You don't have to." My voice is barely more than a gasp.

"I'm glad to hear it because I'll need several doses every single day." He chuckles. "The sensation of gliding in and out of your sleek and slippery pussy is fucking mind-blowing. It's so primal."

"Greedy caveman."

He lets out a feral grunt for show.

I laugh.

"Seriously, Dom, I don't want this with any other woman."

I'm stunned into silence for a beat. "I only want this with you."

"Why the hell did it take us this long to figure it out?"

"We can make up for lost time," I say.

"Damn right."

He moves to my neck, kissing and biting along the way.

I respond by clenching hard against him.

This sensation sends a shiver throughout my body, causing my eyes to roll to the back of my head.

"Your hungry pussy is choking my cock."

He responds by swinging his hips back and ramming right through me, making me cry out.

My bold move sets him off and he lets loose between my legs.

"I'm going to shoot my load so deep inside you, it won't drip out of you for a very long time."

"Oh, God."

A few of my ex-boyfriends dropped a raunchy word here and there, but none of them mastered dirty-talking like Rod.

My plea does little to deter him.

"My cum belongs inside you."

"Yes."

"Say it. I want to hear it, Dom."

"Your cum belongs inside me," I say in a whisper close to his ear.

"Don't you ever forget it." There's no way to miss the possessiveness coating his words.

He pumps my pussy with determination.

When he first pushed my body against the counter, the coolness of the slab helped lessen the combustive heat threatening to melt me like a lava cake. Now, the sheen of sweat glistening down my back makes it easier for him to fuck me deeper every time he thrusts in and out of me.

"Don't stop, Rod."

"Once I coat your pussy with my cum, you'll never want another cock for the rest of your life."

*I'm already there.*

"I'm close, baby. Place the heels of your feet up on the counter."

Although taken aback, I do as I'm told.

I didn't think it was possible, but Rod pushes deeper every time he sways his hips inside me. Each punishing thrust is harder than the last.

He slides a hand over my leg and up to my clit, and begins to rub me with his precision touch.

"I love the way you do that, Rod."

"Baby there isn't much of me left. But, here's the deal, I come once you come."

"Oh, okay."

"You ready to give me what I want?"

The rhythmic pounding of his cock as he continues to rub my sensitive clit sends me into a core-shaking orgasm.

"I'm—"

*Mother of God.*

My head lolls back against the counter as I arch my back, relishing the climactic build-up. The contact of my stiff nipples against his chest pushes me over the edge.

My pussy pulses like crazy.

"Shit, Dom," he says. "Clench my cock even harder. Milk my cum out of me— Oh, Jesus, I'm there."

Rod pulls out and aims his cock over my pussy. He spews an indecent amount of cum, blanketing the little heart sitting on top of my pussy.

He's marked me.

No sooner is he done than he leans forward and wraps me in his embrace, smearing his release all over my stomach.

We stay locked into each other for a long moment, neither

of us rushing to end this. Our heavy breathing is the only sound breaking through the silence.

I don't ever want to let go of him.

"Talk to me, baby," he says, lifting his head up to meet my gaze.

*I'm spent and utterly satisfied.*

"I've never felt this content in my life."

*Crap.*

*I didn't think I said that out loud.*

"Wow, that's a lot to live up to," he says.

"You can manage."

"I'll try hard for you, baby. You're worth it."

I hold him a little closer, closing my eyes to savor every unforgettable second.

"Come on, sweet Dom. Let's go upstairs. I need to wash up my girlfriend before making true on my promise."

"Which one?"

"I promised to sixty-nine you."

"My feet haven't touched the ground yet. Can a girl get a minute?"

"Weren't you the one boasting about how a girl can never have too many sixty-nines?"

"Yes, but—"

"Let's get to it, blondie."

# Chapter 23

## *Roderick*

Dom smiles up at me. "This has been the most incredible afternoon of my life."

When the evening breeze picks up, I wrap my arms a little tighter around her and drop a kiss on the top of her head.

"Though I can't include this evening in that statement," she says.

"Why not?"

"You know why not, Wolfe. Since I've been back from Europe, you've made it a point to rock my evenings."

Yeah, she's been waking up sore every morning this week after riding my cock hard all evening long.

"It's your fault," I saw in her ear, "You're the one who tempted me with your irresistible offer. Once I buried myself balls deep inside your wet pussy without a shield, there was no going back."

Fucking Dom bareback is the hottest thing I've ever done—and I've had my fair share of kinky fun with women—but none of those things come close to knowing no other man has ever taken her this way. Filling her with my cum has become my new favorite activity.

"You're impossible," she says swatting my arm.

Although the evening sky is dark and I can't see her blush, I'm certain her cheeks are flushed.

"So, I did good?"

"Are you kidding me? I love this." She turns in my arms to face me. "When you said you had big plans for our first date, I thought maybe a nice dinner at an upscale restaurant or perhaps you had hired the services of a top catering company for something fancy at your place or mine, but I never expected anything close to this. Everything is perfect."

"We can do dinners anytime. There's only one first date."

"True," she says.

"I wanted to make sure it was an evening neither of us would ever forget."

"Mission accomplished." She smiles.

"I chose this experience because there's a symbolism to this boat ride. One that characterizes us."

"You lost me."

"For years, we've been drifting blind to our changing feelings about our friendship. It took a few detours, but we've finally docked at the same port."

"Look at you, Mr. Poet."

"You like that?" I chuckle.

"I do. It's touching," she says.

I kiss her forehead. "It's from my heart."

She looks up at me, but doesn't speak.

We've been dating for four days now, and the amazing thing is, I'm not itching to get out.

Dom has me by the balls.

I'm tamed. Willingly.

And I love knowing she's mine.

I thought my brothers and Loki were going to give me a hard time, but I was wrong. They're happy I came to my senses. So am I.

When I woke up Wednesday morning with her wrapped around me, I knew our first date had to be memorable. So, I called to the owner of Dark Compulsion. Larkin Gallagher came through for me. One of the club members owns a fleet of charter yachts in California. Luck was on my side. I was able to nab a cancellation on the rental of a 59 ft yacht complete with captain, five-star catered meal and plenty of champagne. It's a lot of boat power for two people, but given the fact I was able to give my girl an incomparable experience, it's worth it. We set sail at three o'clock this afternoon and we've been cruising the Pacific Ocean ever since. Now, we're both standing on the upper deck, soaking in the calmness of the dark sky against the water.

"Turn around," I say.

She squints her eyes at me. "Why?"

"I thought you trusted me?"

"I do, but the way you're looking at me suggests you have something up your sleeve, Wolfe."

"Come on, blondie, stop being so melodramatic."

She studies me for a beat.

"Okay, but you better not try anything sneaky."

"Everything is aboveboard."

"Sure. I have my eyes on you," she says before pointing two fingers from her eyes to mine.

When her back is facing me, I rummage through the back pocket of my jeans until I find what I'm looking for.

"I wanted you to have something to remember this night by," I say, slipping the necklace around her neck.

She gasps. "What are you doing?" She tries to turn around, but I stop her.

"Hold tight, blondie, I'm not done yet." I finish closing the clasp and I adjust her gift so it's perfectly centered.

Her hands flying to the pendant. "Oh my God!" She turns into my arms. "You're crazy, Rod."

"Yeah, I'm crazy about you."

She blushes. "What is it? I can't make out the shape."

"Let me help." I pull out my phone and tap on the front-facing option on the camera app. "Here you go." I turn the phone towards her.

"Sweet baby Jesus are these diamonds?"

"As if I'd buy you something cheap."

"No way."

"I've bought you jewelry in the past for all of your milestone birthdays."

"But nothing with diamonds," she says.

"You weren't my girl then."

She bites on her lower lip and stares at me through her lashes. "I kind of like it a lot when you say that."

"Get used to it because I'll keep saying it a lot." I offer a warm smile.

"Still, Rod, this looks like it cost a fortune."

I knew this would be a tug-of-war. I'm used to it. Dom's a giver. It's a challenge for her to receive. It was the same song and dance four years ago when I bought her a house she couldn't stop talking about in Venice Beach. She wouldn't have it. She thought it was way too extravagant for a gift. In the end, I had to compromise. Although the house is under her name and paid in full, she insists on paying me back—with interest—a little every month. You can never accuse her of taking advantage of people. She doesn't know it, but I made sure to buy StreamTunes shares under her name. We'll probably end up fighting over it, but it's not like there's anything she can do about it.

"Are you saying you aren't worth it? Because I beg to differ."

"You sweet talker, you." She swats my arm again.

"I'm warning you, Dom, there will be no compromise. I want to see this around your neck."

"Fair enough. I won't fight you on this one. It's too gorgeous. Although, I still can't make out what it is."

"I bought it at Cartier—"

"Rod—"

"Didn't you just make me a promise?"

"Okay."

"It's called *'Juste Un Clou'*. In other words, it's a fancy and creative design of a nail."

"Really?"

"Really. The designer basically molded a nail in a circular shape and left a small gap. I thought the rose gold version would look beautiful against your skin complexion."

"I absolutely love it. Other than to take a shower, I'll never take it off," she says, lifting her chin up and giving me a definitive nod.

The significance of her words fills me with pride.

"I'll always be with you." *Just as it should be.*

"I'll always feel safe," she says before falling into my arms.

I bite the question burning my tongue.

I guess I slept like a rock the first night we were together because I didn't hear her talk in her sleep. Dom has this nightly mantra, 'I'm safe, I'm safe, I'm safe'. It took every bit of my self-control not to drill her in the morning to find out what was troubling her. I promised not to push, and I haven't, but now, it's increasingly difficult to keep quiet.

I have to know. "Is there any reason for you not to feel safe?"

She looks up at me. "No." She smiles.

"No one can hurt you anymore. Jarreth is dead."

"I know. I'm okay, really." Her shivering body betrays her words.

From the first day I came to her rescue, Dom became the rock in the utterly chaotic world Mom's poisonous aura cast over me. Dom gave me a reason to care and attend school. I never imagined I'd come to her rescue twice in the span of a few months.

Dom's tattoos aren't a sign of rebellion or badassness. And they're not to ride a growing trend. They aren't meant to shake up the status quo. They're to cover some pretty bad scars left behind by one of her mom's douchebag boyfriends.

After her dad left, her mom went on a dating binge. Every time I'd drop Dom off at her place after school, I was always suspicious of some of the men coming in and out of Natasa's rented house. One day, as I was waiting outside her last class of the day to walk her home, a few of her schoolmates told me she'd left early in pain. That time of the month, they said. I set off to her place to make sure she was okay. As I was nearing her house, I heard a horrible scream. As I turned the corner, I saw Jarreth Howard—Natasa's latest mistake—dragging my best friend over the asphalt against shards of glass, rocks and God knows what else. He had both hands around her right wrist, leaving the left side of her body exposed. Her jeans protected her lower part, but her tank top did little to save her upper body.

Jarreth was in his boxer briefs. Dom was screaming bloody murder. I didn't think twice. I bolted towards them. The asshole jolted when he saw me, but it was too late. One punch and he was out. By the time I was able to calm Dom down, the police had arrived. I guess a neighbor made the call.

Jarreth was using Natasa's beat up backyard shed as a place to lure, drug and molest young boys. Dom caught him because she got home much earlier than usual. He received a record sentence after a staggering number of victims—all boys—came forward. He was supposed to rot in prison forever. To Dom's consternation and mine, Jarreth's prison bride—a former legal clerk—almost got him out early last year based on an alleged oversight from the prosecution's office. Some of Jarreth's inmates took matters into their own hands. Now, he's six feet under.

I stroke her lower lip with the pad of my thumb. "No one else has hurt you since Jarreth, right?"

I've never prayed for a *no* so much in my life.

She doesn't answer.

"Dom, I don't want to push you, just tell me, please."

"I feel safe with you, Rod," she says, nestling her trembling body against mine.

I could blame the evening breeze, but I'm no fool.

Her evasive answer feels like someone slugged my chest with a sledgehammer.

*Goddammit.*

I had my suspicions, but now I'm certain she's keeping something from me. I swear to God, if I ever find out someone hurt her, I'll go fucking ballistic.

## Chapter 24

## *Dominika*

In the month since we've been dating, this is the first time we'll be apart. I'm leaving later with my team for three and a half days to shoot in Miami.

*One month.*

I still can't believe it.

To my surprise, Rod didn't push further to find out if someone had hurt me after our first date. I'm grateful.

These last four weeks have been more blissful than I could have ever imagined. For the first ten days, we used my house as our kinky nest. That's until Rod started missing his massive Manhattan Beach mansion. So, I packed a few bags and moved to his place. I thought I'd miss being in my own space, but nothing compares to falling asleep and waking up in his strong arms.

I smile and hum to myself for no reason these days. Half the time, it's like I'm walking on sunshine. Temperamental artists are a hell of a lot easier to handle because my utter happiness shields me from their capricious and irrational demands. After years of feeling defective, Rod brings out a whole new lexicon of emotions in me.

I'm whole.

Complete.

Unbroken.

Perfect just the way I am.

It's like he's repaired the jagged crack in my heart left behind by my parents and my assailant.

I'm unapologetic in admitting this relationship makes me feel part of something greater than myself. Something I thought would elude me for the rest of my life. Something I didn't deserve. Him being a sex god is bonus. Thanks to my boyfriend's remarkable prowess in bed, I went from a shy and insecure lover to a much more confident one. I wouldn't call myself a maneater just yet, but I can hold my own and more importantly, I can satisfy him. It's mind-blowing to hear him roar my name as he climaxes and to know I'm the one responsible for taking him over the edge.

*Wow.*

Other than my dreamy relationship, work has been pretty amazing. I've acquired a lot of new clients. Word of mouth is a powerful thing.

As for Joel's proposal.

The British rock star is persuasive and incredibly generous. He showered me with extravagant flower arrangements and obscenely expensive video equipment for days in his attempt to sway me. He only stopped when he found out Rod is now my boyfriend. Johanna, Elsa and Isobel think it's an amazing opportunity. Even Rod has been nudging me to accept. In the end, the decision was taken out of my hands—for now, anyway. Brawn Impulse's latest hit exploded in the UK, Japan and Korea forcing them to postpone their American tour. Joel's offer is still on the table.

Rod has a jam-packed day of meetings. He was gone before I got up this morning. Since he's insisted on driving me to the airport, we'll have time to catch up before I fly out, but I wouldn't mind stealing a kiss. I'm lucky we work next to each other.

I grab my phone off my desk to text him, but decide against it.

"Some things are best delivered in person," I say out loud.

I still have a few things to knock off my list before calling it a day, but I could use a break. Not to mention, word has it Loki was in a giving mood this afternoon and stopped by Sugar Glaze Shack. There are donuts and then there are *donuts*. Sugar Glaze Shack's are way up there.

I stand up, smooth down my hair, and straighten the lower part of my dress to make sure I still look presentable. I changed and touched up my makeup not long ago because when we arrive in Miami, the team and I will be whisked away to a celebrity party. Traveling in jeans and Chucks won't do this time.

I pass my staff—who is so immersed in their work they don't even bother looking up—and head to Pending Inference. As I stride through the industrial space, I smile at a bunch of familiar faces on my way up to Rod's office. A short elevator ride later and I'm on his floor.

"Hey, Marissa. Is Rod still in a meeting?"

"He is." His executive assistant squints her blue eyes at me. "He's in the large fish tank with a few stuffy guppies from a big recording label and his shark-ally, Loki."

I laugh. "You kill me."

She smooths down her blonde hair. "That conference room looks like a giant aquarium and those idiots in there with them don't look too smart—hence the analogy. It shouldn't be much longer. Mr. Wolfe should be out any minute now."

"In that case, I'll stick around for a bit."

"FYI," she says, "I hope you know your dress will turn heads and don't think I didn't catch sight of the killer black heels." She sighs. "If only I could walk in those without looking like a drunken sailor, I'd make the hubby very happy. I'm so pathetic at it, he's given up on buying fuck-me heels. Bless him." Marissa has a unique sense of humor. "Miami men won't know what hit them. Oh, bite my tongue, you already have a man. The boss might veto your departure." She grins from ear to ear.

"Really?"

She cocks an eyebrow.

I only have eyes for one man, but I'm tickled pink by her compliment.

"Where are you hiding the donuts?" I change the subject.

"Oh, so this little visit has nothing to do with a man, but everything to do with dessert," she says.

My staff and Rod's know we're seeing each other. It's amazing how many people weren't surprised by the news. I guess my boyfriend and I were the only ones who were oblivious.

"I'm glad to see you have your priorities straight." She laughs.

"You're crazy, Marissa."

"Yeah, tell me something I don't already know."

"So, are you going to tell me where you're hiding the goods?"

"Loki went a little nuts, so I had to display *the goods* in the small conference room near his office. That way." She points to her right.

"Can I bring you one?"

"God no. I've already had three. They're addicting. One more and I'll have to kiss my girlish figure goodbye."

"They're sinful. The shop is a little out of the way, so I have no intentions on holding back."

"Go for it."

When I walk past the large conference room, I catch sight of something dark and delicious. I'll be honest, I'm always weak at the knees when Rod wears a suit. Today, he looks good enough to eat. Gorgeous. Sexy. Domineering. Fierce. And mine.

*Damn.*

I stare at him.

I'll miss him over the next few days.

After a steady dosage of his hungry cock, I'll have to go without.

*How will I survive?*

A series of steamy scenes flash in front of me as I replay last night's toe-curling embrace. My body heats up to dangerous levels.

My gaze locks onto a pair of dark chocolate eyes and my cheeks burst into flames. His glance is so intense, I look away. I have to. The lust emanating from those smoldering brown eyes is enough to make me reconsider my business trip.

*Double damn.*

# Chapter 25

## *Roderick*

*Is that Dom?*

There's no mistaking the beautiful blonde staring at me.

*What the hell is she wearing?*

*Damn.*

*Does she have any idea what that dress is doing to me?*

*Christ.*

My brain was going numb from all this boring legal talk when a vision appears in front of me. I always liked the concept of the all-glass conference room, now, I curse it.

How cruel is it to see something—someone—I can't have.

Dom looks like a tempting seductress in a red dress that molds her body to perfection. Her smoky makeup accentuates her blue eyes, which are peering back at me like expensive aquamarine stones. And then there are those delicious fucking lips. When they part, I shift in my chair to adjust myself. I do my darndest not to think of how amazing those lips felt wrapped around my cock last night as I fucked her pretty mouth, but it's a catastrophic failure. I can only picture her on her knees looking up at me, begging me with her huge vulnerable eyes.

*I'm so fucking screwed.*

If I feel like this right now, how am I going to make it until Friday? Three and a half days without her is unbearable and to think I wasn't even able to devour her this morning.

*Fuck.*

Considering how hot and heavy things have been between us since we started dating, I doubt I'll be able to jerk off enough times to compensate.

"Rod?"

I'm vaguely aware of someone calling my name. I'm too mesmerized to care.

Dom smiles at me and I have to force myself not to respond.

*Damn, woman. What are you doing to me?*

"Rod?"

Loki's voice cuts through my inappropriate daydreaming.

*Shit.*

*Focus, Wolfe.*

"I apologize. You were saying?"

He frowns, before shifting his squinted eyes to where my girlfriend is standing and back to me.

"I *said* there are certain terms about this contract that need to get the blessing from the legal team."

"Yes." I nod. "It's best if we're all on the same page." That's a pathetic attempt to save face.

Loki stares at me like I have two heads.

I smile.

He swings his scrutinizing gaze to the two men sitting across from us. "We've been at it for three hours. I vote we call it a day. Let's reconvene when the legal team gives us the green light," Loki says. "Jude Solomon, my executive assistant will be in touch."

Thank God one of us still has his head in the game.

"Rod, you're okay with that?" Loki turns his attention to me.

"I am," I say, looking forward to getting the hell out of this room.

I chance a glance in Dom's direction, but she's gone.

*Damn.*

Once the customary parting greetings are over and done with, I set off to find Dom, but not before Loki gives me a piece of his mind.

"What the fuck?"

"Sorry." I wince. "I got a little distracted."

"A little? Rod, you were practically eye-fucking your girlfriend. Thank God Jude and Solomon were too consumed by the contract to notice."

"Sorry. It won't happen again." I meant to stop at that, but for some reason, my mouth keeps running. "I'm not used to this."

Loki narrows his eyes at me. "The relationship?"

"No. I can't get enough of her. I can't get her out of my fucking system."

Loki's eyes widen.

"And God knows I've tried." *Many, many, many times.*

I chuckle under my breath.

Our nightly sex marathons are proof.

Loki shakes his head. "Roderick Wolfe has been brought down to his knees by his best friend. If I wasn't this happy for you, I'd give you a hard time." He pats me on the shoulder before pulling me into a bro hug. "You're a lucky guy. She's pretty hot."

"Is she ever?"

"Go find her." He winks.

He doesn't have to tell me twice.

I step out of the conference room and head to my left.

"She went the other way," Marissa says when I pass her desk. "She was looking for you, but settled for a sugar fix instead. Less trouble."

"You think you're funny?"

"As a matter of fact, I do."

"Get back to work," I say.

"Yes, boss. Whatever you say, boss." She laughs.

I take a right and resume my mission.

When I enter the small conference room near Loki's office, I find her.

*That fine ass.*

"I object to that dress," I say.

Dom turns around to face me. "It doesn't look good on me?"

Now that there's nothing obstructing my view, I can fully take her in. The light bounces against the gold chain of her necklace. The pendant is hidden—resting near her heart. It fills me with pride every time I see it on her. The neckline of her crimson-colored dress dips to accentuate her slender neck. I was right. The fabric clings like a kid glove to her gorgeous tits. I'm proud of her for displaying her ink without shame.

My eyes travel down, taking in the rest of her.

The hem falls below the knee. What a sexy as hell length. It elicits all sorts of raunchy thoughts. The demure cut and the fiery red hardens my cock. It's like the damn thing is an invitation for misbehaving.

I close the gap between us. I'm about to answer her when I spot a dot of chocolate glaze on her chin. Without thinking, I lower my head and lick it off.

"Rod..." Her voice comes out in a tremor.

"To answer your question, it looks too damn good on you. So much so, I'll have to add it to my bank of recurring filthy fantasies."

She flashes me a bright smile. "Thank you."

"The vibrant colors against your blonde hair..." I say, caressing her face. I drop my eyes to her feet. "Are those new?"

"Yes."

Those shoes were designed to destroy a man.

"Tsk. Naughty Dom. When you get back, I might have to demand you wear them so I can fuck you wearing nothing else but those strapped to your feet."

"Oh." She blushes.

"Please. Don't play innocent with me. You wore this dress for one of two reasons. One, you want to make sure I have some juicy material to jerk off to while I miss you desperately. Two, there's a lucky bastard in Miami who'll have the pleasure of peeling it off you tonight to find out what you're hiding underneath."

She tilts her head back and laughs. "Silly Rod, there's only you."

*Fuck.*

And if her declaration doesn't do something to me.

"Say it again." I tug at her hair.

"There's only you, Rod. I don't want anyone else."

I was content with that first part, but that second part has my heart doing this weird trippy thing again. It's been happening a lot lately. "I like the sound of that."

"As for discovering what I'm hiding underneath... there's plenty of time for *you* to find out."

*Holy Jesus.*

"Is that an invitation?"

"Only if you're game."

"Someone is playing with fire."

She gives me a one-shoulder shrug. "Maybe I don't mind getting burnt."

I love this newfound confidence. It wasn't there at first, but I coaxed—and fucked it—out of her. In some small way, I'd like to believe I helped her blossom into this woman who goes after what she wants.

As I consider her bold proposal, I do a quick inventory of the spaces in this building where I could have a little alone time with her. It's the middle of the afternoon and our options are limited, but I'll be damned if I'll allow her to get on that plane without making up for this morning.

I grab her hand into mine. "Let's go."

She doesn't protest.

I stride down the hallway until I reach a heavy door.

I open it and gesture for her to step through first. I'm right behind her.

Our studios are located inside a renovated three-story warehouse in Culver City. This stairwell goes straight down to the street. Unless there's an emergency, nobody ever uses these stairs. I can fuck her as hard as I want and no one will be any the wiser.

*Good.*

The door closes behind me with a heavy clang.

"What have I gotten myself into?" Dom dances from one foot to the other.

"Save it, blondie. What did you expect when you threw fuel on a raging fire?"

A dangerous glee lights up her eyes. "A passionate quickie before I leave?"

I wasn't prepared for her answer.

*Fuck me.*

My cock twitches at her words.

"Oh, you're going to get passion. You're going to get so much of it, you won't know which coast you're on."

"I guess you're game." Her wicked grin is delicious.

I press my lips against hers and dig my fingers into her long hair, forcing her to walk backward until I pin her body against the wall.

"Dom..." I grunt as my cock throbs against her stomach.

"Rod..."

I love hearing the desperate note in her voice. Her hands mirror mine as she fists the back of my hair. The roughness of her action sends a tingle to my balls.

"I want you so much, baby."

I pull her dress up along her thighs and bite off a loud growl when my fingers brush against the lace edge of her panties. Dom loves delicate lingerie. Lucky for her, I'm a generous man.

"Oh God, how am I going to survive all those days without you... and without your cock?"

"I'm in the same boat, baby. Your pussy is an addiction I don't know how to break." I groan into her mouth as my fingers stroke the warm and wet material between her legs.

She responds by running her tongue over my lips, and that makes me wild.

"My God, I can't believe we're doing this," she says as if it's only now it hits how far we've taken things.

"Second thoughts?"

She smiles wide. "Hell, no."

*That's my girl.*

I tighten my hold around the fabric of her panties. "What color?"

"Don't you want to find out for yourself?"

"I've got some pretty badass skills, but I can't hold you and peek at the same time."

"Noted. It's the sexy leopard skin combo you bought me a couple weeks ago."

"Darn. I *liked* those."

"Liked?"

I rip her panties off her body.

Her eyes widen. "Holy shit, are you crazy?"

"Shhh." I place a finger against my lips. "I need something to remember you by."

"And the drawer full of panties I have at your place isn't enough?"

I shake my head. "None of them smell like you."

I crush her lips before forcing my tongue into her eager mouth.

She groans when I slide two fingers deep inside of her.

"How is it possible you get wetter every single time I fuck you?"

"I think I'm wet the *second* you touch me."

I finger-fuck her hard, my thumb rubbing vigorous circles on her clit.

"Rod, you're driving me out of my goddamn mind," she says, her voice juddering with my frantic thrusts. "I need your cock inside me."

"Greedy girl." I pull my fingers free and slide them through her folds to her clit.

"Fuck," she says, "Please, Rod. I want you so much, I'm not above begging."

*Well hell.*

I make quick work of undoing my belt and shoving my pants to my thighs, releasing my swollen cock. I'm so fucking hard, it's almost painful.

"Yes," she says, biting at her bottom lip and eyeing my cock like it's her last meal on this earth. And fuck, I can't wait to send her to heaven. I lift her up in my arms and no sooner are her legs wrapped around my waist than I thrust inside her like a savage.

Her groan is so loud it echoes around the stairwell.

*Jesus Christ.*

I'll never get used to how amazing it feels to be inside her pussy unsheathed – flesh against flesh as her tightness chokes me. I could fuck her twelve times a day and it still wouldn't be enough.

It doesn't take long for my heavy balls to tug. I slow the pace to hold it off. "Baby, I'm almost there. Are you close?"

"Yes," she says, clenching around me. "Oh, God." Her breaths are ragged. "Oh, God, don't slow down. Fuck me."

She moans and shudders and bites into the shoulder of my jacket as I take control of this dance. I pump into her hard and fast against the wall, praying she doesn't bruise too badly.

And then, I stop.

Her eyes fly open.

"No," she says, panting.

"Just changing it up a gear." I slide my desperate cock all the way deep.

Her long groan is so fucking sexy.

And then, I go to town, gripping her tight and fucking her so fast, it feels like we're about to burst into flames.

"Jesus!"

"Too loud, baby," I say, still pumping her hard. "You want an audience?"

She doesn't reply. Eyes hooded. Body trembling. She's on the cusp and so am I.

"Milk my cum out of me." I whisper my command against her mouth.

And she does.

With a breathy groan she clenches hard.

*Holy Christ.*

"Come for me, Dom."

I slam into her.

My balls tighten, ready for lift-off.

There's no holding back.

It feels like her pussy is melting around my savage cock and it's fucking divine as I drive in and out of my girl.

"Ohhhhh..."

And there she blows. One last hard thrust and I send her flying, convulsing in my arms as I as I pour my release deep inside her pussy.

*Fuck.*

Our heavy breathing fills the stairwell. She's struggling as much as I am.

"That—that was amazing," she says, her chest rising and falling.

"That was off the charts."

As much as I'd like to hide here until I'm ready for round two, it's unreasonable. She has a flight to catch and I have a company to run.

"Let's get dressed and presentable," I say, squeezing her ass and dropping a kiss on her lips.

"Okay, but I'm not sure about the presentable part," she says. "I think you pretty much destroyed that possibility."

"I guess you're right." I chuckle.

I drop her to her feet and place a tender kiss on her forehead. I pull my pants and boxer briefs up, tuck away my cock and zip up. Once I'm done, I turn my attention to her. I smooth down the fabric of her dress and comb her hair with my fingers. It's a paltry attempt at hiding the telltale signs of our raunchy session.

"Let's sneak back to my office so you can use my private bathroom."

"Yikes." She pats her hair with the palm of her hand. "The damage is irreparable?"

"Let's just say you look like your boyfriend banged your brains out."

"Oh, no. That obvious?"

"A bit." I chuckle.

"We can't go anywhere yet."

"Why is that?"

"I'm pantieless." She points at her thong lying on the floor.

*Oops.* "Sorry."

"You aren't sorry at all, Wolfe."

"Not really."

"And... and... I can feel..."

"Feel what?"

My girl blushes.

"Tell me, baby. What do you feel?"

"Dribbling," she says. "I can't believe you'd put me in this predicament."

My hand dips under her skirt.

"What are you doing, Rod?"

I wipe away the dribbles. "Looking after my girl," I say. "Now, let's get to the bathroom before you leak some more."

"You're..."

"Amazing?"

She laughs. "That's one word for it."

I grab what's left of her lace underwear and shove it into my jacket pocket.

"They'll be right here until you get back."

She arches a brow. "Like you're going to jerk off to them?"

"Nah, nothing that sordid. It's a little memento for when I need a shot of your heady scent."

"Unbelievable." She shakes her head.

Her beautiful blue sparkling eyes smile at me, reminding me how much of a lucky bastard I am to call her mine.

I wrap my arms around her, pulling her little body close.

"Three and a half days sounds like an eternity," I say.

Her hands drape around my neck, and she drops her head against my chest. "I'll miss you so much, Rod."

"I'm in love with you, Dom."

I've made peace with the fact my recurring heart palpitations have little to do with the threat of a heart attack, but everything to do with something so new and so profound, I hesitated to put it into words until now.

She pulls away from me, her eyes wide as her jaw drops open. "You— What?" She squeezes her eyes shut and opens them again. "Rod? Really? No way."

Her flushed cheeks are so endearing.

This is unexpected for both of us.

I lean in and brush my lips against hers. "I'm in love with you."

"Oh, my God, Rod." Tears swell in her eyes. "I think I'm going to pass out." She fans her face with her hands. "Is this really happening?"

"Believe it, baby."

I wipe away the few tears trickling down her beautiful face.

"Stupid tears." She laughs.

"I'm in love with your stupid tears and every part of you," I say. "You're the only woman I've loved other than Nana. Every guy in my entourage knew you were off-limits. Protecting you was a vow I took so seriously, I locked you away in the friend zone. You were untouchable, even to me. I don't know when it happened—probably well before you left for your training, which would explain why things were so weird between us—but I'm tired of denying it. You stole my heart, Dom."

"I'm so in love with you, I didn't know what to do with

myself before leaving LA. I was so afraid my growing feelings would change our relationship. I was scared it would push you away if it wasn't mutual. It took me by surprise, but loving you is the best feeling in the world."

"Same here, baby." I place a gentle kiss on the tip of her nose.

I never thought I could love someone this much, but I do. She's right. It's a pretty amazing feeling.

# Chapter 26

## *Roderick*

Neither Dom nor I were looking forward to her departure. Saying goodbye to someone has never felt this cruel. We made promises to text and call each other every day, but we know it won't compare to hanging out on my deck after dinner, catching up on the highlights of the day. For years I was content falling asleep alone in my king size bed. I doubt it'll be the case in the coming days.

I stroll back to my office carrying a plate with two cookie and cream donuts in one hand and a latte in the other. Since meetings ate up my morning and Dom is away, I decided to work later tonight.

"There you are," Marissa says when she sees me.

"I just got back from LAX."

"You have a visitor." She approaches me. "A *very* charming one."

"Aren't you married?"

"I'm am, but it doesn't mean I'm blind," she says. "Not to mention, when a man is as observant as your visitor, it perks a girl's ears."

I frown. "You lost me."

"My new hair color."

"Blonde as usual?"

"No. I got my hair done yesterday and the hubby has yet to notice, but your visitor did."

"Who's the—"

"I went from a dirty blonde to an ash blonde—a more youthful, bright tone. I love your girlfriend's golden blonde—"

"Is there a point to this?"

"You're like my husband," she says.

"Marissa, I don't have all day. Dark? Light? Regardless. Your hair looks great. Now, who's the visitor?"

She lets out a loud huff. "Mr. Gideon—"

"Gideon Wilding? He's here? In LA?"

"Yes and yes."

"I can't believe it. I haven't seen him in such a long time."

"Well, he's in the building."

"Holy shit. Did he have an appointment I forgot about?"

"No. He just dropped by. I thought it was a little peculiar, but given who he is, I didn't give it a second thought."

"He could've made an appointment. He's lucky I wasn't caught in a meeting or traveling."

"I'm sure he's eager to catch up. I've read so many stories online about him and how instrumental he was in your career, but I didn't know he was such a gentleman. It's so rare in the music industry."

"Did you put him in the conference room?"

"I put him on the second floor. I still have to tidy up the aquarium, and the other conference room on the third floor is under siege—donuts," she says, dropping her eyes to my plate.

I laugh. "Good call."

"I didn't know how long it would take you to get back from

the airport, so I made sure he had coffee and donuts while he waits."

I can't believe this. I haven't seen the guy in five years. I was going to knock off a few things on my list, but seeing an old friend trumps work.

~

After dropping the donuts and coffee in the kitchen, I take the stairs two by two. As I approach a conference room, Gideon's loud voice booms from the door that's ajar.

"What the fuck are you talking about, Peter?" he says. "I didn't fly overnight from London for you to come empty-handed. I have a fucking company to run."

*Whoa.*

"Is that your excuse? Why the fuck do you think I pay you such outrageous fees? You're the lawyer. Figure it out."

*It doesn't sound like he's having a good day.*

"Make the problem or problems go the fuck away, Peter. If you don't, I'll fire your ass and find someone who will. Call me back the minute you have something. And don't waste my fucking time until you do."

*I'm not sure what he's dealing with, but when lawyers are involved, it's heavy shit.*

It feels weird to knock on a door in my own building, but for some reason, I feel compelled to do so.

I enter the room. "I can't believe my eyes." I approach him.

"Rod Wolfe. How are you doing, man?"

We exchange a bro hug.

"Can't complain." I step back and take a good look at him. "You're unrecognizable."

Gideon's fitted jacket and shirt are practically ripping from his bulging bicep and chest muscles.

"I'm fifty-seven, if I don't keep in shape, I don't get any pussy. I guess I should say the kind of pussy I like. There's a hell of a lot of subpar pussy out there, but it doesn't get my dick hard."

*Too much information.*

"Come on, you're exaggerating," I say.

"Money isn't enough anymore with women. They're looking for washboard abs, sparkling personality, a stud in bed—who sports a ten-inch cock—and a pro at eating pussy. When did they become so fucking demanding?" He laughs. "In any case, when I moved to New York five years ago, I started working out with a personal trainer. When I moved to London three years ago, I hired a new one. I juice to help me bulk up faster and trim off the fat."

My eyebrows knit together. I've been training long enough to know he isn't talking about kale, beet, or carrot juice.

"Really?"

"Yeah, I had to resort to steroids to keep up with young pups like you."

His candid response surprises me.

"I also had to get on the Viagra prescription to keep it up longer. Aging fucking sucks," he says.

*Whoa.*

"Enough about me. Long gone is the poor kid with big dreams from the Fashion District. You're sitting on top of an impressive empire," he says, opening his arms and pivoting around.

"Nah, it's a little side business," I say. "Let's sit down."

"Good idea."

My gaze slides to the untouched latte and donuts before landing on him. "You're on a no carb, no sugar diet?"

He laughs. "You're quick. I forgot that about you. The

donuts look tempting and I planned on eating one. I got caught up on that stupid phone call."

"Is everything okay?"

"You know how it is. Success fosters envy in some people and brings out the ugly green monster in many sore losers. I'm dealing with some shit right now. Nothing my legal team can't handle."

"I'm sorry to hear that."

"Don't worry about it, Rod. At this rate, you'll be standing in my shoes soon. Just make sure you have shark lawyers on your side."

"Noted," I say. "It's great to see you, Gideon, but how did you know where to find me?"

"I bumped into Holt three months ago at an event in London and he told me all about your amazing success. I remember Googling your company and the catchy name stuck. Since I arrived in LA yesterday, I thought I'd look you up. You know me. I like things up close and personal, so I decided to drop by instead of calling."

"I see."

"I'm sure you're a busy man. I hope it's not a problem."

"Not at all. It's a great opportunity for us to catch up."

"My sentiments exactly. Speaking of which, I'm still blown away by your CEO title. A lot of artists get lost once the spotlight isn't shining bright on them anymore."

"Oh, I got lost. Remember my rehab days?"

"Who in this city doesn't go to rehab?" He chuckles. "That's behind you now."

"Yeah, I wouldn't be here without a great network of family and friends."

"Well, I'm proud of you. You were worth taking a chance on." He smiles wide.

"Thanks for believing in me."

Dom shot, edited and uploaded the videos that caught Gideon's attention. They say show business is one part talent, three parts luck. I'm living proof of that. Patrick Dreiser was the band manager for Random Misconception. Their drummer had to bail out because his father was running—and rumored to have pretty good chances—for Governor of California and he didn't want to lessen his chances by having his son involved in the wild music business. Gideon knew Patrick well. An introduction and a few auditions later, and I joined Holt, Beckett, and Jace as the fourth member of Random Misconception. My bandmates grew up in an upscale part of LA I was never privy to—until Gideon showed up in my life.

"You turned out great despite your parents. Is your dad still in hiding? I'm surprised he never came out of the woodwork, even in your heyday."

"He's dead. So is my mom."

Gideon blinks. "I'm sorry for your loss."

"This may sound cruel and heartless, but it wasn't a loss for me, or my brothers."

Everyone knew Mom had a vendetta against Dad, but no one thought she'd be willing to die for it. It took a while, but Mom got her act together. She even got a decent job—she didn't want to mooch off me. My brothers cut her out of their lives well before they enlisted. I covered a few of her expenses and gave her money every month. We didn't have much to say to each other, so we didn't talk often. One day out of the blue, Mom declared she was going to Buffalo on vacation. I was a bit taken aback by her choice of destination considering she'd never even set foot outside of California. Two weeks after she left, I got a call from Buffalo PD. Rachel Chalmers T-boned her rented SUV into River Wolfe's pickup truck, killing both of them on impact. After her death, as I was sorting out her affairs, I came across a trail of papers showing Mom had hired private investigators to track my father. She had methodically planned the murder-suicide for a year.

"We don't get to choose our parents."

"No, we don't."

"Glad to see you've moved forward. How are Rory and Roark?"

I'm about to answer, when there's a knock at the door.

"Come in," I say.

Marissa pops her head in. "Am I interrupting anything? Well, this will only be a minute." She doesn't give me a chance to answer. "Since the boss left his afternoon treats upstairs, I thought I'd bring them down. I also brought a fresh latte for Mr. Wilding... in case the first one was cold."

"That's thoughtful of you," I say. I was looking forward to a sugar and caffeine high.

Marissa enters, carrying a tray. She places a piping hot latte and donuts in front of me and a cup in front of Gideon.

"You're a doll." Gideon smirks at her, his eyes traveling over my executive assistant's body almost... sexually? "If Rod doesn't want you anymore, call me."

"You're such a smooth talker, Mr. Wilding. The hubby would never forgive me if I left the boss. He likes Rod, and my boys love his music."

"Fair enough. Remember, the offer stands." He winks.

She blushes.

*Okay.*

"Best if I leave you two music execs at it," she says.

"Thank you, Marissa."

"Yes, thank you," Gideon says.

Gideon watches Marissa leave the conference room, fascinated. It's like he's never seen a woman in his life. She's attractive, but given his line of work, he's surrounded by beauties all the time.

Confusion about that strange interaction clouds my thoughts when I speak. "She's lighthearted."

"She is." He almost licks his lips.

*What the fuck?* "And she's happily married and she has three boys, Gideon."

"I saw the hard-to-miss ring on her finger and she did point it out. I don't touch what belongs to another man. Not to mention, she's way too old for me, but she's a curvaceous blonde, so that plays in her favor. What can I say? I'm a big ol' flirt." He flashes me a wolfish grin.

"Still on the same steady diet I see." The harshness of my words surprises me.

"If it ain't broke..."

"Right," I say. "To answer your question, my brothers are trailblazers. UTV.com is breaking new ground. Major networks and cable stations don't like how they're shaking up the status quo."

"Wow. They're behind that?"

"They're more low profile than me." I laugh.

"We can't all be rock royalty."

I smile. "Rory's wife is the one responsible for their impressive roster of in-house produced programs and films. Her idea paid off. That's what sets them apart from their Goliath competitors."

"Good for them." Gideon nods. "Wow, Rory put a noose around his neck. Did she put a gun to his head?"

"No, Rory has always been the stable one. I was the wild card with anger management issues and Roark was kind of in between."

"Did Roark lose his balls as well?"

"You mean is he married?"

"What else?"

"No, he's still single."

"I don't have to ask about you. I'm sure you're wrecking pussy everywhere you go—"

"I'm in a committed relationship."

Gideon's eyes bulge out of his skull. "A what? Please tell me that's a disease."

"I'm seeing someone."

"No shit?" His eyes drop to my left hand.

"I'm not married, but I'm off the market."

"Jesus Christ. I leave LA for five years and it all goes to hell. Who's responsible for castrating you?"

"I still have my balls—"

"Was there a state—or nationwide—mourning among women when you announced your cock would have to lower its standards and fuck only one pussy until you came to your senses?" He snorts.

I fail to see the humor.

I can't tell if he's joking or if he's being serious, but his tone irritates the fuck out of me.

"Gideon—"

His phone rings.

He picks it up without apologizing.

"Talk to me, Peter."

*Well, this turned out to be a strange reunion.*

"What the hell? You're a moron, Peter."

I flinch at his sharp tone.

*Jesus, he's ripped that guy a new one.*

"I don't even know who that is." He lets out an exasperated sigh before shifting his eyes to me. He pulls his phone away from his face. "One second."

"Sure." I shrug.

He returns his attention to the conversation. "For fuck's sake, Peter, you're useless. I'll be there asap." Gideon ends the call.

"Sounds serious," I say.

"Goddamn incompetent lawyers. They charge a fortune, but can't solve shit. I wanted to go out for dinner, but I'll have to take a rain check. What about tomorrow?"

After witnessing his outburst, I'm not certain I feel the need to spend any more time with Gideon, but to be fair, I've had my dimwit moments in the past.

"Tomorrow night works for me."

"Great. Give me your number and I'll text you where we'll meet."

"It doesn't have to be anything fancy, we can head to—"

"Rod, it's my treat. Relax," he says and pats me on the back.

"All right." It's incredible how tense I am around him.

# Chapter 27

## *Roderick*

When I got home last night, I texted Holt. I wanted his take on things. He was also surprised by Gideon's *Mr. Universe* appearance and his abrasive attitude.

At least I'm not the only one.

Gideon is nothing like I remember. Maybe he changed over the years and I never picked up on it. Then again, I met the guy when I was seventeen. I worshipped the ground he walked on because he allowed me to escape from the shit hole I grew up in. I owe him so much. Getting me signed with Random Misconception was a coup for Gideon. As our career hit new heights, he received an offer he couldn't refuse. He became the CEO of Streamify—a leading music streaming service—and moved to New York. Who knows? Maybe the Big Apple's fast-paced life made him a lot more hardcore.

I pass the security gate at the Labyrinth Lounge and drive my Maserati up the driveway to the restaurant. I've never been here before, but I've heard of it. It's a members only restaurant—part of the umbrella of restaurants and clubs owned by Carl Zorion.

I follow the hostess to Gideon's table.

The place is packed for a Tuesday night.

The décor also is opulent and matches the upscale note of the exterior of the building. Every detail has been weighed. One glance at the patrons, and it's as plain as day, they're dripping in money.

When we arrive at the table, I thank the hostess.

With a nod, she scurries off.

Gideon and I give each other a bro hug before sitting down.

He adjusts his tie. "Did you find the place okay?"

"I did. It's a little top-secret. Thank God for GPS."

"It would kill the whole notion of privacy if it were too obvious."

"No doubt. I guess you've been a member since the beginning?"

"I've been part of Carl's circle since the days when he used to have these hush-hush underground parties where you'd receive the location three hours before things kicked off. It was all word-of-mouth. Now, he has a fleet of locations that cater to people like me. The restaurant is a nice front."

"I see."

"I'm surprised you never became a member here no matter how many times I tried to get you to join."

"Dark Compulsion works well for me." *I like kinky. Not freaky.*

"Pity. You're missing out on so much, Rod."

Rumor has it the Sanctuary is where the unspeakable happens. Like Dark Compulsion, it's an adult club for the rich and famous, but unlike my club, the Sanctuary only caters to those looking for hardcore BDSM—weird-ass fetishes, extreme erotic humiliation, masochism, and the list goes on. If you have a cool seventy-five thousand dollars burning a hole in your pocket, you're guaranteed a filthy good fuck, no strings attached and no drama post-fuck. No thanks.

"I hope you were able to sort things out with your lawyers," I say changing the subject.

"Ah, you're referring to yesterday's phone call. I wish I could say I had, but unfortunately it's still a thorn in my side."

"I'm sure everything will work out in your favor."

"I sure hope so because it's fucking annoying and a huge time-sucker," he says.

"I can understand."

"Enough of this uninteresting legal talk, we're here to catch up. Let's get you a drink and we'll order some food."

"That sounds good."

~

The meal was outstanding. I can't say I expected anything less.

An hour later, the restaurant is a lot more animated than when I first arrived. When Gideon talked about catching up, I guess he meant sharing every detail of *his* life in London. He hasn't asked too many questions about me, and I haven't offered to fill in the blanks.

Gideon drops his napkin on the table. "Do you still hang out with your bandmates?"

"They're like brothers to me. We hang out as often as we can. But you know how it is, we've gone in different directions and we each have a business to run. However, no matter how crazy, we'll spend the week between Christmas and New Year's on Catalina Island. We each have a home there, so it's great. We haven't missed one yet. Holt still makes it back every year with his daughter."

"That's good," he says before taking a sip of his Bloody Caesar Geisha.

*I have no idea how he stomachs that thing.*

"Keep your boys close," he says. There seems to be more to his statement. "Whatever happened to that girl who pretended to be your shadow? Tsk—" He snaps his fingers together, trying to remember.

I arch an eyebrow. "Who?"

"Donatella? Diandra? Danika?" He squints his eyes. "The blonde who used to follow you around like a lost puppy."

"Dominika?"

"Yeah. The Polish chick."

"You mean my *Austrian-born* best friend."

"Poland. Austria. Same thing."

*Mexico. Costa Rica. Same thing. Not.*

"She's still hoping your fame will brush off on her?"

*Whoa.*

"Gideon, Dominika isn't that kind of person. She never expected anything from me. She has her own successful video production company now and her own studio—adjacent to ours. She's made a name for herself in the industry on her own merit—not by riding my coattail. In fact, she's brushed off my offer to help numerous times."

"So, she got her act together?"

"She was never lost. She always knew what she wanted to do with her life."

"Maybe I confused her shyness for being a bit lost."

*Not sure how that happened.*

"She's always been well grounded."

"Humph. Really?"

"Really."

"She must be all grown up now."

*There's something about how he said that.* "She's twenty-five."

"She was cute before—blonde, slender waist with good size

tits, and a hell of a mouth... she must be quite the piece of ass now."

*What the fuck?*

My right hand curls up into a fist at Gideon's crude, disrespectful, and offensive remark. "Excuse me?"

"It's no secret, Rod, every guy in your entourage had eyes for her—"

"Remember yesterday you asked me a question and I wasn't able to answer you before Peter called with some bad news?"

"Sorry, Rod, a lot has happened since yesterday. Which question?"

"Dominika is my girlfriend, so watch your fucking mouth."

He frowns. "Seriously?"

"Seriously, you better not talk about her like that ever again."

He lifts his hands in a truce. "Oh, okay, sorry." His tone suggests the contrary.

A long stretch of silence elapses between us as I struggle to calm down.

He clears his throat. "You've been together long?"

"We've been steady for a month. It's still new, but we've known each other for so long. It's stupid it took us this long to clue into our feelings."

"Feelings?" he says. "What a dirty word. Never thought I'd live to see the day where a former rocker and certifiable bad boy pussy-magnet like you would say that kind of shit."

"Things change. People change," I say.

He's changed as well, but not for the better.

"Hey, if you don't mind being in a boring relationship, more power to you," he says. "More pussy for guys like me who still have their balls attached to their cock," he says with a laugh.

I glare at him.

Most people would say congratulations, way to go, or, it's about time. Gideon is almost dismissive. I'm not sure why it irks me so much considering he's in and out of LA, but it does.

For the next few long seconds we sip our drinks, avoiding each other's gaze. The tension swirling between us is overwhelming.

"I have a play room at the club," he says breaking the awkward silence between us. "I was hoping we might hang out after this. You're way more handsome than I'll ever be and I'm hoping it'll tip the pendulum in my favor." He laughs.

*Didn't he hear what I just said?*

"My dick is dying to punish a willing pussy. All this legal shit did a number on my dick, but a nice young, tight ass would help. Maybe we can share a few girls?"

"I have a girlfriend."

"I don't see her around." He shrugs. "It's just us boys." He play-punches me.

"Bros before hoes?"

"Exactly. And don't you ever forget it."

*Idiot.*

"Aren't you a little old to still adhere to that kind of thinking?"

"I know where my loyalty lies," he says.

*Misguided fool.*

"My loyalty lies with my girlfriend."

"Rod—"

"Just because Dom is out of town for a few days doesn't mean I'm going to fuck another woman behind her back."

"I was thinking more along the lines of two or three wet pussies." He laughs at his own joke.

I stare him down. "Same thing, Gideon."

"You know the rules. What happens at the club stays at the club."

*He doesn't get it.*

"I wouldn't set foot in any private club in LA—or anywhere else in the world—without Dom."

"It'll be our little secret, Rod," he says. "She doesn't have to know. It'll do you good to dip your dick into something fresh for a change."

*What's wrong with this guy?*

"I'll know, and I'll have broken her trust. You'll know, and you can use it against me—"

"I wouldn't."

*Sure.*

"It doesn't matter. That's not the kind of relationship we have, and I don't want another woman."

"For fuck's sake, Rod, you could've done so much better. Dominika? Really? Wait 'til you get tired of her and realize you're better off without her."

My mouth drops open in shock.

I cast an incredulous gaze his way. "Do you have a beef with Dom?"

Gideon lifts his hands up. "Not at all. I'm just giving my opinion."

"In that case, drop it."

"Come on, Rod—"

"I never asked for your opinion or blessing, Gideon. What right do you have to waltz back into town after five years and tell me who I should or shouldn't date? I'm a grown ass man."

"At some point in time, my opinion mattered," he says.

"That ship has sailed. Your opinion no longer counts."

"I'm sorry you feel that way. I only want what's best for you, Rod."

*No, seriously. Who the hell does he think he is?*

"And Dom isn't?"

"I don't think she's good enough."

*What an arrogant statement.*

"You know nothing about her," I say, a little too loud.

"You should be with a woman who elevates you," he says.

"Rich coming from a guy who doesn't even believe in relationships," I say. "You know what, I think it's time for me to go." I get up, dig my hand into my pocket, pull out my wallet and drop four hundred dollars on the table. "That should cover it."

"I can't believe you'd choose a woman over me. This is LA, Rod, there's plenty of ass… none of it worth damaging a long-standing friendship."

I study him long and hard.

The mentor I once knew and admired is dead to me.

"If we didn't have a history, I'd punch you in the face for those crass remarks about Dom—*my girlfriend*." My jaw works. "Don't let it happen ever again."

I walk out of the Labyrinth Lounge without granting Gideon a second glance.

# Chapter 28

## *Dominika*

"Let's take ten, people," I say to the crew.

"Hey, Dope D, good call on the extra lighting." Kool A gives me two thumbs up.

This yacht has more voltage shining bright on it than a nuclear power plant.

It wasn't my call. It was part of his long list of requests.

"The video will look slick once we get it right," I say.

"Word has it you're the best, Dope D."

*You may have a stage name, but I don't need one.* "Word would be right." I offer him a small smile.

"And she's funny too," Kool A says to his entourage.

That elicits a few chuckles.

"Time is ticking. You should start your break now," I say.

"Can we take twenty instead of ten? I need to send off a bunch of text messages to my peeps. You know how it is when you're on top," he says with a cocksure grin.

"We can take as long as you want. When the record label gets the bill, you'll have to explain why it's so high."

"Ten it is," Kool A says.

"We're on the same page?"

"Yes, ma'am."

*Good.*

Morgan, my 1st Assistant Director, approaches me. "I didn't like those last shots."

"Neither did I. We'll try a couple more takes and call it a day. I'm confident we have enough footage to edit the perfect scene when we get back to LA."

"All right, you're the boss," he says. "I'm going to get some coffee. Want one?"

"Thanks, Morgan. But I've hit my quota."

"All right. See you in ten."

"See you."

A night shoot in Miami sounds like a dream. This one is anything but. Between rapper Kool A's ridiculous demands and the slutty half-naked girls gyrating like strippers on this rented 74 ft yacht, it's quite the spectacle. But there's no backing out now because the label paid me a hefty fee. Luckily, the rest of this video will be shot in Rod's studio and the girls will be replaced by male background dancers.

I drop my camera on top of one of our travel trunks and distance myself from the crew. Even though it's ten o'clock at night, it's still so hot and humid. As I slick back my hair, I can't help but laugh. Isobel was right. Only in Miami can my super straight hair get a bit of a curl. It's more frizzy than curly, but I'll take it. I can imagine how wild her curls get down here. I close my eyes and welcome the warm breeze blowing against my face.

*Life is pretty sweet.*

As I bask in bliss, my phone vibrates. With rushed hands, I pull it out of the Louis Vuitton sling bag I keep it in when I'm on set.

Rod: Still working hard?

I can't help the smile stretching my lips.

Dominika: I am. What about you?

Rod: Same. I'm still at the office. How's the shoot?

Dominika: He's a rapper with an overinflated ego who thinks he has a talent for directing. Need I say more?

Rod: Got it. I miss your voice. Can I call?

Dominika: I have about seven minutes.

Rod: I'll take it. I'm dying to hear your voice.

Dominika: You're so demanding.

Rod: You're right.

Dominika: You're lucky I love you so much.

*God, I love writing those words.*

So much has changed between us. I'm no longer afraid to tell Rod how I feel about him. Knowing it's mutual is the most empowering feeling in the world.

Rod: Calling now.

"Hey, baby. I miss your sexy ass."

I grin from ear to ear. "I miss yours too."

"You like my ass?"

"Stop it."

"Are you blushing thinking of my sexy ass, Dom?"

I hate that he knows me so well.

I still can't believe we went from best friends, to lovers, to something so much more intimate and permanent.

We're in a good place.

I never thought my wish would come true.

"Did you call me to put dirty images in my head?"

"It's hardly fair I'd be the only one in this predicament."

"You're an idiot, Wolfe."

"Yeah, but you still love me."

"I do."

"Almost done?"

I let out a loud exhale. "Yeah. Day one is going so-so."

"Will you have to stay in Miami longer?"

"No. I'll wrap things up by Thursday night. There's way too much going on in LA for me to stay an extra day in Miami. We'll piece something together with what we shoot."

"So, you're still flying back early on Friday?"

"Yes."

"Sounds like it'll be an all-work-no-fun stay in Miami?"

"Other than the party last night, I've been stuck behind the camera. We fly out at six on Friday morning, so I can't even sleep in on my last day here."

"But you get to sleep—naked—in my arms Friday night. You know what that means?"

I shiver at the delightful, sexy thought.

I grin again. "I can't wait."

"Neither can I."

"How are things with you?" I change the subject.

"We have another meeting with Veemonth Records on Thursday. I hope we can come to an agreement so we can start working with a few of their artists. More work for us and more work for you."

"They'd be crazy not to want to work with us," I say.

He chuckles. "They'd be off their tree to think any other studio video production company or producer could revive their old-timers."

"Right?" I laugh.

"Oh, guess who's in town?"

"Why don't you tell me? I might be here all night trying to guess."

"Someone we haven't seen in so long, I didn't even remember what he looked like."

I frown at the phone. "Holt is back in town?"

"No. Gideon is."

*Wh—what?*

My world comes crashing. Horrific memories come flooding back at the mention of my aggressor's name.

I feel light-headed as a wave of nausea bubbles up from my stomach. I hold onto the ramp to avoid falling to my knees.

I swallow the sick feeling rising in my throat. "Gideon Wilding?"

"The one and only. Wild, huh?"

"Wild," I say in a small voice. Panic surges through me. "He moved back to LA?"

"No. He's still posted in London. He's been in town for a few days. He's dealing with something that involves lawyers, so I assume it's serious."

"I see. Did he call you?"

"He showed up out of the blue at the studio yesterday. In fact, he was waiting for me when I got back from driving you to the airport."

"Oh. You saw him?"

"I did. I saw him again tonight. We just had dinner."

"That's good." I keep my tone casual.

"Not really."

"What happened?"

"He's changed, Dom. A lot. He's a bit of a douchebag now."

*He's always been one in my book.*

"Why do you say that?"

"He spent most of the evening talking about himself and then he wanted to convince me to accompany him to his private club."

A lump forms in my throat. "Did you go?"

"No. I told him I wouldn't set foot in a club without you."

"He knows about us?"

"Like I said, he spent most of the evening talking about himself. I had a small window of opportunity to mention we were together. In any case, he's not worth another breath."

"How long is he here for?"

"I'm not sure and I don't care. I suspect once his legal troubles are behind him, he's out of here."

*Thank God.*

My heart is beating so fast, I'm surprised I can still hear his answer.

"Rod, I have to go."

"Oh shit, seven minutes went by already? I can't believe I wasted all that time talking about Gideon. Okay, I'll call you tomorrow night."

"That sounds good."

"I love you, baby."

"I love you, Rod."

I hang up.

I've never been so thankful to end a phone call in my life. The worst part is, it was with the man I love. The man I've been hiding a big secret from—one that could unravel this relationship faster than ice melts under the sun.

Breathe.

Needing time to gather my emotions and compose myself, I

walk to the other side of the boat and stare out into the dark horizon, reliving the terrifying moment when Gideon stopped being the guy Rod trusted to watch over me—when he was on stage or running from one interview to another—to become a monster capable of the unspeakable.

*'No, please don't do this. Don't hurt me.'*

I can hear myself begging for Gideon to stop.

I can still picture the evil glee in his eyes as he forcefully entered me.

I can still see the expression on his face when he grunted he was going to take what he wanted from me.

I still remember how he smirked, insulting Rod for being too much of a wimp to pop my cherry first. He was man enough to defile me and claim the prize.

My hands are trembling.

A river of tears rolls down my face.

*You're safe. It's behind you. You're safe.*

I repeat the comforting words in my head, but they never reach my heart.

I draw in a shaky breath and wipe my cheeks. I blink, and I'm back, missing the blissfulness I left behind in LA before Rod's troubling phone call.

Do I tell him?

*This would destroy him.*

I doubt I could handle it if he looked at me differently, and treated me differently.

*This would destroy* me.

How can he possibly deal with me being soiled and tainted?

*This would destroy* us.

Breathe.

I love Rod so much I can't risk bringing up the past. Not to mention, Gideon is passing through. His life is in London now—far away from me.

Breathe.

Just when I was willing to allow myself to ignore the shadows of the past, they come looming back into my life, threatening to shatter a perfect relationship. A perfect love.

# Chapter 29

## *Roderick*

"It's good to be us," Loki says before bringing his glass to his lips.

"Damn right."

We're sitting in a booth at Vego's Lounge finishing off a second glass of champagne.

"I can't believe you managed to impose that clause in the contract and Veemonth Records' lawyers agreed."

"They need us more than we need them," I say.

"You're right. A few edgy videos could double their downloads overnight."

"Dom is excited and her head is bursting with ideas."

"I'm not surprised."

"Yeah, my girl's pretty creative." I wink.

"Your girl," Loki says. "I can't believe how much this relationship has changed you, Rod."

"She's changed me for the best."

Those words feel sorely inadequate, though I'm not sure how to phrase how this woman makes me feel.

"Wow," Loki says, "I'm blown away. I don't know if I'll ever be able to get over this."

"You have plenty of time. Things are pretty great between the two of us. She's a keeper."

"If *you* can be tamed, anything is possible." He chuckles.

"Don't be so down on yourself. There's a woman out there who would be willing to accept all of your many, many, many flaws."

"Fucker."

He laughs. "Changing the subject, have you heard back from Gideon?"

"No."

*Thank God for small favors.*

"I still can't believe all the terrible things he said."

"It's more than what came out of his mouth. It's his whole demeanor. I don't hold a medical degree, but I doubt it's a good idea to mix steroids, Viagra, alcohol and a shitty personality together."

Loki laughs. "If he's juicing as much as you say he is, chances are he can't get it up without Viagra. I have no explanation for the booze or moronic personality."

"Enough about Gideon. I doubt I'll hear from him ever again. I'm sure he got the message."

"You're right. Do you want another drink?"

I check the time on my watch.

"It's nearly eleven. I'm going to head out soon to pick up Dom."

She got back this morning and other than a quick kiss, she's been locked inside her studio working. If I don't pull her away from her iMac, she'll still be there on Monday morning.

"Talk about dedication," Loki says. "Any plans for the weekend?"

"Dom looked exhausted when she got back this morning.

Twelve hours of hard work later, I'm sure there isn't much left to her. I doubt she'll have the energy to do much more than hang out at my place."

"Why don't you guys come over for a barbecue tomorrow night? I'll invite—"

A text flashes on my phone. I lower my eyes, expecting to see Dom's name.

"The girlfriend is ready to go home?" Loki chuckles.

I grab my phone and frown when I see the name on the screen.

"It's Holt?"

"He's texting you? Isn't it the middle of the night in London?"

I shrug. "I have no idea." I do a quick Google search. "It's seven o'clock Saturday, London time. He's up early for a weekend."

"I guess you don't have a choice when you have a kid," Loki says. His phone chimes. "Holt texted me as well."

"Did someone hack—"

"Rod, you need to read Holt's message," Loki says

I open the message and read it through. "This must be fake news."

"Didn't you say Gideon had changed?"

I frown. "He's an asshole, not a predator."

"Rod, I know you wouldn't be sitting here if it weren't for that man, but this is fucked up. Gideon always came across as a decent guy. This article paints him in a different light."

I stare down at my phone and re-read the first headline again.

*'SEX SCANDAL: GIDEON WILDING RAPED ME THEN TRIED TO PAY ME OFF TO SHUT ME UP'*

Dom comes to mind.

"Listen, Loki, do you mind if we cut this short? I'm going to pick Dom up. If I don't, she'll be cross-eyed soon. I'll call Holt while I'm waiting around for her since I'm sure she'll beg for a few extra minutes."

"Sure. Tell me what Holt says."

"I will."

"I can't wrap my head around this."

"Neither can I. We'll talk tomorrow morning about dinner at your place. I'm sure it's fine, but I want to confirm with Dom."

"Sounds good."

I leave Vego's Lounge troubled and confused.

Only a dickless prick would force himself on a woman.

Gideon might be a lot of things, but these accusations seem unbelievable.

## Chapter 30

## *Dominika*

I'm glad to be home, even if I barely saw my boyfriend.

Part of the reason is work. The other part is the news he dropped in my lap on Tuesday. It's ridiculous to think because I've been able to move past Gideon's assault, I could keep it a secret from Rod forever. Since we plan on spending a quiet weekend at his house, I'll tell him the truth.

Isobel and I had long chats about it for the past two evenings, and she convinced me it's best if Rod knows. She's right. Keeping this buried any longer will be the demise of our relationship. I need to be open and honest with the man I love.

"I'm hungry," I say out loud, rubbing my eyes. "And tired."

I've been hunched over my iMac for so many hours, I lost count. I sent the team home hours ago. Everyone is exhausted. I guess I shouldn't complain too much since it gave me something to focus on instead of the rattle of my nerves. I may have made the decision to tell Rod, but it still doesn't mean I'm not scared shitless.

I head to my small kitchen to get some food. Rod asked Marissa to order some wraps so I wouldn't starve.

The man is so attentive.

As I walk by the reception desk, the office phone rings.

*Who's calling at this time?*

Only in LA.

I pick up on the second ring.

"Upon A Star Productions. Dominika speaking. How can I help you?"

"Wrong number," the muffled voice on the other end says. The call cuts off before I have time to respond.

*This has been happening a lot lately.*

Jenny, our receptionist-slash-intern, has been complaining about dropped calls for the past couple of days.

*Strange.*

I drop the phone in its cradle and resume my mission.

I grab a wrap from the refrigerator. I'm already salivating. I take a huge bite and chomp down.

*God, this is delicious.*

I'm about to take another bite when the roar of the engine of a car catches my attention. It's followed by the sound of screeching tires and then the explosion of glass shattering.

I jump in fright.

Footsteps crackle against glass.

*What the hell is going on?*

I drop my wrap and pat my body in search of my phone to call 911.

*Crap.*

I left it in the editing room and there's no phone in the kitchen.

"Where are you, bitch? I know you're in there." A voice I'll never forget hits my ears with splintering pain.

*This is not happening.*

My heart is pumping so hard, it hurts.

*Oh my God.*

I look around, but there's nowhere to hide.

No back door to escape through.

No secret passage out of here.

I'm trapped.

As I try to figure out how to save myself, the sound of the footsteps grows louder.

*No, no, no.*

Then, I see him.

A face I was hoping to never see for the rest of my life.

I'm so terrified, I freeze on the spot.

"Gideon?"

There he stands.

The guy who sexually assaulted me right after one of Rod's biggest concerts, without an ounce of remorse.

Memories of my attack assail me.

I can't breathe.

My chest rises and falls as I became more and more aware of my predicament.

"You didn't expect to see me, did you?" A sneer curls the corner of his mouth.

"Wh—what are you doing here?"

"Sweet little Dominika," he says in a low, mocking voice. "Did you miss me half as much as I missed you?" He smirks, taking another step forward.

I take one back.

"Your boyfriend told me you had a little studio right next to his, so I thought I'd stop by for a visit. Nice digs, by the way. Sorry about the window. I just had to see you."

*Asshole.*

I don't clue in at first, but when I blink again, I flinch.

Gideon's beer gut has been replaced by a flat stomach. His t-shirt stretches across his broad muscular shoulders revealing a buff-looking physique.

His hair is now sprinkled with even more silver strands.

His eyes are still black as tar. As dark as Satan's.

He catches me staring and smirks.

I snap out of my trance and blink at a furious pace.

Gideon's intimidating size blocks my path to safety.

*Breathe.*

"You're looking good, Dominika." His gaze rakes down the length of my body, making me feel dirty. "Really good." His eyes are fixated on my breasts, rising and falling.

"Get out!" I point.

"Not a chance. You and I need to catch up. I'm glad to see you're back to being a blonde. I hated it when you dyed your hair black. Good thing I held onto a lock of your hair for safekeeping after we made love. I jerked off so many times smelling your perfume. You know how much blondes make me hard?"

For a long time, I thought my hair color had provoked Gideon's savage assault. Men have fetishes. Maybe that was his. I died my blonde hair jet-black soon after that tragic night because I never wanted another man to hurt me ever again. I was grasping at straws to explain why a man I trusted would violate me.

"We never made love. You raped me."

He takes several steps forward.

Vomit rises up from my gut.

*How do I get out of here?*

"So, you're the bitch trying to bring me down?"

*Huh?*

"Did you go to that reporter to start spreading nasty rumors about me because you don't remember what happened between us that night?" The muscles in his jaw clench and he narrows his eyes.

"Wh—what?" I'm confused.

"I never raped you, Dominika." His demonic eyes fill with

irritation and... hatred? "This stupid reporter keeps telling me an idiot bubblehead claims she has proof I hurt her. Is that you?"

"What reporter? What are you talking about?"

"You were begging for my dick."

Each word slices through my soul.

"Not to mention the slutty outfit you were wearing that night sent a clear message—you looked like a virgin desperate to be treated like a whore."

"You're a filthy pig. There was nothing wrong with my clothing. I was wearing a jeans skirt and a t-shirt from Rod's band."

I don't know why I thought he deserved an answer.

"You weren't wearing a bra—your nipples were staring at me—and your skirt was so short I could practically see your dripping pussy."

He's lying. I've been wearing bras since I was twelve. My skirt hit me mid-thigh and my t-shirt was too large for me.

"I gave you what you wanted, Dominika. Plain and simple. You're still a tease now. Nice little top." He licks his lips.

"I never wanted you. I never wanted to be hurt, humiliated, or raped."

"That's your story now? Is that why you're after a quick pay off, or maybe you're pining for your fifteen minutes of fame?"

"I don't know what you're talking about."

"You're a fucking liar." The words come out with such venom, I flinch.

"Please, leave me alone. I never talked to any reporter. You told me not to tell and I haven't. Nobody knows."

"So, your boyfriend still doesn't know we made love?"

I cover my ears. "Stop saying that. Stop saying that. Stop saying that."

Gideon lets out a roaring laugh. "Rod still doesn't know I

took something precious from him? Something he'll never have. He may be the one fucking you now, but you came all over my cock before his."

"A victim doesn't enjoy being assaulted."

He takes another step and he's standing right in front of me.

*Please, God, save me.*

"You liked it rough, bitch. We both know it." He brings a hand up to my hair.

My head jerks back. "Don't you fucking touch me."

He ignores me and caresses my hair with the back of his hand.

I'm so scared right now, I could die of fright.

"Remember how you moaned when I came inside your tight virgin pussy? I can still smell your innocent cunt, Dominika."

I flinch away from him.

"You fucking animal."

"Why don't we have an encore, so I can show you how much of an animal I really am. I've learned a few new tricks since we were together."

"Don't you dare touch me." Every part of me is shaking like a leaf.

*God, please save me.*

His eyes blaze with fury. "I'm going to do a lot more than touch, you fucking whore. I took your pussy, let's see if your boyfriend has already taken your ass. My guess is, you're still a virgin there."

A sob catches in my throat and tears fill my eyes.

*He's going to hurt me again.*

Panic strikes.

There's no escape, and I know he won't hesitate to use force to immobilize me. Now, he's much stronger. I can't allow this to happen. I won't survive this time.

*I need to get away from him. Now.*

I try to run, but he grabs me by the arm.

*I'm no match for him.*

"Let go of me, you fucking asshole."

Gideon shoves me up against the fridge so hard, the impact steals my breath.

*I have to fight for my life.*

I try to run again, but I don't get far. This time he grabs hold of my tank top and the strap of my bra, pulling against both with force. My top rips exposing my breasts and my bra goes flying across the room.

"Look at those huge, juicy tits. Did you get a boob job?"

His eyes flash something evil as I try to cover myself.

"Don't be shy, Dominika."

I coax myself to calm down and not freak the hell out.

Think.

Focus.

Breathe.

I use this moment to my advantage and kick him in the shin.

"I was going to be nice, but now I'm going to fucking rip your ass in half," he says, coming at me.

*He's going to rape me, and then kill me.*

*God, please don't let this happen.*

Something inside me shifts.

*I can't die.*

*I won't die.*

*I can't die.*

*I won't die.*

*I can't die.*

*I won't die.*

I didn't have the strength or courage to fight him off eight years ago, but this time, I'm not going down without a fight.

From the corner of my eye, I spot a tripod leaning against the wall. Gideon makes a grab for me. I duck, run, and swipe up the tripod. I use all the rage and pain I've buried for the past eight years and lunge at the bastard, swinging as hard as I can.

I hit him right on the chin.

The blow is so hard, his head snaps to the side and blood splatters all over the place.

He makes a chocking sound.

I swing again, and this time, I hit him in the chest.

He stumbles back before landing on his ass, the wind knocked out of him.

*Run, Dom. Run.*

Adrenaline fuels me and I take flight. "Help! Somebody help me!"

# Chapter 31

## *Roderick*

I called Dom a few times on my way to her studio, but she didn't pick up. It doesn't matter because I'm not too far.

*She gets so lost in her work.*

As I zoom down LA's streets, I flash back to the shocking headlines Holt texted us. I still can't believe the accusations. The allegations of sexual misconduct seem so out of character. Gideon a rapist? No way.

I turn into the parking lot to my studio and drive the short distance to Dom's. I pride myself for having insisted she rig the area with cameras. This is an isolated part of LA at night since the buildings surrounding us are all old warehouses converted into offices and studios. It's a different story during the day, but most everyone is home or out partying this late on a Friday night. You can never be too safe.

As I approach her studio, I'm baffled by what I see. A large window is smashed in by a car.

"Whoa."

Since the driver's door to the vehicle is still open, I assume whoever caused this accident is inside the building.

I hope no one is hurt.

I park, get out of my car, and hurry to Dom's studio. I don't bother closing my own door. I take in the scene, baffled, my eyes darting around the space, searching for answers.

*Holy shit. There's glass everywhere.*

"Dom?" I rush inside to make sure she's okay.

"Help! Somebody help me!"

It's Dom. My blood runs cold at her shrill voice.

She emerges from the kitchen. Her top is ripped and her breasts are exposed.

*What the hell?*

"Rod! Help me! Help me!"

Her scream takes ten years off my life.

*Jesus.*

She comes crashing into me. I catch her.

I grip her shoulders and shake the hell out of her. "Dom, what's going on?"

"Please, help me!" She's hysterical. "Don't let him hurt me again."

She's crying so hard, I don't recognize her beautiful face.

"Who is in there?"

She wriggles out of my grasp and runs to hide behind me. I feel her shaking against my back. I adopt a fighter's stance, ready to protect her. This is one time I regret not being a gun owner.

"Come back here, you filthy whore!"

*Gideon?*

He steps through a doorway, and I do a double take at the sight of his bloodied jaw.

My eyes widen. "What the fuck is going on here?"

"Hey, Rod." He attempts to smile, but he grimaces instead. I assume from the pain.

He takes a step forward.

"Don't come any closer," I say, lifting both hands in front of me.

"Rod, it's me. I'm your friend. Your mentor. You can't turn your back on me."

"Gideon, I don't know what's going on, but you better not take another step."

"Rod—"

"The window is nothing more than dust, Dom's top is ripped, she's exposed, she's shaking like a leaf, and she's crying. On the flip side, your face is covered in blood and there are some pretty scary things written about you on the internet."

He tilts his head to the side. "What things?"

"There are some serious accusations, Gideon."

"All lies." Something dangerous—demonic, even—flashes in his eyes. "I can't believe you'd believe those sluts who are out to get me."

"I don't know what to believe anymore, Gideon."

He takes a step forward despite my warning.

"I said don't come any closer."

"This is how you repay me after everything I've done for you, Rod?"

My nostrils flare in my attempt to regulate the violent pounding of my heart.

"You'd be a broke son of a bitch, with nothing more than a high school diploma to wipe your ass with, working a shitty warehouse job, living in a crappy part of LA, driving a piece of junk. *I* made you, Rod. Without me, you'd be a loser. I mean, look at your parents."

*Asshole.*

"I made you who you are, but you choose to believe women trying to take me down?"

*So, he's aware of the accusations.*

"You can't trust women, Rod. They're nothing but bitches

and whores." He tilts his head to the side, his eyes shifting past me.

Dom clings even harder to me.

"They're backstabbers. They manipulate you and then cry wolf. Your bitch is no different."

*I don't even know who this guy is anymore.*

He takes another step.

I point at him. "Stay where you are."

"You'd really hurt me, Rod? I thought the other day was all talk."

"I'll do whatever it takes to protect Dom."

"You're such a fool. You believe them over me. Thanks, bro. Whores like yours are trying to ruin my life by running their slutty mouths to reporters. I'm here to teach yours a lesson."

He's not making any sense. "What are you talking about?"

"She thinks I don't know, but I figured it out. She's plotting to bring me down by spewing lies about me—like that shit on the internet you're talking about."

"You're not making any sense, Gideon."

"She's a lying bitch."

It takes everything in me not to drive my fist into his jaw and break it so he never opens his stupid mouth again. "What is she lying about?"

"She's blowing everything out of proportion," he says.

"You raped me, you lowlife!" Dom's words land with the same impact as a bomb.

I do a double take.

*Jesus Christ. Please, God, tell me I misheard her.*

"He raped me, Rod."

It's a struggle for me to take in air and breathe.

"He raped me," she says, her voice low. Defeated.

"Wh—wh—what?" I stutter.

"She's a lying bitch," he says.

"Gideon, did you... touch her?" I can't say the word. Not in relation to the woman I love.

Gideon's lips curl up in a condescending sneer. "It wasn't my fault, bro. *She* came on to *me*. She begged me to fuck her. She said she was tired of waiting around for you to do the honors."

"Stop twisting things around." Her nostrils flares and her whole body radiates with rage. "You raped me!"

Reality descends like a ton of bricks.

"He... hurt you, Dom?" My gaze remains steady on my former mentor.

"For fuck's sake, Rod. You're—"

"He did!" She starts crying again. "I was only seventeen and a virgin, but you didn't care, Gideon. You wanted to take something from Rod. You kept repeating it over and over again. You said it again tonight. You've always wanted to be Rod. You're just a worthless piece of shit who preys on young girls."

*The stuff on the internet is true?*

"I trusted you!" She points a finger at herself. "Rod trusted you!" She turns that finger my way. "You hurt me." Dom jabs a finger at Gideon. "Then, you threatened to ruin Rod's career if I said anything to anyone."

"Get over yourself, slut. You wanted my dick, begged for—"

With a growl, I charge towards him and slam my fist into his jaw with such force, teeth go flying out of his mouth.

He falls back like a felled tree, his head landing with a crack.

He's out cold.

*Not good enough.*

I dive to the floor. "Goddamn, motherfucker," I say, lifting my arm over my head.

"No, Rod, please don't!"

I hesitate for a long moment, debating, with my fist ready to beat Gideon into the next life.

I can't even speak. Rage boils inside me like lava.

"He isn't worth it," Dom says. "You can't go to prison on his account. I love you too much, Rod. Don't break my heart. Please, don't do this."

It takes every ounce of willpower I possess to hold back.

I turn to face her. I'm breathing so hard, I fear I might have a heart attack.

Dom stares down at Gideon's lifeless body, her eyes widen in panic. "Is he dead?"

*I can't tell.*

*Shit.*

Adrenaline pummels my temples like a jackhammer.

I place two fingers against his neck to check his pulse.

The motherfucker is alive.

I shake my head. "He isn't."

"Thank God," she says in a whisper.

"Did... he? I mean..." My words fade off. I can only wave a finger at her ripped top.

She looks down then back up. She shakes her head. "No. I was trying to get away from him.

"You were... seventeen when he...?" I can't say it.

"I'm so sorry." Dom sobs, running to me.

She throws herself at me, and I catch her.

"You didn't do anything wrong, baby."

"I should've told you."

*Jesus Christ.*

*He did hurt her.*

The agony of knowing I didn't protect her when she needed me the most is enough to bring tears to my eyes.

I look down at Gideon and it's hard to justify why I shouldn't end his miserable life right now.

*Piece of shit.*

"Shhh. It's okay," I say, getting up with Dom still cradled in my arms.

"I'm sorry." She repeats the words like a prayer in between hysterical fits of tears.

I want nothing more than to take her pain away, but I can't yet.

"Give me a sec," I say.

I reach into my back pocket, fishing for my phone. It's missing. I look around. It's on the floor. It must have fallen out in the chaos.

I grab it, smearing Gideon's blood all over it.

*Goddammit.*

I dial the number and wait.

"911, state your emergency."

# Chapter 32

## *Dominika*

It's a little past six in the morning by the time we walk into Isobel and Rory's Santa Monica home. We remain quiet as we follow Rod's oldest brother inside the house. The weight of the tragedy silences us all.

"Let me start breakfast," Isobel says when we enter the kitchen. "I'm sure everyone is starved."

"Good idea," Rory, says. "I'll help."

"Let me get Dom into the shower first," Rod says.

"I'll grab her some clean clothes," Isobel says.

"Rod, I'll do the same for you," Rory says.

"We'll leave them in the guest bedroom near the bathroom that only has a shower," Isobel says.

"Thanks," Rod says.

"Rod—" I'm about to tell him I'm okay, but the look on everyone's face shuts me up.

Rod called his brothers and Loki after he called the police. They arrived at the studio in record time and stayed all night with us. When Gideon came to, the police demanded answers, but he couldn't speak. Between my blow and Rod's, his jaw was broken. He could only point an accusatory finger at my boyfriend. Rod smirked back at him. Thank God, everything was caught on camera.

Isobel consoled me while Rod talked to the police. I cried to the point where I had nothing left. It took a few hours before we were allowed to go to the hospital—there was so much to report. Paramedics had checked me out to make sure nothing was broken. I only had a few cuts and bruises. I was more terrified than anything else. Still, the police and Rod wanted me to get further medical attention. I insisted I was fine, but Rod refused to listen. The wait was excruciating, but I have peace of mind there's no internal damage. Rod showed up at the right time to save me. A few more minutes and Gideon would've gotten his filthy paws on me again.

"Come on. Let's go," Rod says, extending his hand.

He drags me up the stairs and down the hallway to the bathroom.

"I can take a shower by myself," I say when he opens the door.

"I know," he says. "I need one too... And I need to hold you in my arms." His voice is so smooth now. It's lost its edge.

I choke back tears.

"Okay." I nod.

He strips me of my clothes. The paramedics gave me a blanket to cover my nakedness, but Isobel came with a top. As much as I want to burn the clothes staring at me from the floor, the police asked me to hold onto them—they might be part of the police investigation.

Rod peels out of his clothes, steps inside the shower, and adjusts the water temperature. "Hop in," he says.

I get in, and he wraps his strong arms around me.

My body tenses.

I'm certain he's going to demand an explanation, but he doesn't. He holds me, kissing the back of my head.

He brushes my wet hair away from my face. "Too hot?"

"No. It's perfect," I say before closing my eyes.

Rod likes to take hot showers. Today, I don't complain. The scalding heat makes me feel like I'm cleansing my soul.

It's cathartic.

*It's finally over.*

"He blindsided me," Rod says.

I nod.

There's nothing more to say.

Gideon was always quick to tell Rod he would watch over me like his own daughter. We all bought the lie. He was a convincing shyster.

"Let me wash you," Rod says after a few long minutes of silence.

"Okay."

Rod lathers my body with shower gel. He scrubs every last part of me. The steam helps permeate the cleansing scent of lavender. He then moves onto my hair. Feeling his strong hands against my scalp is so soothing. He's so good at this. Once he's done, he soaps his body and washes his hair. I'm mesmerized. He didn't spend any time on himself, yet he pampered me.

He shuts off the water. "Let's get out." He steps out of the shower, grabs hold of a towel, wraps it around my shoulder, and uses the end to gently dry off my face. The whole time we exchange furtive looks, never locking eyes with each other. He grabs another towel and hands it to me. "For your hair."

"Thanks."

He wraps another towel around his waist. "Let's go."

Before I know it, he picks me up in his arms.

I have no desire to fight him on this. Instead, I drop my head against his muscular chest and close my eyes.

He steps into Isobel and Rory's guest bedroom and sets me on my feet. "Will that work?"

I follow his gaze to the bed to the pile of clothing. We each get a t-shirt and a pair of shorts. "Yes."

"Good."

We lock eyes onto each other.

His eyes radiate such compassion and tenderness.

"I'm sorry," I say.

"Dom, there's nothing for you to apologize about. End of story."

I nod, holding back another wave of sobs.

Since Isobel is much taller than I am—and we aren't the same size—the clothing doesn't fit. It's a small price to pay considering I don't have to wear anything that's been in contact with Gideon.

"Come on," Rod says. "You need to eat."

Then, it hits me.

"I haven't eaten anything since lunch," I say. Other than the bite I took from my wrap before my past came crashing into my present.

"I figured that much."

When we reach the kitchen, Isobel and Rory have a feast displayed on the table.

"This looks so good," I say with a wary smile.

"Sit over here." Isobel points to a chair. "I want you between Loki and I," she says in a motherly way.

I look at her confused.

So does Rod.

"I want you between your brothers," she says.

He arches an eyebrow.

"Don't pretend you don't know what's about to happen. We need to talk, and God knows how you'll react."

"You knew?" Rod's gaze shifts to mine.

I lower my eyes to the floor.

"I did," Isobel says, "which is why I think I might need Rory and Roark's help."

Rod frowns. "You think I'd hurt her?"

Her lips flatten in a thin line. "Don't be ridiculous."

"Then, why are you dictating where I sit?"

"I'm afraid you might be tempted to track down Gideon and end his life. Not that I condone killing another human being, but I would understand. Trust me, the thought had crossed my mind dozens of times after Dom's attack. And again after you called Rory last night. Gideon Wilding shouldn't be allowed to walk this earth, but I'm not God and neither are you."

A shiver runs across my body.

Her words are frightening and touching at the same time.

Rory sighs, placing his hand on Rod's shoulder. "Sit. Down."

He does, but not without grumbling something under his breath.

"Let's eat," Isobel says.

Rod's stare on me is heavy.

I'm not courageous enough to stare back.

~

Breakfast is tense to say the least.

No one even attempts to make small talk.

We all eat in silence.

On any other Saturday, I'd be able to appreciate how delicious the food is, but today, I'm filling my stomach.

"How did it happen, Dom?" Rod says out of the blue.

I jump in my seat.

It's stupid because I knew the question was coming. It's unlike Rod to hold back. I assume he didn't want to barrage me in the shower.

When my eyes lock onto his, my stomach twists with nerves. His gaze is still burning with rage. My fear is once he finds out all the details, he might not want to look at me at all.

*You can do this.*

"Well..." I sigh. "It happened after the biggest concert of your career at the Staples Center. You guys had sold out the arena in less than an hour. It was insane. The buzz was so high—"

"Weren't you backstage with Gideon? I remember seeing you."

"It was after you guys had left."

Rod frowns, then nods. "The interview."

"Yes. You, Holt, Jace, and Beckett were rushed to MTV's studios for the LIVE Q & A with your fans for their MTV Music Special. They had asked to keep it to only the band members and your manager. I stayed behind with Gideon."

"Fuck." Rod exhales a deep breath, his eyes filled with anguish. "It was crazy that night. It was the height of our career, but I couldn't take you with me. They were pretty strict about it since so much can go wrong when shows are live. I still remember how many screaming fans were waiting for us outside their studio. I also remember how happy I was you wouldn't be caught in the chaos and you were somewhere safe. It put my mind at ease."

"Gideon counted on that."

Rod pinches the bridge of his nose. "I trusted him. I told him no one touches you."

"I think he took it as a personal challenge," I say. "He isn't man enough to own it, so he waited for when he knew we'd be alone and there was no way you were going to be close enough to save me. No one could. Gideon made sure we were in a remote area of the arena. I was too naïve to pick up on his evil plan."

"What do you mean?"

"He promised a big screen TV, popcorn, pizza, and dessert. I just wanted to see you shine. We headed to one of the tour buses parked way out in the VIP area." Rod and his band had a few tour buses on hand regardless of the city. They were more like game rooms on wheels than anything else, but they were far cozier than most hotels. "Gideon opened a bottle of champagne and poured two glasses. I reminded him I was underage—"

"What a douchebag," Loki says.

"He wanted me drunk," I say, looking at him. "He waved off my protest, stating that it was a big celebration. A little bubbly wouldn't hurt. One glass turned into a few too many, and I started feeling lightheaded. I told Gideon I wanted to go back to Isobel and Rory's place and wait for Rod there. But he cajoled me into staying a little longer. After a while, I was feeling uncomfortable being around him, so I got up to grab my phone. That's when he turned into someone I didn't recognize. He snatched my phone from my hands and threw it on the floor. For good measure, he stomped all over it, smashing it to pieces. I was so confused. The champagne had lulled my senses. I tried to run to the door to escape, but he laughed and blocked my way. When I looked into his eyes, I saw a monster."

Isobel slides her hand between mine and Loki rubs my shoulder.

"I wish I'd known you were still around," Loki says. "I must've been somewhere packing equipment. I was certain you'd gone with Rod since you guys were always together. I didn't know you were in danger."

I place a hand on his arm. "It isn't your fault. I had no idea I was in danger. I didn't know I was supposed to fear someone who had become a friend." I inhale a shaky breath.

"What happened next?"

My gaze slides to Rod's. "He wrestled me to the floor."

"Fucking asswipe," he says.

"I fought back, kicking and screaming, but I wasn't strong enough. Then, he punched me and knocked me out—"

"I should've ended the motherfucker's life." Rod points a finger at me.

"Calm down," Rory says. "Let her finish."

Rod huffs.

Rory nods my way, and I continue my sad story.

"The next thing I remember is him over me—" I let out a low shaky sob.

"Jesus Christ," Loki says. He pulls me into his embrace, and I drop my head against his chest. "I'm so sorry, Dom."

"I'm going to fucking rip his goddamn head off before castrating the son of a bitch by ripping his balls from his body before stuffing them into the mouth of his decapitated head." Rod leaps out of his chair.

His brothers are quick to restrain him.

"Sit the fuck down, Rod." Rory says.

"The motherfucker deserves to die." Rod wrestles to free himself from his brothers' hold.

Rory sighs. "You want to end up in prison for a pee on?"

"He violated her. I can't sit here and do nothing," Rod says.

"You need to calm the fuck down." Rory grabs Rod's wrist. "That's what you need to do."

Rod doesn't budge.

"Get your ass in that chair now or I'll force you to sit down." Rory's tone is razor sharp. "Your choice."

Rod pulls out of Rory's grip and does as he's told.

Rory and Isobel exchange a glance.

I knew Rod would lose it.

"You ending up in a cell isn't going to help Dom," Roark says. "Your girlfriend needs you to keep your head on your shoulders. *Not* turn into a murderer like Rachel."

Rod points at his brother. "Don't you fucking compare me to her."

Roark sneers. "Keep at it and you'll become her."

Rod shoots his brother a slicing glare. His body is tense and in defensive mode for a while before he concedes. He crosses his arms over his chest and sinks into his seat.

He looks like he's about to burst an artery.

"Go on, Dom," Isobel says.

"When I came to, he was hovering over me. In a panic, I realized that my skirt was up around my waist and my underwear had been pulled down to my knees. He'd covered my mouth with his hand to prevent me from screaming. The next thing I know..." I stop, unwilling—and unable—to provide all the sordid details of my attack.

Rod drags his hand down his face, his remorse as tangible as his pain. "I'm so fucking sorry, Dom."

"Don't blame yourself," Rory says. "I felt as powerless—and remorseful—when I found out. I wasn't even in town when it happened and I hate myself for it."

Rod's eyebrows hit his forehead. "You knew?"

"Down boy. I didn't. I was out of town. Isobel told me everything on the way to Dom's studio after you called. Trust me, I wanted to kill him with my bare hands. Gideon is a vile piece of shit, but you can't stop an evil force, Rod. And, as I've told you a million times, you can't protect Dom twenty-four seven."

My eyes move to Isobel's stare, who seems as shocked, confused, and hurt as she did when she found me sitting in front of the stadium crying, with blood running down my legs, with a split lip and a bruised chin where Gideon had punched me.

I offer her a shy nod.

She nods her understanding.

"Dom called me when she was able to borrow someone's phone—"

"Didn't that person call the police? She was hurt," Rod says.

"It was a couple," I say. "I told them I had spoken to my mom, and she was going to take me to the police station. They stayed with me until Isobel showed up."

Rod's nostrils flare.

"I drove so fast, I was sure I was going to get arrested," Isobel says. "Rory was in Houston at a conference, so I took Dom to my aunt Celeste's house—"

"She's the doctor?"

"Yes, Rod. She worked at a Beverly Hills clinic—still does—and suggested we head there. It was the middle of the night, but she insisted on documenting everything and grabbing as much evidence as possible. I never left Dom's side. My aunt had packed a change of clothes for Dom since she kept everything she was wearing that night. I wanted to call the police. Dom panicked and begged me not to say anything. She explained why. And I had to respect her wish even though I didn't agree with her decision not to expose the asshole. She was protecting you, Rod."

Loki angles his body so our eyes lock. "What did Gideon threaten to do?"

"To end Rod's career," I say. "Rod came from nothing and he finally got a big break. I didn't want Gideon to take that away from him. I believed he had the power to make it all disappear, so I kept my mouth shut."

"The guy deserved to be beaten to a pulp for what he did to you, Dom," Roark says. "Glad my brother got a swing at him. He might not have killed the asshole, but he hurt him real good."

I nod.

"Why didn't you tell me when I told you he was back in town?"

I meet Rod's dark gaze.

"Don't say you're sorry again, Dom. I want an explanation." He knows me well.

"The longer time passed, the harder it was to confess what had happened to me," I say. "And as time passed, I knew Gideon no longer had a hold on your career, but I was ashamed and humiliated, and I felt so... soiled." I pause, taking a breath. "Once he left LA, I figured I'd never see him again. I was wrong. I was going to tell you this weekend. I knew he was in town and I was freaked out about it, but I never thought Gideon would come after me again."

"Dickless coward," Roark says.

"Fucking predator," Rod says.

I no longer have to carry around the huge burden that's been weighing me down for so many years.

"Gideon is repugnant," Loki says, "but his reign of terror is about to end."

Isobel leans forward. "What do you mean?"

"After Rod left Vego's Lounge to head to Dom's studio," Loki says, "I was so freaked out by the allegations, I kept doing searches until Rod called me to tell me about the attack. While we were in the hospital, I stepped outside as often as I could to follow as the scandal exploded in London. In fact, Holt and I have been back and forth. He knows about what's happened."

I don't follow. "What scandal?"

"Holt sent us a few links to developing news in London," Rod says. "They were all about Gideon. . . and some pretty scary shit he did to women. After reading the headlines, I rushed to your studio. I had a bad feeling."

"Holt is as shocked as we all are," Loki says. "Since the first victim came out, so many others have stepped forward. Some of the things these women are accusing Gideon of are atrocious. He allegedly raped a thirteen-year-old girl. She was ripped apart so badly. . . front and back. He, well, I'm sorry to say this, but the bastard fisted her after fucking her."

We all gasp at that.

"She's an adult now, but she still carries the scars," Loki says. "Understandably so."

"Just like I do," I say.

"Men like Gideon disgust me," Loki says. "There are so many grown women who would willingly have sex with him. Why violate innocent girls?"

"Motherfucker," Roark says.

I slap my palm against my forehead. "Now, I get it."

Loki narrows his eyes. "What do you mean?"

"He kept yelling at me that I was trying to destroy him by talking to a reporter and spreading lies. I was confused—"

"I guess you aren't his only victim in Los Angeles," Rod says.

"Given the media frenzy in London," Loki says, "I bet there are a lot of women who will step forward once the news hits the US."

*My God.*

Rod gets up and circles the table.

Worried, I turn to Isobel.

She slides her puzzled gaze to her husband.

"Rod," Rory says.

"What are you—"

"Leave it, Roark. This is between me and my girl," Rod says. "Baby." He calls for my attention before falling to his knees next to me.

Loki and Isobel pull their chairs back before getting up all together.

My boyfriend's handsome features are etched with so much pain. He cups my face in his hands and stares at me. His eyes swell with emotion.

I flinch at the sight.

And then, to my utter shock, the love of my life bursts into tears. "I'm sorry he hurt you, baby. I'm sorry he stole a precious part of you. I'm sorry he blackmailed you. And by God, I'm sorry you kept silent for so many years to protect me," he says in between tears.

"Oh, my God, Rod. Don't say that. It wasn't your fault. Please don't cry."

"I swore after Connie and her gang of bullies in high school and after rescuing you from Jarreth, I'd always keep you safe. I'm sorry I wasn't there to protect you when you needed me most. I'm sorry I failed you."

"Don't you dare blame yourself for Gideon's actions. He's worse than a venomous snake. My Roderick Wolfe has always been there for me. Always," I say, looking straight into his teary eyes.

He shakes his head.

I'm not sure if it's because he doesn't believe me or he's still unable to process what's happened.

I've never seen Rod cry before. For me, he's always been this larger than life superhero who managed to triumph despite life's shortcomings. He's the warrior who's never afraid of a fight—no matter the size of the adversary. To see him broken on my account makes me love him more.

"I have to ask, Rod." My throat tightens and tears spill from my eyes. He wipes them away.

"What is it, baby?"

"After all this... You might... I mean..."

"You can ask me anything," Rod says.

His eyes are so red.

"Do you see me differently? Maybe..." *You don't want me anymore.*

"No. You're still my sweet Dom. Nothing's changed for me."

"Really?"

"I love you, baby. All of you."

"I love you so much, Rod."

"No more secrets."

I nod. "I promise."

"I'll never let anyone hurt you ever again. You mean too much to me—you always have. I'm nothing without you, Dom."

Tears flood his gorgeous face again.

I don't have time to wipe them away because he tucks his head between my breasts.

*My God.*

It breaks my heart to see him like this.

My own tears roll from my eyes onto his hair as my lips rest against the back of his head and I cradle his body.

I feel like I have since we started dating.

Complete.

Content.

Blissful.

*It's over.*

*I'm safe again.*

I embrace him a little tighter in my arms, closing the door

on my dark and painful past. I can let go of the troubling shadows.

Shame.

Humiliation.

Guilt.

There's no more room for those feelings in my life or in my future with the man I love.

# Chapter 33

## *Roderick*

*Four months later*

Dom lifts a hand up. "And… cut!"

Morgan clasps. "We got it!"

"That's a winner." Loki fists pumps. "My bet is on over one hundred million views within three days and God knows how many paid downloads."

Applause erupts in the room.

"If we achieve anything close to that, you guys get a cut of what we make," Scott says approaching Loki. "To be able to top the charts again as a band, is priceless." Scott Deen is the lead singer of Flooding Dynasty—one of the rock bands on Veemonth Records' label that went into obscurity. Dom's video will mark their comeback.

"You better pull out your checkbook." The confidence in Loki's gives me wings. "Dom nailed it."

Both men turn to look at her.

Scott nods. "You're an incredible director, Dominika. I was a little wary about your age, but you have amazing vision."

"I'm flattered," she says.

There's another collective cheer.

I look at Dom and wink. "Good job."

Her cheeks flush. "Thanks."

I love that I can still make her blush.

A small crowd forms around her, congratulating her and her team. Her wide smile says it all. I'm happy to stand back and watch her bask in her glory. She deserves it.

As people scatter and go back to their jobs, I pull out my phone.

Rod: I want you in my private bathroom in the next two minutes—no panties.

She drops the camera she was holding on a table, pulls out her phone, and reads my message. She turns around and looks at me. She cocks an eyebrow, a teasing smile flirting on her lips. Since she's still standing there staring at me in disbelief, I decide to provoke her.

Rod: What are you waiting for, woman?

Dominika: You're kidding, right?

Rod: I'm as serious as my hard-on... which is huge by the way.

Dominika: We're still at work.

Rod: So?

Dominika: You're a very dirty man, Wolfe.

Rod: For all of your holier-than-thou attitude, you'll be the one benefiting from my dirty mind. Joel Banner is taking you away and I won't see you for the next two weeks. I'll be damned if I don't fuck the hell out of you before you leave in a few hours.

She was still hesitant the second time around, but I pushed her to accept Joel's incredible offer. She'll be going on tour with him for the next six months. I'll be flying out to be with her every single weekend. Unfortunately, this coming weekend, I'll be in New York, so I have to make up for it.

Dominika: You're greedy. And jealous. Ha ha.

Joel is no longer a threat. He makes it a policy to never go after another man's girl. I respect that about him.

I grin and tap out another text.

Rod: You want to play hard to get, blondie? I'm game.

Dominika: There's no end to your dominant nature?

Rod: You mean there's no end to my insatiable hunger for you?

She looks up at me.

I wink.

Her grin is so fucking wide right now.

Dominika: What if we get caught?

Rod: Don't even pretend you wouldn't love that. Who keeps pushing me to go back to Dark Compulsion any chance we have?

Her cheeks turn beet-red.

Rod: Enough back-and-forth. My private bathroom. Drop the panties. Go. Now!

Dominika: Yes, sir!

Without looking my way, Dom heads toward the stairs. I wait a few short minutes before following her. With each step, my cock throbs in anticipation. This isn't the first time we've sneaked around—in fact, we're pretty good at it by now—but the challenge of not getting caught is such a rush, it heightens everything.

I'm so turned on, you'd never know I fucked her thoroughly last night. I can't get enough of her. Every day she wakes up nestled in my arms is testament to that. There's nothing like a passionate morning fuck with the woman you love to get your day started on the right foot.

The first month after her attack, intimacy was off the table. I didn't push. I was ready to wait as long as it took. I never allowed my desire for her to supersede her readiness. Gideon opened up some painful wounds when he crashed back into her life and she needed time to heal.

The dipshit came back to LA to cover his tracks after a reporter contacted him about a woman who alleged he had forced himself on her. He was desperate to find out who it was and to shut her up. Little did he know, he had a shit storm brewing in London. Soon after Dom's attack, the media tsunami rolled into the US. Women in Los Angeles and New York came out with their own accusations—carbon copies of the heart-wrenching stories reported in the British press.

As I walk by Marissa's empty desk, I let out a sigh of relief.

*The less she knows, the better.*

I enter my office, lock the door, and head straight to my private bathroom. I slip inside and lock that door as well.

Dom turns around. "What took you so long?"

"For someone who was hesitating, you sure are impatient."

"You got me all worked up," she says.

"Good." I pin her with a hungry stare.

She's gorgeous.

She's wearing a classy navy dress that doesn't quite hit her at the ankle. Her nude-colored heels draw the eyes up to the slit, accentuating the opening at the front of her dress.

I offer a wolfish grin. "Where's my prize?"

"What prize?"

The devilish glee in her eyes tells me she knows what I'm talking about.

"Your panties."

A naughty smile curves the corner of her mouth. "You mean these?"

I let out a little growl when I catch a glimpse of the patch of silk fisted in her hand. "I didn't expect purple."

"They complement the dress," she says.

"And they complement the woman."

She smiles at that.

I was in London last month for a meeting with Holt and I might've gone a little crazy at Agent Provocateur.

It's for her pleasure as much as mine.

"You're full of flattery, Wolfe."

"And soon, you'll be full of me."

She explodes in laughter. "That's cheesy."

Yeah, she's right.

"Get your fine ass over here."

She sashays in my direction, her panties swinging from her finger, each step sassier than the last.

*Damn.*

"Tease." I grab her panties and tuck them in the back pocket of my jeans.

"Not again," she says. "Rod, you keep doing that."

"Don't I buy you new ones every time?"

"It's so embarrassing walking around without panties."

"Not for me it isn't."

She swats my arm.

"I guess I should thank Joel for saving my panties since you'll only be able to steal them or rip them apart on weekends when you come out to see me."

"Smartass," I say as I pull her to me. "I'm going to miss you."

"I'm going to miss you too," she says.

I take her mouth in a heart-stopping kiss. Our tongues swirl and dance.

I grab a handful of her silky hair, fully aware I just fucked up her fashionable updo. I kiss her with fervor, unapologetic, raw. Desperate, even. I'm fueled by the sad notion I'll have to go without her lips for a long time.

I break our embrace, conscious we don't have much time left before she has to leave for the airport.

I release her hair. "How do you want it?"

"I get to choose?"

"I get final say, but I'm willing to indulge you."

"You're too kind."

"Are you going to answer my question?"

"Decisions... decisions." She taps her chin, her eyes shifting left to right.

"Tick tock," I say.

She's still debating.

"Choose, or I'll decide for you, Dom."

"Okay, how about this... I want you to fuck me hard enough so I feel your cock inside me for the next two weeks."

She's come a long way in the last five months. Sometimes, I'm taken aback by her newfound brazenness. Still, I love knowing I'm responsible for bringing out the dirty girl in her.

"That's not a good enough answer, Dom."

She huffs. "Demanding much?"

"You need to be precise, baby."

She frowns.

"You want me to take your ass or your pussy?"

Something dangerous veils her blue eyes.

She folds her lower lip between her teeth.

She's thinking harder now. "Here?"

"Why not? The door is locked. It's not like anyone is going to walk in."

"I guess you're right."

"So, what will it be? Dirty or filthy?"

She flashes me the biggest smile I've ever seen. "My ass."

"So, you want it filthy?"

"Yes, I do."

"You're sure?"

"All talk, no action, Wolfe. You having second thoughts?"

"Not on your life, blondie."

She laughs.

I had to be patient with her, but once Dom discovered how good it was to get her ass fucked, she's never looked back. We've never been this bold before, but then again, I've never had to live without her since we've been together.

"Then fuck my ass, Wolfe."

"With pleasure." I grin. "Turn around and assume the position."

She does.

I stand behind her, gripping her hips with both hands. I meet her gaze in the mirror.

We grin at each other like fools.

I tilt my hips forward and grind my hard cock against her back. "This is for you, baby."

"I'm so lucky." The mischievous glint sparkling in her eyes is arresting.

"Damn right you are." I take a step back. "Now show me your beautiful pussy."

I don't have to repeat myself twice.

With her heavy-lidded gaze still on me, Dom inches up the hem of her dress, revealing her smooth, bare thighs and her perfect ass. She pulls the fabric over her head and hands it to me. I grab it, walk to the door and place her dress on a hook with care. Her bra hits the floor by the time I'm back standing behind her. She flashes me a seductive look as she places both hands on the counter. She gets on her toes and pushes her ass out, wiggling it.

*So fucking tempting.* "Good girl. Now, arch a little more for me, baby."

She does.

I cock my head to the side, admiring the sinful view of her glistening pussy lips.

"You like what you see?"

"I like it a lot."

My cock swells with hunger.

I lean into her. "I smell your arousal."

"Too bad there's not enough time for you to taste it."

"I should redden your ass for that remark."

"Too bad there's no time for that either," she says.

"Damn you, my cock was hard before, but now it's begging to be let loose between your legs."

"What are you waiting for, big boy?"

*That smart mouth.*

I redden her ass.

"Ouch. What was that for?"

"You're too cocky for your own good and it's a reminder so you know who you belong to while you're on the road."

"As if I could ever forget."

I kiss her neck, caressing her arms. "I love you."

"I love you so much, Rod." Something flashes in those blue eyes. "Now, fuck me before I die."

"Yes, ma'am."

I take a step back, unzip my jeans and lower them and my boxer briefs to my knees. With quick hands, I pull my t-shirt over my head and fling it behind me.

"My boyfriend is a freaking hunk," Dom says.

I return her smile.

I fist my cock and stroke it as I approach her. "Hold on tight, baby."

"Hit me with your best shot, rocker boy."

She's in a playful mood.

"Don't worry, I will."

I circle her waist with my hands and ram into her pussy with such force, she stumbles forward as her hands slide against the sleek countertop.

"Oh, God," she says.

"Christ, I'm going to miss your pussy."

I fuck her relentlessly, forcing her hips to slam against the counter. Needing more, I grab her shoulders, pulling her closer into me, letting out a feral growl.

"More, Rod. More."

Her pleading intensifies our carnal ride.

"You like it when I fuck you hard?"

"God, yes..."

I lift my head and stare into her blue eyes.

"Fuck, baby, you look like a woman whose boyfriend is taking really good care of her."

"He is," she says, panting.

I plunge my thumb inside my mouth and then move it to her ass. I slide it inside her tightness.

"Oh, fuck, yeah." She clenches her asshole around my intrusion.

"Christ." There isn't a better sensation in the world, unless she's gripping my cock.

I resume my mission, fucking her sweet pussy while pumping her ass.

*Jesus.*

I'm pounding her so hard, her tits are bouncing and seeing them swing with each one of my forceful thrusts is so fucking hot.

My heart is beating loud.

The build-up tugging at my balls lets me know this is going to be a short ride.

*Damn.*

I pull out of her and remove my thumb from her ass.

"Why did you stop?"

"So I can fuck your ass," I say.

"In that case, carry on."

I shake my head at her.

"Baby, I need you to take a step back and rest your elbows on the counter."

"Okay."

She does as she's told.

"This might be a little bumpy," I say.

"I don't mind."

I dig into my pocket for the little bottle of lube I brought from home.

She narrows her eyes at me. "Bastard! You knew I'd ask to get my ass fucked."

"Not at all. I was hopeful, but I was okay either way. It's always good to be prepared." I wink at her.

She smiles back at me.

I pour a generous amount of lube into the palm of my hand and coat her ass before slathering my cock with the slick liquid. I slide my cock between her slit and tilt my hips back and forth, rubbing my hard cock against her. Without having to ask, Dom presses her ass against me.

*Damn.*

Needing more, I fist my cock and rub it from her hole to her clit, grinding between her cheeks.

Dom's mouth falls open.

When she closes her eyes, I halt all movement.

Furious blue eyes stare at me in the mirror.

I cock a brow. "You want me to continue?"

"Yes, I do."

"Eyes on me, baby."

"Sorry," she says.

The next few long seconds, I tease her with my cockhead, by painting slick circles against her puckered hole, spreading the lube all over.

Her head drops and she moans for me.

Dom's body trembles under my caress, involuntarily tensing every time my cock grazes the tight rosebud of her ass.

I stop long enough to spread more lube between her ass cheeks before I massage her rim, loosening her. I take my time preparing her before sliding two fingers deep.

She lets out a long sigh. "So nice," she says.

I twist my fingers left to right, stretching her hole.

Her head drops. "So, so nice..."

I can't resist gently finger-fucking her tight hole. She way she groans and trembles makes my cock swell.

"Enough, Wolfe. Fuck me now," she says, moving forward so my fingers slide free. She even wiggles her ass at me.

My cock throbs.

*Dirty Dom.* "You're going to kill me."

"What do you think you're doing to me?"

I pour a healthy amount of lube on my palm and then fist my cock, the view of my girl ready for me and my own slick hand rubbing me is almost enough to push me over the edge.

"Your safe word?"

"Balloon."

We went all the way on her birthday earlier this year. The memory makes me smile.

"Good girl. You tell me to stop, and I'll stop. No questions asked. Okay?"

"Why do you say that?"

"I have to learn how to live without you for two weeks. I can't promise I'll be gentle with your ass."

"Oh."

"You use your safe word if you have to. Got it?"

She nods. "Yes."

"Fuck, you're perfect." I trace the cleft between her ass cheeks.

She gasps at my touch and her knees go a little weak.

"Ready?"

"I am."

I drop the bottle of lube on the counter and start caressing her back as I push my cock head against her tightness, giving her time to adjust.

Dom pushes back into me like the greedy girl she is, forcing my cock inside her all the way until I'm balls deep.

"Finally," she says.

I narrow my eyes at her.

Even though this isn't the first time, her ass still grips me so tight, it's enough to make me come without thrusting into her. I take several deep breaths, before I'm sure I'm not going to shoot my load too early. I take a few beats to savor her ass properly. It's always a treat.

*Slap!*

"Don't ever do that again unless you want to kill me," I say, once I find my composure.

"That was hardly a punishment. Is that all you've—"

I find her clit and work it.

She sucks in a sharp, needy inhale.

"Look at that. No smart retort."

She lets out a little whimper and her eyes roll to the back of her head.

"I want your eyes on me the whole time, Dom. You hear me?"

"I don't think I can."

"Then, you don't want my cock."

Beautiful blue eyes stare at me, indignation swimming in them.

*Someone had a change of heart.* "I'm going to destroy your ass, baby."

"Yes, please."

I withdraw a couple of inches, and then, push into her like a beast.

I lose it.

I thrust in and out to the sweet sound of her pleading sobs.

In and out of that perfect tight little ass.

I relish the perverted sound of my slick cock pumping her.

Dom does this twerking thing where she flaps her ass cheeks together as they swallow my cock.

It's a beautiful thing.

It's so hot, it's enough to force me over the edge.

Unable to contain myself, I grope her ass and squeeze hard.

She cries out.

But I take little pity on her.

I'm fucking her so hard, my balls slap against her pussy. She moans so beautifully for me.

*Fuck.*

I glance at my reflection and to my surprise, my chest is covered with a fine sheen of glistening sweat.

"You like the way I use your hole, baby?"

"God, yes." She presses her ass against my hips, leaving me no other choice but to be buried to my balls. "Fuck, I love your cock."

"You're such a good girl for letting me have my way with your tiny hole."

"God, Rod," she says.

"Do you like my cum in your ass, Dom?"

"Oh, yes. I do."

"Ask me like a good girl to soil your hole."

"I love having your cum deep inside my ass."

"Who are you talking to?"

"You, Rod."

"Better. Now, say please."

"Rod, please, come inside my ass."

"Are you ready for my cum?"

"So ready."

Seeing her like this drives me out of my fucking mind. Knowing I'll soon coat her ass with my cum fuels me.

"Oh, God, Rod."

"You close?"

"I am. I am."

I grip her hip with one hand and circle the other around her body until I reach her dripping pussy.

"Help me out. I need you higher on your toes."

She nods. "Okay."

I dip my fingers between her pussy lips until they're skating over her hard clit again. I place all my focus and attention on her little ball of nerves, pressing the pad of my finger against it in earnest, circling her in the hard way she likes.

"Oh," she says, tilting her head back. "Rod..." I love how my name is nothing more than a whimper.

I thrust deeper inside her ass, stroking her clit in punishing circles.

"Mother of God—"

"Shhh. Not so loud, baby."

Her eyes meet mine in the mirror, but she's so far gone, she can only offer a feeble nod.

*Fuck, I'm holding on by a thread.*

I press my finger against her clit as I pound her with more urgency.

Harder.

Faster.

Merciless.

I shove my length into her sweet ass over and over again until I have nothing left.

*Christ, her ass is so damn slick, so damn tight.*

I lean my naked chest against her back, close my fingers around her clit, and bring my lips close to her ear. "Give me what I want, Dom."

"I— Oh— God—"

"Come for me, baby." I press harder against her clit as I slam into her one last time.

"I'm—" Her head drops. Her body is trembling.

"Head up, Dom. I want you to look at me. Do you hear me?"

She flings her head back.

Whatever was holding her hair in place goes flying.

The look of ecstasy painted on her face is unbelievably hot.

"Oh, Rod—"

She clenches her ass hungrily around my cock.

*Fucking hell.*

My girl comes apart.

The styled hair is long gone, leaving behind a beautiful woman babbling an incoherent string of curses as she gives in to pleasure. With her eyes fixed on mine, she chants like this for a few long seconds until she utters two core-shaking words.

"I'm yours. I'm yours. I'm yours."

That does it.

Lost to her sweet revelation, I go crazy.

I'm rough now, gripping her hips and slamming into her.

I'm like a wild man, chasing my release as she keeps clenching against me, still navigating her way through the aftershocks of her own climax. She closed her eyes a while ago. I can't even reprimand her. Right now, I can only focus on not allowing my heart to stop. I slow my cadence, and she squeezes me so hard, she leaves me no choice but to follow her.

"Oh, baby." *I'm done.*

A tidal wave washes over me and I release my cum inside her, growling and slamming into her as my balls empty out.

*Jesus Christ.*

I come so hard, it sends a thunderous ricochet shuddering through my body. I come and come and come until there's cum dripping from her ass down my legs.

It has no end.

*God.*

For a few long minutes, you can only hear our heavy breathing as we both attempt to recover. As my vision clears and my senses return, so does my ability to speak.

"Damn that was hot."

"It was." She laughs.

She lifts her head and our eyes meet.

"You're the best thing that's ever happened to me," I say for the millionth time.

"I never thought it was possible to miss someone before you even leave."

"I'm in the same boat, Dom."

"I don't think I'll survive the next two weeks," she says in a soft voice.

"I won't."

# Epilogue
## Roderick

*Two years later*

"Christmas Eve is so magical." Dom sighs, allowing her head to fall on the headrest.

"It is," I say.

"It's been such a busy year, I'm looking forward to seeing everyone. And I'm also looking forward to not working."

"Same here."

"I'm exhausted," she says.

"As much as I love how our companies have grown in leaps and bounds, I have to admit, it's been a draining year and December's breakneck pace was unbearable. Thank God for the holidays," I say.

"Ten days of chillin' and relaxin'. I can't wait."

I hired a chauffeured car for the trip to Long Beach. We're catching the helicopter for the fifteen-minute flight to Catalina Island. I have a private charter waiting for us. My brothers, Loki, Jace, Beckett, and Holt chartered a yacht yesterday, but I needed an extra day.

"Neither can I."

Dom brings her hand to my cheek, her finger running against my trimmed beard. "The best part is, I get to spend more time with you."

I grab her hand, bring it to my lips and kiss it. "I'm going to milk these next few days because who knows, come January, my girlfriend might be too busy for me."

"Nonsense." She giggles. "You'll always be number one."

"You say that now, but when you're an award-winning music video director, you might change your tune, blondie." I wink.

She grins. "Never."

Joel's tour across America was a huge success. This was a major game changer for Holt's company. Joel's band played to sell-out arenas and stadiums from coast-to-coast. Dom captured every riveting and showbiz-worthy moment. The members of Brawn Impulse even went back to Woolwich, London to retrace their humble roots. Dom followed them. She pieced together a documentary tracing the journey of a bunch of guys with big dreams who started life in the dumpster. The parallel with my own life is uncanny.

On the night of the premiere, there wasn't a dry eye in the theater. When the documentary ended, Dom and the band received a standing ovation.

Well deserved.

Dom extracted parts of the two-and-a-half-hour long documentary and compressed it into a shorter version for television, cable and other specialty channels. The strategy was a winner. *'Shattered Windows'* was nominated for a Golden Globe Award at the upcoming January ceremonies. There are even rumors of a possible Emmy Award.

I couldn't be prouder of my girl.

"Being amongst friends is exactly what I need after this trial," she says.

We lock eyes.

"I agree."

Gideon's trial has been a heck of a shocker.

Dom was lucky he used a condom. In recent years, he hasn't been as careful to cover his tracks. He got three girls, aged thirteen to fifteen, pregnant when he raped them. He denied the kids are his. DNA says otherwise. The four kids were placed in loving homes. One of the girls had twins.

*Scumbag.*

The news left everyone speechless. For years, Gideon paid off those poor girls to keep quiet, but with the hefty cost of the trial here and in London, his money started running dry and his victims decided to out him.

With everyone's support and love, Dom testified. I was there with her every step of the way. One of my brothers, Loki, or one of my former bandmates was always with me because the desire to kill Gideon grew stronger every time I had to look at his ugly face. The ironic thing is, his sex club, the Labyrinth Lounge, was his demise.

Owner Carl Zorion's sixteen-year-old daughter had dreams of becoming a singing sensation. She had talent. Over summer break a few years ago, Carl sent her to London so Gideon could mentor her and help build her team. He never suspected he was sending his daughter straight into the arms of a serial rapist. She came back from London depressed and borderline suicidal. Carl never understood why. Neither did his wife. When all of this exploded, Cassie came out. Gideon threatened her by saying he had proof her parents were involved in human trafficking of young boys and girls for Carl's clubs. The asshole even claimed he had proof that would put the Zorions aw[illegible] the rest of their lives, leaving Cassie somewhat of an [illegible]

All lies.

Cassie was too young to know anything about her father's business. Carl went after Gideon with a vengeance.

The massive media exposure gave other women the courage to step forward. There were victims in New York, LA, Miami, London… and as far as Russia—Martina Kekovna had big dreams when she moved to London at nineteen. None of them involved being raped. Throughout the years, Gideon left a devastating trail behind him. He targeted young, innocent and impressionable girls and then twisted things around in his favor. The trial went on for over a year. But he never went to prison for his crimes.

"He was man enough to rape us, but not man enough to take responsibility for his horrific actions."

Gideon took his own life a few days before his sentencing.

As much as I would've loved nothing more than for the coward to stand in front of his victims and get what was coming to him, knowing he'll never be able to hurt another girl or woman is justice in itself.

"We're here," I say when the chauffeur takes a right turn before driving down the road leading to the helicopter.

"Bring on Christmas!" Dom says.

The car slows to a halt. I thank the driver, get out and circle the car to help Dom out. A blonde and two men are waiting for us.

"Good afternoon, Mr. Wolfe. Miss Jacek," Shayla Marnell, the manager at Chopper Luxe, says. "Derek and Peter will take care of your luggage."

"That sounds great," I say nodding at the two men.

They grab our luggage and head inside the building.

"If you'll follow me," Shayla says with a hand gesture. "We have to go through the building and out the other side to reach the other helicopter."

"Oh, that's new," Dom says. Her eyes shift to the gray helicopter sitting on the tarmac to our left.

"With the Christmas holidays, it's been crazy busy," Shayla says. "The second tarmac accommodates the surplus of flights at this time of the year."

"I see," Dom says.

I don't say a thing.

We follow Shayla.

"I don't think I'll ever get used to flying in a helicopter," Dom says, "It feels like there's nothing between me and this big void."

"Don't worry, sugar plum, I'm here. Hold on to your strong, masculine boyfriend for safety," I say.

"Shut up, Wolfe."

I chuckle.

I look ahead and spot the kickass black and gold helicopter through the glass door. As we approach the door, my heart is racing. I can't wait to see Dom's face when she sees what awaits her.

A tall black guy opens the door. Shayla thanks him before stepping outside of the building. Dom also thanks him and follows Shayla. I'm next, stepping outside with a huge grin on my face.

Dom stops in her tracks. She looks left, then right. She even turns around in a circle.

She turns to face me. "What's all this?"

"What does it look like?"

"Rose petals?"

I shake my head.

"They aren't rose petals?" Confusion paints her beautiful face.

"It's much more than that, baby. Four thousand four hundred and eighty-three white rose petals, to be precise."

They're spread from here all the way to the helicopter. "It's the number of days we've been best friends—twelve years and one hundred days since I've loved you. And there are nine hundred and thirteen red ones—two and a half years since I fell in love with you."

"What's going on, Rod?"

I approach her. "I don't want to leave LA with my girlfriend."

"Huh? You don't?"

Her eyelashes bat like crazy.

"No. I want to leave LA with my fiancée." I take a step back and drop to one knee.

Her hands fly to her mouth. "Oh my God." That comes out muffled. "I don't know what I did to deserve you, Rod Wolfe." Tears fall freely and her whole body is trembling.

I reach out and pull her right hand into mine. "You got it the wrong way around, Dom. I'm the one who's at a loss as to how come I'm the lucky guy who gets to love you, care for you, and protect you."

"Stop it! You're going to make me cry."

"I think we're well past that."

She responds with a vigorous nod.

"I can't picture my life without you—"

"Neither can I."

"But this dating thing is getting old."

"Are you saying what I think you are?"

"Why do you think I'm on one knee?"

She cries a little harder.

"Right after our first night together, I remember telling Loki and Roark, I didn't think it was a good idea to pursue things further because I thought you'd want more... and I didn't know how to give more." I pause. "You taught me how to love and how to be loved, Dom. I never thought our love could fulfill me like this. Thank you."

She looks down at me, bewildered. "I don't even know how to respond to that, Wolfe."

*As if I'm done.*

"The last two and a half years together have been the best of my life. Before we started being honest with each other, I always thought I had it all, but our first kiss made me realize I had nothing. I've said it before, but I'm nothing without you, Dom. You're my everything," I say before choking up. "I want to spend the rest of my life with you."

"Oh, Rod."

"And I want to have beautiful babies with you. Lots of them. Lots, and lots, and lots of them."

She laughs through her tears.

I let go of her hand, fish inside the pocket of my jacket and pull out a red box with gold filigree. I open it.

She gasps, blinking even harder now. "That's breathtaking."

"Just like you."

I bought my girl a stunning oval-cut Cartier ring with brilliant diamonds that extend to each side of the ring.

"I've never seen anything remotely this beautiful."

"I got a little help from Isobel," I say. "We nailed it?"

"You could've given me a piece of string and you would've nailed it, but yes, it's perfect."

I grin wide. "Dominika—"

"I think I'm going to pass out."

"Wait it out a sec, baby."

"Okay." She smiles wide.

I return her smile. "You're the only woman who knows me from the inside. Dominika Lianna Jacek, will you be my wife?"

"God," she says.

"Marry me, baby."

"I want to be your wife more than anything in the world, Rod."

"Is that a, yes?"

"It's a hell yes!" She does a happy dance.

"You've made me a very happy man. Let me seal the deal."

I stand up and slip the ring on her finger.

Seeing the large stone on her finger sparkle under the sunlight fills me with pride.

"It's incredible," she says. "Oh my God, we're going to get married."

"Damn right." I lift her in my arms and swirl in a circle.

She shrieks and laughs.

I stop and look at the camera. "She said yes!"

Dom looks at me confused.

"Say hello to the gang on Catalina Island."

"What?"

I point to Shayla.

She's holding my backup phone and filming every magical moment. The black guy is a professional video editor. His name is Darrius. Morgan recommended him. The other two guys who grabbed our luggage work with him. It's all part of the ruse. Our friends and family will be waiting for us on Catalina Island, but I still wanted them to be part of the celebration.

I drop her to her feet.

I pull out my phone from the back pocket of my jeans, enter my password, tap on the camera app, and hand my phone to one of the guys stand next to me.

He grabs it from me and gives me a thumbs up. "We're rolling."

I wave. "I'm off the market for good, guys."

"You're crazy, Wolfe," she says and swats my chest.

"I am. For you." I kiss her lips.

"I love hearing that," she says.

"Sweet Dom. My best friend. My lover. My girlfriend. My soon-to-be-wife. You're all mine now, baby."

"I was always yours."

"Dom and Rod forever."

"Forever." She smiles up at me.

I embrace her in my arms, pulling her close to me. "Fair warning, I want to fuck you wearing nothing but that ring on your finger tonight."

"Rod Wolfe—"

"Yes, Mrs. Wolfe-to-be?"

# The Next Book Boyfriend

## Lochlan

Rod and Dom haven't stopped smiling since they arrived. Joy radiates from them. Rod popped the question and his princess said a resounding yes. What a way to end a stellar year.

A bunch of us arrived early this afternoon to kick off the Christmas holidays. Instead of being huddled at someone's house, we've all congregated to the Catalina Island Inn. Rory and Roark are throwing a little party to celebrate the happy couple. After all, it's a big fucking day. Rod's brother took it one step further by flying in Dom's cousin Johanna and a few other cousins and aunts from Europe. Even Natasa, Dom's mom, is here. Rod didn't leave her much of a choice in the matter. Since she arrived, Natasa has been guarded. It's more than the language barrier. She doesn't seem happy to partake in celebrating this new chapter in her daughter's life. The rest of Dom's family is bouncing off walls with excitement.

Isobel catches me staring at an awkward exchange between Dom and her mom. She rolls her eyes.

I shake my head.

*Unbelievable.*

Neither Dom nor Rod lucked out when it comes to parents. It's such a contrast to my own childhood and the relationship I have with my parents. They showered my sister and I with love and attention... something Dom nor Rod can spell.

Our buddy Levi Aldridge and his pregnant wife are also here. Dom catching the bouquet at their wedding a couple years ago is still a running joke.

After a round thanking family and friends, and showing off Dom's dazzling engagement ring, my business partner stalks towards me, champagne glass in hand.

"You did it, Rod." I lift my champagne glass in salute.

He returns the favor.

"Yes, I did."

"You broke the oath, bro," I say.

He knits his eyebrows together.

"Once a bad boy, always a bad boy..."

"Dom made me want to retire," he says. "Someone else can have my title."

Even though he shared his plans months ago, I'm still in awe he didn't run at the last minute.

"I think that guy over there claimed it." I jerk my chin towards our friend Collin Dennison.

Rod laughs.

"Collin is holding on to his single status for dear life," I say.

"He'll be eighty and still chasing pussy," Rod says. "His stride might've considerably slowed down by then, but yeah, Dennison will be a certified manwhore for life and a long-time subscriber to Viagra."

"Jesus, that's funny." I laugh. "Glad to see you're no longer in Collin's league," I say. "Rod Wolfe in love, in a committed relationship and soon to be walking down the aisle..." I shake my head, "...incredible."

"I guess I have you to thank."

He chuckles.

"I'm not joking, Loki."

His expression turns serious. "What did I do?"

"You dragged my ass to Vego's Lounge for an intervention with Roark after my tantrum over Joel Banner paying Dom too much attention. God, I was pissed off at you for treating me like a child—"

"You were acting like one."

"I won't argue," he says. "You challenged me. And, since I don't back down from a challenge, I had big decisions to make. I didn't know shit about relationships and even less about love, but I knew not exploring things further with that beautiful woman other there," his gaze shifts to his fiancée, "wasn't an option. I went after her with all my baggage and she didn't close the door in my face."

I pat his shoulder. "Thank God you opened your fucking eyes. If I was the culprit, then I expect your first born."

"Fucker," he says, grinning.

A moment passes between us.

"I'm going to be a father," Rod says. "And a heck of a better one than my deadbeat dad."

My eyebrows hit my forehead. "Dom is—"

"No. Not yet. But I want a family. Beautiful little girls who look like Dom and little boys who are as hardheaded and stubborn as I am."

"Jesus, Wolfe, you sound pussy whipped."

"Watch your fucking mouth, asshole, that's my future wife you're talking about." He laughs.

I chuckle.

"Funny..." He shakes his head.

"What is?"

"Between the two of us, you're the one who's always had his shit together. This should've been your engagement party."

I ponder on my response.

I may not have Collin's reputation and I sure as hell never wrecked as many pussies as Rod did back in the day, but there's a reason the press calls me Naughty Loki.

"I haven't met a woman yet I wanted to date long-term, let alone take the next step with."

Rod's eyes slide to mine, his stare incredulous. "You're sure about that?"

*Her* beautiful face flashes in front of my eyes. "She's off-limits."

He rolls his eyes. "This again."

"There's a girl code as much as there's a bro code. You don't mess with your buddy's little sister and you sure as hell don't mess with your baby sister's best friend."

*Even if three years ago, you were a breath away from saying fuck it and taking what you've wanted for far too long.*

## *Bonus Scene*

For a bonus scene about Rod and Dom (we travel ten years into the past to when Rod and Dom meet as teenagers), subscribe to my newsletter.

**www.MyRomanceAddiction.com**

### ***Who's The Next Book Boyfriend in This Scorching Hot Series?***

Lochlan (Loki) Berkshire comes across as the one who has all the answers... that's until he bumps into *her*—the woman he's been obsessed with for three long years... his baby sister's best friend.

She was a girl when she left LA. Now, she's a drop dead gorgeous sexbomb strolling back into town, threatening to bring poor Loki down to his knee. And she's armed with a few secrets...

**Binge-read now: Always Destined**

### ***Reviews are a beautiful thing.***

It only takes a few minutes to leave a review, which makes a huge difference for an indie author like myself.

**Here's the link to leave a review for:**
**Always Mine**

# My Own Experience

Until a trip to St. Lucia, I really didn't know what it meant to be sexually harassed or violated. I'm fairly tall. At 5'9, I always felt I could stand on my own. Add many years of serious weight training sessions, training four times a week at a high performance gym since January 2018 where I do competitive indoor cycling three times a week—I'm usually at the gym for two hours at a time—and a couple of years of *real* boxing (not boxercise) with former professional boxers—men who've knocked out opponents many times and who believed in training their handful of female students on how to get hit in the head and stomach. Basically, I always felt I could defend myself.

As many of you know, living in the Great North is challenging for someone who dislikes winter. Going to paradise, aka a Caribbean island holiday, is the highlight of my year because truth be told, it can never be too hot in my book.

My paradise holiday in St. Lucia in late April 2018 was absolutely spectacular. The first few days were amazing. It was super hot, sunny and beautiful. In other words, the exclusive resort was a dream. The first four days were magical. All that changed on the fourth night.

I was leaving the piano bar with three other guests—all Brits—and going back to my room when a group of four male resort employees wearing their uniform approached us. One of the guys started singing, and seeing as I walked on by, he got my attention by letting me know he was singing for me.

Since I was on holiday and I didn't want to be rude, I stopped. The other girl and the couple kept walking. The hotel employee approached me and his colleagues scattered. He started making small talk. He asked for my name. He gave me his. He also wanted to know when I was leaving. I answered his questions. After a few minutes of small talk, I informed him I was going up to my room.

That's when the whole conversation took a different—and unpleasant—turn.

He took a step forward. I took one back. He then asked me if he could come up with me. I was shocked. I said no. I was going up to my room *alone*. He insisted. I said no, I wasn't interested. As I was starting to get incensed by the back-and-forth, I decided it was time for me to walk away. He grabbed me, slammed my body against his and proceeded to inform me that before the end of my holiday, we *would* get together. I twisted my way out of his embrace and ran. I didn't even bother taking the elevator, because I was afraid he'd be able to see which floor I got off. I sprinted up the four flights of stairs.

I was frightened and I didn't know what to do. The only thought that came to mind was I'd have to endure his unwanted attention for the rest of my holiday. I know, it's absolutely crazy, but that is actually the first thought that came to mind.

After taking a shower, I went to bed. I had a horrible night's sleep. The reason I didn't go to the concierge's desk and report the incident after it happened was because I was overwhelmed and confused. I was trying to process it all because it didn't make any sense. I didn't even know the guy until he approached me.

I remember seeing the employee in question working at the bar, but I'd never spoken to him. I never even said hi. I never made eye contact. So I was trying to understand how he even thought I was interested. The only reason he stood out was because he was the only employee who was wearing prescription glasses. Everyone else seemed to have 20/20 vision.

The next morning I woke up angry. I was livid. Then I started panicking at the idea he might actually take things further and force himself on me. This guy frightened me and he refused to take no for an answer. Who says he won't make true to his promise? I'd be putting myself in danger if I didn't report it. After taking a shower, I marched to the concierge's desk and demanded to speak to whoever was in charge. I recounted my story to an assistant manager. Her face dropped when I reenacted how the employee touched me. She simply said, "That's sexual harassment."

I agreed.

She asked me if I could share my story with the resort manager, as unpleasant as it was. I told her I would. The manager couldn't believe my story. The shock on his face was evident. So was the confusion. He was as incensed as I was that an employee would step outside of their boundaries in such a grotesque way. The resort manager asked me if we could go to the spot where the incident happened because there were cameras all over the place—unfortunately there were none where this happened. I wondered if the employee knew that. The resort manager asked me to reenact everything again. I did. He took the name of the employee and assured me he would take action.

The resort acted quickly.

They removed the employee from the premises and assured me he wouldn't be back until the end of my holiday. I shared my story with a few other women at the resort and that's when I found out I wasn't the only one who had been targeted by this guy. He preyed on single travelers and those who were traveling with an 'older' significant other (May-December relationships). Yeah, I know. In the end, the hotel terminated his employment.

It was a frightening experience because I realized this man had decided in his head something was going to happen between us, regardless of how many times I blatantly told him I wasn't interested. My wishes and desires weren't important to him.

Of course, my story isn't nearly as dramatic or traumatic as Dom's or the many women who have been raped, violated and brutalized, but for the first time in my life, I was able to understand the sense of powerlessness that courses through you when you're dealing with a predator.

My heart goes out to anyone who's been in Dom's shoes.

# Scarlett's Book Banter

Dear Sexy Reader,

Thanks so much for coming along on this emotional ride.

Out of the countless books available, I'm grateful you selected mine and read it all the way to the 'Scarlett's Book Banter' page.

You ROCK!

I'm honored beyond words.

The intensity of Rod and Dom's romance took me by surprise.

I was a bit nervous to push things into a darker storyline, but I'm happy I did. It was hard at times and I'll be honest, my heart was beating so fast when I wrote the chapters around Dom's tragic secret, but something stronger inside compelled me not to skim the subject, but deep dive... so I went for it.

And I ugly cried.

Frankly, I was a mess all over my laptop even when I edited those chapters.

But again, I had to go there.

I hope you loved Rod and Dom's story as much as I enjoyed writing it.

Rod and Dom's love story is the second scorching hot romance part of an incredible line up of page-tuners. As I'm sure you know by now, each romance is *unique* and filled with passion.

Before we move on to the next book boyfriend, I want to highlight Rod's name.

The kickass readers inside my (former) Facebook readers' group (Thank you asshole hacker for making me lose the group I cherished so much) were instrumental in helping me select cover models and designs, and also the names of my alphas.

Most times, they help me select between a list of names I've already spent time brainstorming.

However, in Rod's case, Melody Furman came up with his name. It wasn't a name on my radar, but when she suggested it, that was it.

Roderick is smoking hot.

That name also influenced the name of Rod's brothers, aka Rory and Roark. It even influenced the name of Rod's parents, aka Rachel and River. I wasn't planning on giving the Wolfe clan names that start with the letter R, but the names were great ones for each character.

A huge thank you, Melody.

***Who's the next book boyfriend on the list?***

Loki is really good at giving Rod sound relationship advice, but is he as good at taking his own words of wisdom?

It's easy to be stoic when you're not the one so consumed by a woman, you can barely think straight.

Bad boy Loki comes across as the one who has all the answers... that's until he bumps into her—the woman he's been obsessed with for three long years... his baby sister's best friend.

She was a girl when she left LA. Now, she's a drop dead gorgeous sexbomb strolling back into town, threatening to bring poor Loki down to his knee. And she's armed with a few secrets...

Trust me, Loki is your next book boyfriend.

**Binge-read now: Always Destined**

That's it for me.

I'm diving right back into the next book.

Much love,

*Scarlett Avery*

P.S. Reviews make my heart sing.

P.P.S. I keep writing because of your hunger for my stories. Thank you for your fervor, love, and loyalty. I'm humbled and incredibly grateful. Without you, there's little reason to keep coming up with new stories.

P.P.P.S. For access to the Bonus Scene, go to:

www.MyRomanceAddiction.com

If you've already signed up to my list from previous books, you can visit the same page to download the Bonus Scene and/or Storyboard for this romance.

## It Was Always You Series

These sexy as sin book boyfriends are notorious bachelors forever... that's until they cross paths with the women who bring them down to their knees.

**Always You** (Levi and Jules)

**Always Mine** (Roderick and Dominika)

**Always Destined** (Lochlan and Kyla)

**Always Forever** (Holt and Everly)

**Always Us** (Jace and Eliana)

**Always Love** (Jagger and Stasia)

Holt's baby brother, Beckett, kicks off an illegally hot series.

The Moguls are part of the It Was Always You's world. Each book in the spin-off is filled with explosive passion.

These darn right delicious The Moguls go after the women who steal their hearts with guns blazing.

## The Moguls Series

**Bossy Mogul** (Beckett and Arianne)

**Off Limits Mogul** (Rhys and Keira)

**Ruthless Mogul** (Phoenix and Michaela)

**Damaged Mogul** (Gage and Lily)

You'll find **all my books** and **reading order** on my site: **www.ScarlettAvery.com**

# About Scarlett Avery

Two-time *USA TODAY* and Amazon TOP 21 bestselling author Scarlett Avery unapologetically brings book boyfriends to their knees. Only smart, sassy, and vulnerable heroines are brave enough to unravel these heroes.

Scarlett's love stories are intense and passionate, emotional and steamy, layered with some delicious angsty scenes that always leave you begging for more.

She writes romance because with every story, she goes through the beautiful adventure of falling in love.

*On a personal note...*

Scarlett lives in the North Pole (aka Canada).

*The Thomas Crown Affair* (1999) is her favorite love story.

*Love Actually* is her all-time favorite Christmas movie.

She's a polyglot who'll gladly listen to the same audiobook in multiple languages when it's available.

She could live off elaborate cheese boards accompanied by

French or Portuguese bread and a fantastic glass of white wine. Same goes for a mezze platter with Greek pita bread.

She has a serious love affair with Italian gelato and ice cream. During summer months, you're sure to catch her sipping on an Aperol spritz because, OMG those are so amazing.

Printed in Great Britain
by Amazon

51429021R00209